PITTSBURGH THEOLOGICAL MONOGRAPH SERIES

Dikran Y. Hadidian
General Editor

12

THE EMERGENCE OF CONTEMPORARY JUDAISM

Volume Two: Survey of Judaism
from the 7th to the 17th Centuries

THE EMERGENCE OF
CONTEMPORARY JUDAISM

by

Phillip Sigal

Volume Two:
SURVEY OF JUDAISM
from the 7th to the 17th Centuries

THE PICKWICK PRESS
Pittsburgh, Pennsylvania
1977

Library of Congress Cataloging in Publication Data

Sigal, Phillip.
  Survey of Judaism from the 7th to the 17th centuries.

  (His The emergence of contemporary Judaism ; v. 2)
(Pittsburgh theological monograph series ; 12)
    1.   Judaism--History--Medieval and early modern
period, 425-1789.   I. Title.   II. Series.   III. Se-
ries: Pittsburgh theological monograph series ; 12.
BM180.S53   296'.09   77-831
ISBN 0-915138-14-X

To my beloved mother

Sophia Weingarten Sigal

to whom I owe a lifetime of appreciation
this book is dedicated with affection and gratitude

PREFACE

The task of writing a preface and an introduction to a second or third volume of a multi-volume work before the first volume is completed is a difficult one. Nevertheless, it must be executed.

The format of this series of volumes designed to survey the evolution of Judaism is two-track. The text is designed for uninterrupted reading. The extensive notes, sometimes running into brief excursi on specific themes, together with all the reference and bibliographical material are provided with several purposes in mind. The first is to provide assistance to the reader who is seeking in-depth amplification and is interested in a more extensive treatment of the subject. The second is to give the student access to bibliographical material to facilitate the writing of term papers and graduate theses. The third is to suggest possible themes in unexplored areas. Finally it is hoped the teacher or scholar can put this material to good use and in turn expand upon it. Wherever possible original sources have been used. These include published geonic sources, responsa, and other documents found mainly in the works of Jacob Mann, Louis Ginzberg, S. D. Goitein, B. M. Lewin, and in the various collections of responsa. In addition, all rabbinic literature, allusions, and references have been derived from, or checked against the primary sources, both tanaitic and amoraic, the agadic midrashim, geonic sources, the medieval commentators, and the halakhic digests.

A word is in order regarding the chronological termini of this volume. All chronological limits are the arbitrary selection of an author as he conceives the nature of his work. The question that presented itself was: What is medieval Judaism? The reply that suggested itself was that the term "medieval Judaism" is indefinable. I found, furthermore, that the volume can only be executed partially on the basis of chronology and partially on a thematic basis. This would in turn involve chronological over-lap. Thus, in the case of Karaism the material even touches upon the eighteenth century. On the other hand in Kabalism we reach back into pre-geonic mystical antecedents. Then again, the "medieval" questions of the relationship between Christian scholars of Judaica, Humanism, and the Protestant Reformation are being left for the next volume. These subjects will then be combined with themes that bring the sixteenth and seventeenth centuries into a sequence with the "modern" era, the eighteenth century, and even the nineteenth century.

Every book has many facets to it, each very important. A manuscript must be prepared for a publisher and there are many practical tasks and monetary costs that have to be under-taken. It is therefore appropriate at this time to offer tokens of appreciation to those who have helped make this book a reality.

Firstly, although the book was originally conceived as a text for a course at Duquesne University it has moved some-what beyond that limitation. Nevertheless, it remains appropriate to offer my appreciation to that university, its theology department and its chairman, Father Charles Fenner, who have been most encouraging to me and where I have been privileged to teach in recent years. I am also thankful to Dikran Hadidian, Librarian of the Pittsburgh Theological Seminary and General Editor of the Pittsburgh Theological Monograph Series who has been most graciously supportive in the issuance of this projected multi-volume series as a full survey of the biblical religion of Israel and post-biblical Judaism. The typing of the draft manuscript was facilitated by a special grant. For this I extend my appreciation to Congregation Rodef Shalom of Pittsburgh which was of significant assistance through the good offices of Rabbis Solomon Freehof and Walter Jacob, and the Executive Secretary Vigdor Kavaler.

This work could not have been undertaken had I not recently withdrawn from full-time rabbinical work to devote myself to study, research, and writing. This also required reinforcement, and for the continuing friendship and courtesy extended to me during this transition period by my colleague and former classmate, Rabbi Solomon Kaplan of Congregation Tree of Life in Pittsburgh, I am deeply grateful.

Additionally I offer my appreciation to Professor Jakob Petuchowski of Hebrew Union College-Jewish Institute of Religion, whose encouragement has been most gratifying.

The glossary was prepared by one of my students at Duquesne University, Cheryl Keith, to whom I am indebted for her diligence and kindness. I thank the library staffs at both Duquesne University and the Pittsburgh Theological Seminary for their unfailing courtesy and assistance, to my typist

Kathy Herrin for her expertise, and Jo Anne Sieger for her creative contribution of the art on the cover of this book. Finally, I am appreciative of the hours and energy put into helping me with the preparation of the manuscript, the indices and bibliography by my daughters, Sharon and Sabrina, and my wife, Lillian. To those three I am also inexpressably grateful for the encouragement and inspiration to do what I am doing generally, and in the composition of this work specifically.

This volume is being dedicated to my mother, Sophia Sigal of Toronto, Canada, to whom I owe an ineffable debt for many long years of self-sacrifice and maternal love during those significant early years when the student embarks upon his academic, intellectual, or religious dreams.

Surely I will be indulged a poetic ending to a narrative of religious history. As I complete this book walking the beaches and gazing out at that incredible phenomenon which, as the author of *Job* says, God ordered

> Thus far shall you come and no further,
> and here shall your proud waves be stayed,

I cannot help but think of that great paean to Creation, Psalm 104. And while emotionally, physically and intellectually absorbing this majesty of the Creator I reflect upon the theological appropriateness of the tradition to recite this psalm on Sabbath afternoons in the waning hours of the day that celebrates the cosmos. And then with the psalmist I can only pray (104:33-34):

I will sing to the Lord while I live,
I will sing to my God while I am;
May my meditation please Him
As I rejoice in the Lord.

Falmouth, Cape Cod
August, 1976

CONTENTS

APPENDICES

INTRODUCTION

This volume spans over a thousand years and three continents, geographic areas stretching thousands of miles from the
Atlantic Ocean to the Euphrates River, and from the North Sea
to the Dead Sea. It relates to civilizations spawned by two
great religions, Christianity and Islam, as well as to the
ancient Hellenic and Graeco-Roman cultures which infused both
of them. Jews lived in that space for all of that time and
participated in all the rich variety of those three civilizations. But this volume will not do more than occasionally
refer to how they lived or what they did for a living. It
will rarely mention all of those aspects of civilization which
are currently common to histories: food, dress, entertainment,
economics, socio-political events, civic and communal systems,
growth of communities, professions, and the lives and deeds of
political or military leaders. Certainly all these facets of
history apply to Jews. But it is my conviction that a genuine
history of Jews must be one of the religious and literary life,
of scholarship and religion. This is therefore not a "history
of Jews", but a *survey of Judaism*, and an exposition of the
varieties of Jewish religious experience.

The chronological termini as well as the themes and the
personalities covered, by nature of the work, had to be decided arbitrarily. Not everything could be included, as desirable as that may be. And at some future date that desider-

atum may be fulfilled with the expansion of this volume into several. But at this time the limitations of space required careful selectivity. The personalities emphasized, therefore, are those who are among the scholars of Judaica who have had a major impact upon the direction of Judaism. The literary compositions described are of two types generally. Firstly those that have played the most significant part in the curricula of Judaic studies up to the modern period receive main attention. And secondly major attention is accorded those works, such as writings of Maimonides, that have been the sources of religious life, especially of the halakha, during the last three or more centuries. This seemed to be appropriate for a multi-volume work entitled *The Emergence of Contemporary Judaism*: the purpose being to examine where the Judaism of today comes from, how it came into being, who were among the major moving forces and what were the interacting aspects of the non-Jewish milieu.

This book is written from a point of view. I conceive of Judaism as a religion, and that those who adhere to this religion in any of its variegated manifestations are members of the faith community which is currently called the Jewish People. "Peoplehood", a term in wide vogue, is understood as a religio-theological designation. On the one hand, therefore, it would appear incongruous for one who does not believe in any of the doctrines of Judaism or commemorate its theological celebrations to be considered a Jew. On the other hand, however, since "heresy" is indefinable, it is a moot point whether one ever ceases to be a Jew short of his voluntary disassociation from Judaism through the process of af-

firming an incompatible faith. As will be seen in the course
of this book, not even the affirmation of Islam or Christianity
is sufficient to terminate one's Judaist obligations and prerogatives. It is not, nevertheless, my task in this volume to
explore the ramifications of this unusual theological phenomenon: the difficulty of ceasing to be a member of the faith
community of Judaism. Rational and scientific judgment, however, precludes a racial or ethnic explanation. Jews of the
modern world who are part of this faith community simply do
not have the same blood or ethnic origin. Countless Jews are
descended from mediterranean origins, countless others from
the slavic-oriental mixture that constituted the Khazars,
countless others from a wide variety of intermarriages with
Europeans of every tribe and clan that trace themselves back
to Celts and Gauls, Visigoths and Franks and what-have-you.
There is simply no other explanation for the continuity of
one's membership in Judaism until one ceases totally to be a
part of it and raises one's children in another faith, than
the compliment paid to Christian and Islamic monotheism and
the theological grace that made heresy and expulsion nearly
impossible.

This book proceeds then by perceiving Judaism from a
theologico-halakhic standpoint. It also sees Judaism as a
multifaceted faith with no genuine "orthodoxy" and rare
"heresy". History substantiates this despite also showing
that from time to time efforts were made to establish the
hegemony of a certain school of thought or pattern of observance. Judaism was never monolithic. Lines of authority
were never severely drawn. There was no hierarchy and no

centralized authority. This is further discussed in the first volume but it is amply documented throughout the medieval period. While some scholars sought to establish authority in the past, resistance was always successful, and religious authority repeatedly re-emerged as a contemporary and local affair.

The Judaism encompassed in this volume shows great variety not only in ritual observance, but also in theological conceptions. Halakhists from the time of the Talmud to the present have not agreed with precision on what practices take precedence or are mandatory, nor on how they are to be executed. The same lack of precision was true of the philosophers regarding doctrine. This multifaceted nature surfaced again in the juxtaposition of rationalism and mysticism. Despite both Kabalism and rationalism verging on the borders of paganism coming from different directions, in the opinion of some, both were incorporated as valid theological expressions.

The choice of "Circa 1650" for a description of the religious practices of Judaism is related to the historical and intellectual reality of the time. Historically, East European Judaism had come into its own. It was already progressing to that point which made it the most intensive center of Judaic studies and religious life in the entire history of Judaism. There was emerging a "pretender" to "orthodoxy" in the form of the religious life advocated in the Shulhan Arukh, a comprehensive digest of halakha compiled by R. Joseph Karo of Safed, Palestine. This gained in hegemony when it was supplemented by the notes and glosses of R. Moses Isserles of Poland. When eighteenth and nineteenth century reformations occurred in

Judaism, the standard against which revision was commonly measured was the Karo-Isserles Shulḥan Arukh, further amplified by local *minhag* (custom) cited by numerous commentators upon the basic text.

Furthermore, though the "modern era" is usually dated from the Napoleonic emancipation of Jews which allowed them gradually to integrate into the civic and political life of the countries in which they resided, its origins should be seen in a different light. Humanism, the Protestant Reformation, revolutions in scientific and philosophical thinking, intellectual movements that bring to mind names such as Erasmus, Copernicus, John Locke, and the French philosophers, all combined to infuse Judaism with changing currents in the earlier part of the seventeenth century. Another volume will have to take up the transition centuries from the sixteenth to the nineteenth. More consideration simply must be given to this transition period. For it is a moot point whether one can begin the "modern" era with the post-Napoleonic Jewish Reformation, or even with the earlier eighteenth century enlightenment of the people and times identified with Moses Mendelssohn when one has such earlier luminaries as Azariah de'Rossi (16th cent.) and Menasseh ben Israel (17th cnet.) to consider. De'Rossi is regarded by a number of historians of Judaism including Leopold Zunz as a forerunner of the nineteenth century "science of Judaism". This is verified indirectly by the many charges against him as teaching what was considered sinful and by the ban issued against reading his writings without special rabbinic permission. He had a strong impact upon both Johannes Buxtorfs. Menasseh was the first rabbinic scholar in the north to undertake the type of literary work he composed, in vernacular and in Latin. He was knowledgeable in the classics and familiar with the writings of the Church Fathers and was perhaps the first rabbi who carried on a widespread interfaith dialogue in correspondence with Christian scholars. These men and others, such as Leon de Modena, were different from both the French and German rabbinical scholars I discuss in this volume, and the Spanish rabbinical scholars and philosophers, as well as unlike the kabalists. They were the precursors of a Moses Mendelssohn and a new era in Judaism which, for lack of a more inspired term, is called "modern", or a mode which, for want of a more sophisticated description, is termed "the science of Judaism". For these reasons I delay treatment of this transition era for another volume in which, though it is chronologically sixteenth century, it will have proper affinity with what occurred in the nineteenth.

Another interesting consideration is the one Salo Baron alludes to in his great *History* (Preface, Volume IX), that the Treaty of Westphalia of 1648 which terminated the Thirty Years' War marked a significant rubicon in religious history Liberty of conscience became a major item on mankind's agenda. Sooner or later its values had to filter through from mutual toleration of Catholics and Protestants to Christian affirmation of Judaism's right to share in a new Europe. But even more, that sixteenth-seventeenth century era ushered in Jewish settlement and resettlement in what was to become the great western democratic societies of Holland, England, France, and above all, North America.

Taking all of these factors into consideration: the intellectual and historical realities of Eastern Europe, the apex of Kabalism being reached in the east, and the spadework beginnings of a great new western center of Judaism, it seemed appropriate to survey the Judaism of 1650 against which the student can measure all innovation and revision.

For a related reason this volume does not take up Christian Judaic studies and the role of Jewish scholars in those studies or the interrelationships between Jewish and Christian scholars, including the English Puritans and continental scholars. It does not consider the work of John Calvin, Martin Luther and others in relation to Judaism. These topics are held over for the transition centuries, for these too are facets of religious history that conveniently relate to the internal developments of Judaism in the eighteenth and nineteenth centuries. From the challenge of an eighteenth century Johann Caspar Lavater to Mendelssohn to accept the Christology, to the very fruitful twentieth century Vatican Council, the seeds of change must be searched for in the sixteenth century. Because the thematic thread of this change in the Christian attitude toward Judaism is best woven as a unit it will be brought together in the next volume. It is there too that the broader question of the relationship between Judaism and Christianity will be taken up. For although what is chronologically called the "middle ages" saw interaction between the two faiths, that interaction was based upon a theological premise of mutual rejection. The "modern" period with its varied antecedents in the sixteenth century is one in which there is an interaction of mutual acceptance.

CHAPTER 1

Reflections

Fanciful images of a "normative" Judaism are often projected.[1] Yet one must be very cautious before judging any particular form of a religion as "normative". Every forest contains many trees. Judaism was never monolithic. During the
first century it consisted of at least six or seven major movements. What finally became "Talmudic Judaism", often called
"Rabbinic Judaism", was the outcome of many centuries of interchange of ideas and responses to challenges. There are those
who have begun a word-play by revising "normative" to "forma-
tive" for the period 200 B.C. to 500 A.D. But here, I believe
we step into the murky waters of correct grammar.[2]

This historic verity, that Judaism was multifaceted, was
also the experience of the middle ages. Much of rabbinic effort and the subsequent literature between 600 and 1100 may
very likely have been a response not only to the highly sophisticated developments in Islam but also to the challenges
of newly emerging groups within Judaism that asserted their
right to a variety of forms of dissent. The best known of all
of these was the Karaite schism which we will take up in chapter four. There is yet needed a comprehensive and detailed
analysis of the debt rabbinic Judaism owes to Karaism, and
consequently the extent to which contemporary Judaism still
expresses certain medieval reactions to Karaism as Talmudic

Judaism reflected first and second century reactions to Mithraism and Graeco-Roman civilization as well as emergent Christianity.

Much progress has been made in these studies since the
days of Solomon Judah Loeb Rapoport of Lwow (Lemberg), a nineteenth century pioneer in Judaic historiography. But the picture is not yet wholly in focus. Just as one cannot truly comprehend the direction of first century Judaism without taking
into account Christianity (and vice versa) one cannot fully
apprehend the direction of geonic Judaism between 600 and 1100
in Babylonia, the "father" of medieval and modern Judaism,
without an appreciation of the stimulus and challenge of Karaism.

There has been no question since Solomon Schechter published a letter from Hushiel of Kairuwan to Shemaryah of Cairo,
hardly two famous historical figures, that by the year 1000
there was a string of centers of Jewish learning stretching
all across Islamic North Africa.[3] This significant historical
understanding further sustains one of the broad theses that run
through this volume with its implications for contemporary
Judaism. I refer to the fact that Judaism enjoyed localist independence, or to put it another way, that rabbis were autonomous within their own communal jurisdictions and for that
reason the multiplicity of Judaisms (note the plural) make it
nearly impossible, certainly unscholarly, to speak of "the"
Jewish tradition or doctrine. In Judaism, *minhag* was the stuff
out of which halakha germinated. And so, as powerful as were
the geonim in Babylonia, with whom we will deal in chapter two,
while yet they wielded their Islamic-granted powers of taxa-
tion and administration, local autonomy and custom, and contemporary authority were making themselves felt in Cairo,
Kairuwan, Fez and Spain. And there were yet other emergent

intellectual forces in France and Germany that grew independently of the geonim.

This brings us to another point that requires early understanding. In modern times we meet with the title "Chief Rabbi". In medieval times there were also "Court Rabbis" and other titled personnel that functioned as mediating representatives between Jewish communities and the secular government. But these men had no intrinsic power indigenously conferred upon them by Judaism. Any power they wielded was secular; it was granted by the secular overlord to a Jewish community council which in turn appointed a communal rabbi. The crux of the matter is that when authority was enjoyed by a rabbi to the exclusion of other rabbis, this authority was not the gift of a theological doctrine of hierarchic authority as may for instance exist in the Roman Catholic Church. No analogy should ever be drawn between the office of Bishop and any known office in Judaism. In Judaism any bishop-like power held by a rabbi would only be that which was imposed by secular law contrary to the historic forms of all varieties of Judaism since biblical days. Religious development in Judaism allowed for local autonomy and equal authority for individual rabbinic scholars. Scholarship, neither wealth nor the canons of political science, conferred authority. A rabbi's writ ran where it was voluntarily accepted, unless otherwise ordained by the secular authorities, Jewish or non-Jewish. The authority of the Chief Rabbinate in modern Israel is simply the most recent example. It rests not upon an indigenous theological doctrine in Judaism but upon the constitutional provisions of the secular government of the Republic of Israel.[4]

Although one must be cautious lest one read a sixteenth century norm back into earlier times, considering the widespread evidence that can be adduced for Babylonia, Spain,

France and Germany from the seventh century on, it is fair to
say that a resolution passed in Ferrara, Italy in 1554 summarizes the medieval experience regarding rabbinic authority and
multiplicity of observance in Judaism. Paragraph (IV) reads:

> No rabbi of one congregation shall interfere
> with the internal affairs of another congre-
> gation, nor shall any of his decisions be
> valid in a congregation which has its own
> rabbi.[5]

These tendencies within the varieties of Judaism we encounter between 600 and the present were largely responsible
for the ability of Judaism to survive the shocks of cultural
integration in modern times.

The term "assimilation" is one that is not highly regarded within contemporary cultural contexts. The current
favor enjoyed by ethnicity and nationalism inspires antagonism
to assimilation which is regarded as turning one's back on
one's heritage. Divorced from emotionalism, assimilation is
merely the process by which human beings adapt the culture of
their environment and minimize differences in appearance and
language and other modes of social life and expression. In a
voluntaristic society this does not imply uniformity or com-
pulsory conformity. There remain broad opportunities for
variety. In any case it need have no implication for one's
theological preferences anymore than for one's political
choices. Judaism has never prevented the Jew from assimilat-
ing in this sense of "acculturation", of members of the Jewish
faith leaving behind the non-theological or non-religious elements of the culture into which they were born as a result of
geography or exclusion, to adopt the culture of the milieu in
which they find themselves. There were often contradictions

and cultural tremors that had to be responded to and harmon-
ized. But such responses were always effective. This was as
true, as we will see in subsequent volumes, in Renaissance
Italy as in the contemporary United States and Canada, or as
was true in the hellenistic world.

What has to be remembered is that Judaism as a religious
expression does not impose separation upon the committed Jew.
Concomitant with that it should be realized that the idea that
Judaism must be insulated from its environment is not sustain-
able by historical evidence. Despite the blandishments of being part of a free society, Judaic learning and scholarship,
fructified by interchange with other philosophies, sciences,
religions and literatures, can flourish in a free society.
This is evidenced from just a cursory review of the giant
religio-literary strides made during the hellenistic era, in
Renaissance Europe, and since the French Revolution. New conceptions and great new movements arose in such societies and
most especially since western Europe opened up the possibility
of integration. One should not underestimate the significance
of modern free societies for the preservation of Judaism. Acculturation and preservation went hand in hand. Aspects of
biblical Judaism were the result of acculturation to Canaanite
and Assyrio-Egyptian culture.[6] Aspects of the variety of
Judaisms that prevailed in the post-biblical period were the
outcome of the tension between acculturation in Graeco-Roman
and Zoroastrian societies and the rejection of acculturation.[7]
The religious renaissance in Islamic Spain and Renaissance
Italy and Holland was the natural byproduct of acculturation
as was the transformation and preservation of Judaism in the
nineteenth and twentieth centuries. Certainly there exists
the counter-productive element of defection and conversion to

the majority faith, but Judaism in all its contemporary acculturated varieties from modern-orthodoxy through the spectrum to
classical reform, is infinitely richer because Jewish scholarship became assimilated to modern scientific methodology and
historicism.[8]

Salo W. Baron, author of the monumental, still-unfolding,
A Social and Religious History of the Jews hinted at certain
ambiguities concerning Jewish history reflected in the title
of his work, which highlights "Jews" rather than Judaism. But
I think he captured the central thesis I favor in one of his
remarks. He wrote, "Only that religion can last 'forever'
which, while retaining its 'eternal' elements, is able to
adapt itself to the changing needs and outlooks of man.
Judaism has obviously been such a religion."[9] This adaptation was possible only because of the theological wisdom that
allowed Judaism to be an open-ended religion. Emancipation
from a central sanctuary and from a hierarchical priesthood,
the innovation of a meritocracy for spiritual leadership,
democratization by publication of successive guides to religious practice, localism, contemporary authority, pluralism,
acculturation, the inability or refusal to define "heresy",
are all descriptive of a historical process still functioning.

The historical judgment is made even by competent scholars
that what is called "antisemitism" has made a failure of integration, and proves that "the world" in a sweeping generalization, regards Jews as an unassimilable ethnic group rather than
as bearers of a religious faith.[10] Others think this becomes
a self-defeating proposition containing the implication that
there can be Jews without Judaism. Perhaps even more corrod-
ing is the attitude expressed by astute spiritual leaders that
anti-semitism, aside from the rare instances where it impels
flight from Jewish identity, stimulates a sense of militant

solidarity. This again omits the element of *faith*, emphasizing *fate*.[11] There can be no doubt that the assault upon Jews during the twentieth century has given rise to serious problems and misgivings about the possibility of integration. But given the nature of the Jewish experience as a covenant people and bearers of a theological tradition with revelation and an eschatology as its termini, the problem of anti-semitism must be brought into a theological focus. Perhaps the Hitlerian holocaust should be singled out as a unique phenomenon and earlier Western Christian anti-semitism restudied within a context of Christian-Jewish theological dialogue that rises above the level of public relations. Such biblical ideas as the dual claim of election by Jews and Christians must be reexamined for their implications in the contemporary world for Jew and Christian alike. It will be no comfort to see the Holocaust from the vantage point of the theological doctrine of *hestair panim*, the concealment of God's presence, but that doctrine cannot be overlooked. What is its mysterious role in history in the function of a God of History?[12]

Christianity and Judaism in their various contemporary forms recognize the "Promise and Fulfillment" theology of the Old Testament. They differ on the nature of the "fulfillment" but have hardly begun the task of examining its ramifications. Hence attention should perhaps be shifted from secular anti-Jewishness to theological considerations. Indeed it would be polyannish to aver that anti-Jewish deeds will disappear. But it would be a measure of desperation to insist that preoccupation with the problem has its value in its role as stimulant to Jewish solidarity. Historically, Jewish solidarity even under the worst of conditions during the fourteenth and fifteenth centuries or in Czarist Russia in the nineteenth, was a communality born of religious fervor and commitment. Joy in

the commemoration of the Passover, the redemptive resurrection
of a despoiled people brought to Sinai where was experienced
the intrusion of God through the Holy Spirit in revelation,
gave the community its staying power and preserved its sanity.
There was a solidarity of theological commitment. A desideratum of the future, may therefore be the reconsideration of the
past, for instance, of the role of the celebration of creation
and continuous re-creation on the Sabbath in the preservation
of Judaism. As will be seen in later chapters, these doctrines
of Creation, Revelation and Redemption are the underpinnings of
all Jewish liturgy and holy day observance.

Abraham Joshua Heschel has observed,

> ...the unique importance of the survival of the
> people is in its being a partner to a covenant
> with God....To be a Jew is...to bear witness to
> His presence in the hours of His concealment...[13]

The question of survival, so intimately bound up with the
problem of the presence or absence of Providence is also closely interlocked with the historical claim of Judaism to a covenantal relationship with God.

As the forthcoming chapters will show, these corelated
issues were high on the agenda of Judaism's response to its environment. Basing themselves upon a doctrinal observation made
by Ezekiel (39:23), "...The House of Israel was exiled for
their sin....I had to avert my Presence from them because they
had rebelled...", for almost two thousand years devout Jews
affirmed the Covenant on every festival during the *Musaph* worship and yet acknowledged "for our sins were we exiled from
our land", applying Ezekiel's words concerning 587 B.C. to 70
A.D. Thereby they implied resignation to the reality of that
concealment to which Ezekiel made reference.[14] Oppression did

not destroy them. Suffering did not undermine their faith or their will. And yet, it was not the *fact* of persecution that gave Jews solidarity, but *despite* the persecution they bore witness. It is not overstepping the bounds of objective intellectual treatment of the subject to suggest that consideration of these historical facts might be the leading need of contemporary Judaic studies.

In the unfolding of the history of Judaism we see the inner strength that enabled it to surmount the moments of concealment of the divine presence because it had faith in the ultimate historicity of the divine promise. In this volume we will be examining the hostile confrontation of Judaism and Christianity during several very difficult centuries between 1100 and 1600. In a forthcoming volume we will ponder the opportunity granted Judaism by the secular powers to flourish after 1800 without regard to whether Christianity conceded its theology to be valid. There we will have occasion to evaluate how Protestant sensitivity to modern currents and Catholic introspection at Vatican II under the inspiration of Pope John XXIII, have opened new vistas for theological discourse concerning the two covenants. This will afford a glimpse at the possible divine role intended for the two plants in all their mutual varieties that grew from the first century religious seeds scattered by the Old Testament and the Apocrypha, challenged and fructified by Hellenism and Mithraism. And finally we will have to examine the new confrontation between Judaism and Islam in the modern garb of nationalist aspiration and consider whether theological discourse might tread where only diplomats and generals camp out in order to bring closer the messianic day.[15]

Running through all of these experiences in the history of the varieties of Judaism is the thread of adaptation, accul-

turation and preservation. The remarkable mystery one finds
in this account of a faith and its bearers is its continuous
luxuriant growth. New ideas were absorbed, new observances
created, old doctrines eschewed, obsolete practices abrogated
or allowed to die. The orchard was consistently pruned and re-
seeded. Our study in this volume opens with a new era. An old
era had passed. The great new literary collection, the Talmud,
had been completed. Judaism had entered a new phase. Its
scholars and spiritual leaders had probably only recently succeeded in preventing any further defection to Christian Judaism and was stemming any further trickle of Jews into remnants
of other ancient sects such as Sadducaism. Karaism had not
yet emerged. The academies in Babylonia were the respected
institutions supported by Jews of other diaspora centers as
well as by Jews of Palestine, as once the Jerusalem Temple had
been supported.[16] As the curtain rises on a new act the center
of interest is in Babylonia.

CHAPTER 2

The Geonim: Halakhic Implications

I. THE SETTING

As a result of the activity of men, each of whom bore the title Gaon, "Excellency", the major primary source for religious authority in Judaism over the next fifteen hundred years was destined to be the Babylonian Talmud.[1] This was a virtual encyclopedia of Judaism, consisting of commentary upon the Mishnah, an earlier compilation or digest of the halakha, the recommended norms of religious conduct expected by the adherents of Judaism. The compilation of the Talmud had been started by Rabbi Ashi (352-427) and was completed by Ravina bar Huna (488-499) at the historic school of Sura on the Euphrates.[2]

The Talmud contains theology, esoteric philosophy, science, mysticism, folklore, medicine, mathematics and astronomy, in addition to the halakhic material governing the religious conduct of the Jew in matters both ethical and ritualistic. Because of this comprehensive nature of its content it became the major textbook of Judaic religious study. Knowledge of the Talmud, competence in using it, has since been the hallmark of one's scholarly rating in Judaism. The scholars who fashioned it are known as Amoraim. Their successors are called Saboraim.

The Saboraim were not a different breed from those who came before or those who came after. All were rabbinic scholars serving more or less the same functions. The different titles should not imply a radical break in continuity. The Saboraim, too, left their mark on the talmudic literature. Primarily, the Saboraim were the "redactors", editors and systematizers of the Talmud during the sixth and early seventh centuries. Although they were not directly involved in the masoretic work, the arrangement of a correct biblical text with its vocalization and correct readings, this work was contemporary. Much of it was accomplished at Nisibis where a Bible-conscious Christian community was engaged in similar work.[3]

The vicissitudes of the Jewish community of Babylonia were closely related to the events that transpired between the Byzantine Empire and Persia, a matter not germane to this volume. Jewish religious development and thought was affected afresh by the new marching hosts of Arabs who began to beat at the gates of Jewish Babylonia in 632. When, under the flag of Islam, the hosts of Arabia moved on the Euphrates and the old city of Bagdad, there were two great historic centers of Jewish learning, one in Sura, the other in Pumbedita. There was fostered talmudic learning, and from there went forth responses (responsa) to inquiries from Jewish communities all over the then-inhabited world from India to the Atlantic Ocean, across North Africa and in Northern Europe alike.

The "responsa" literature becomes a textbook in geography. The replies sent by the geonim in Babylonia to questions of religious history and practice addressed to them, went to the far corners of the Mediterranean world and beyond. It has often been a puzzle why so few responsa went to Palestine, but it is now more clearly perceived that there were two reasons. One was that Palestine had its Gaon. The other was the struggle for authority between the two centers, especially for authority over the Jews of Egypt, which would have tended to reduce harmonious intellectual interrelationships.

As one looks westward, one finds the geonim in communication with Jewish communities in Egypt, Tunis, Algiers and Morocco, the latter three called in the literature of the day Ifrikiya and Maghreb. The greatest of those centers were Kairuwan in Tunisia and Fez in Morocco. Moving further westward, we arrive at the juncture of Europe and Africa where Spain meets the southern continent. On the Spanish peninsula were many flourishing Jewish communities and the religious viewpoints of Babylonian geonim extended over those thousands of miles from Iraq not only to relatively nearby Italy, but to Andalusia, Aragon, Castille in Spain, and Provence in southern France.

The wide diffusion of geonic responsa explains the relative homogeneity of Judaism amidst a definite evidence of diversity. Geography made for variation. But intellectual and religious persistence and productivity of the geonim contributed to the basic unification of worldwide Judaism if not its precise uniformity. On the other hand the ultimate growth of new centers made for their independence. Yet with their autonomy they inevitably built upon Babylonian foundations. Thus by the tenth century, Egypt had a great scholar, Shemarya b. Elhanan, who was hailed as "a sea of wisdom" as far away as Kairuwan and Spain. No wonder then that the Eyptian center began to form its own traditions. The same was true for Spain which we will see more comprehensively in another chapter. Nevertheless there remained a common core of observance and in the next chapter we will see how both similarity and diversity expressed themselves in worship.[4]

II. THE GEONIM

Islam was born in 622 when Mohammed fled from Mecca to Medina. He launched his concept of the *jihad*, "the holy war", which continued after his death in 632. From his small beginnings in West Arabia, his successors conquered Egypt and Palestine, Syria and Iran. All of Mesopotamia fell to Islam, bringing under its flag all the major centers of Jewish learning. When Islam assumed control of Babylonia, the authorities continued to recognize the ancient Jewish institutions and the religious hegemony of the presiding scholars of Sura and Pumbedita. These now bore the title *Gaon*. Whether this title was already in use or came into use in Islamic days is a controversy among historians that will not detain us. Judaism flourished and gained a new richness. It was before 750 that a new Jewish community was organized in Fustat, a suburb of Cairo, Egypt. This was destined to become the ultimate base of Moses Maimonides during the twelfth century and its old synagogue attic was to yield up the precious trove we call the Genizah, a mass of documents without which our knowledge of much of medieval Jewish life, literature and religious thought would be infinitely poorer.[5]

Above all, this Genizah yielded vast new information concerning the responsa, liturgy, collections of halakha and commentaries of the geonim who presided over the academies from 600 to 1100 in addition to an immense amount of raw material from which to gain a new understanding of the internal and international history of Mediterranean Jews and Judaism virtually from India to Spain.

At Sura there flourished a whole galaxy of scholars. We will pause to take notice of only the major contributions to Judaism made by several Suran luminaries. At Sura originated

almost all of the important Jewish religious literature of the
period although its sister community, Pumbedita, was also quite
prolific in responsa. But we will pause to consider, in addition to some of the ramifications and implications of the responsa literature, only two of these major literary remains,
the *Halakhot Gedolot* and the *Seder R. Amram*. The first is a
comprehensive collection of religious practice, the other a
full description of the order of Jewish worship year-round,
and the halakha related to it. Both have influenced every
area of Jewish religious observance and synagogue liturgy as
well as private devotions to this day.

Babylonian religious treatises are the only ones we select
from this period. This too reflects a historical reality. Although we know from the Genizah documents that those who presided over Palestinian Academies which were re-opened under
Islam were also called geonim, they made a far smaller impact
upon Judaism. Literary and spiritual life indeed, continued in
Palestine after the completion of the Palestinian Talmud in the
fourth century, and even after the decimation of Jewish population during Byzantine and Persian wars, into the seventh century. Liturgical composition had a revival during the seventh
and eighth centuries. There is some murkiness about the production of midrash literature there during the seventh to ninth
centuries. But most certainly it is fair to say that whatever
occurred there it in no way, even remotely, approximated the
productivity and the influence of Babylonian Judaism.[6] It is
no longer correct to aver as historians generally have for centuries that pre-Crusader Palestine, from about the fourth century to the twelfth century, or perhaps on to the flowering of
Safed in the sixteenth century, was totally a vacuum in Judaism.
But the sparse findings of the Genizah should not give rise to

exaggeration. It does appear that Palestinian authorities retained an ancient prerogative of fixing the calendar as late as
835, but that hardly attests to a high level of scholarly and
spiritual influence, anymore than does the technical textual
work of the Masorites who flourished during the ninth and tenth
centuries. Possibly the Karaites, of whom we will speak later,
were in the ascendancy in Jerusalem during the ninth century.[7]

Actually during the tenth century, the Palestinian gaonate, as far as we can ascertain, may have been quite arid. Responsa are sparse, testifying to the fact that diaspora communities did not have a favorable impression of the scholarship
there. Some contact was continued with Italy and there appears
evidence that the growing Rhinehand center was in communication
with Palestine around 960. In sum, after his examination of a
mass of literary remains from the Genizah one of the major
scholars of this find concluded that:

> We have reviewed about a century and a half of
> the history of the Palestinian gaonate (about
> 875-1025). So far no literary work of standing,
> produced by the school in the Holy Land, has
> been preserved. The number of responsa is also
> remarkably small....And by the paucity of their
> responsa, as compared with those of the Babylon-
> ian geonim, it is evident that the communities
> in the Diaspora did not fail to notice this
> difference in quality.[8]

That explains succinctly why the Judaism that has come
down to the present in all its manifold forms is Babylonian and
geonic, and the liturgy of the contemporary synagogue is in
general accordance with the Babylonian rite although geographic
variants arose even after the Babylonian rite was diffused.
The Babylonians had a disproportionate number of high-quality
scholars who devoted their careers to the exposition of the

Talmud, the extraction from it of norms for guidance of the
faithful in daily life, and the compilation of these norms
into accessible digests for reference.[9]

III. HALAKHOT GEDOLOT

Possibly the first Babylonian geonic author was R. Yehudai
b. Nahman, Gaon of Sura 757-761 (also given as 760-764). There
has been a high degree of controversy whether he indeed, or a
certain Simon Kayyara, wrote *Halakhot Gedolot*. The technical
discussion conducted by scholars on whether the extant *Halakhot
Gedolot*, a compendium or digest of halakha attributed to him is
indeed the work he wrote or a composite of his work and halakhic remnants of other scholars, will not detain us here.[10] The
work is significant as the earliest compilation of recommended
halakha which we have in our possession in relatively complete
form since the Mishnah was published at the end of the second
century.

A. *Implications*

To a great extent the appearance of this work as the recommended format of Jewish religious practice marked a reasser-
tion of Babylonian claim to hegemony in Judaism and for the
higher authority of the Babylonian Talmud. The geonim reinforced their claim to religious authority independent of Palestine by recalling the historical reality, that Babylonian
Judaism had a continuity as hallowed and as authentic as that
of Palestine. They argued that Babylonian Judaism was the
natural evolution of the Religion of Israel as brought into
the Babylonian exile in 597 and 587 B.C. Geonim argued that

Palestine was constantly in the throes of political anarchy, Jews were alternately dominated by Persians and Romans and their learning was in a bad state. With this they sustained their claim not only for independent local authority in Sura and Pumbedita but for authority over Palestine.[11] This two-track diversity, however, of a separate Babylonian and Palestinian tradition on the one hand, and varying traditions within Babylonia, was the natural historic consequence of post-biblical developments in Judaism wherein a monolithic faith, tradition or practice never took root.

To determine the correct religious practice was not an easy matter. The authoritative source-literature was the Talmud. This was a large, rambling work and it was a near impossible task for one to extract from its pages a quick or explicit decision in matters of complexity, emergency or doubt. Furthermore, the sixth or seventh centuries witnessed some decades of great ferment in the life around them and within the Jewish communities. A wide variety of historical forces were at work similar to those that prompted publication of the Mishnah centuries earlier. These included the clash of empires and socio-political and economic hardships. Among these forces also was the reemergence of sectarians with Sadducean and Christian Jewish background.

While the historical forces may have stimulated R. Yehudai to his literary activity, the nature of the Talmud and the psychological need of his students and his constituency probably influenced the style he chose in which to write his work, or whoever was the author. Like the Mishnah before it, and like every digest of halakha that followed it, the *Halakhot Gedolot* was not designed to be a "code of law" but a manual for easy reference, an aid to the student of the vast talmudic material. It was a historical error to define any of these

compendia as "codes" with all the juristic implications of
definitiveness, legalism and compulsion bound up with that
term.[12]

This compendium was edited for a number of reasons. We
do not by any means have the space to enter into a full discussion of each. A significant factor, however, that may have
motivated the author, was the Karaite schism. We will discuss this at greater length in the next chapter. The Karaite
schism was the greatest internal struggle within Judaism since
the first century. The evolution of events during the emergence of Christianity led to the canonization of the Bible and
the publication of the Mishnah to draw firm lines between
"valid" Judaism and "schismaticism" or *minim*. Similarly it is
highly probable that R. Yehudai or Simon Kayyara published the
Halakhot Gedolot for similar reasons. The author's projected
aim was probably the establishment of an "authoritative"
regimen of practice and the consequent delineation of Karaism
as being "heretical". He endeavored to give the student and
scholar as well as lay-people a picture of the academically
preferred halakha and to clarify the differences between
geonic-talmudic or "rabbinic" Judaism and Karaism.

Assuming for our purposes, in order to refer to a specific
author for convenience, that it was R. Yehudai, we may surmise
that he succeeded in a way he had not clearly intended. He
did not stem the emergence and growth of Karaism. But he set
some interesting precedents for halakhic writing which had been
taken up from time to time by a wide diversity of scholars and
are espoused even today in those quarters where the revision of
traditionalism is carried forward. Among the innovations in
his style and format that have had far-reaching consequences
were:

a. He omitted all agadah (folkloristic material, homilies, etc.) from his compilation. By so doing, he indirectly furthered the weaker status of agadah in the hierarchy of Jewish religious values. Doctrines, concepts and motifs that find their basic expression in the agadah have not received the priority of dogma in Judaism. It may not be correct to say "one can take them or leave them", for that would be an oversimplification. Yet it is undoubtedly fair to argue that what does not have firm root in the halakha has a far weaker claim on Jewish credulity and commitment. This is not to say that agadah is not vital to Judaism, nor to deny the significance of faith and the confession of belief in what would be agadic statements.[13] But there are ambiguities in the field of theological doctrine (agadah) that are not present in behavioral theology (halakha) demanding a person's commitment to the miraculous and mysterious. By omitting this aspect from his compendium, R. Yehudai not only set a precedent for future labors in the vineyard of halakha, but also released his readers from the onerous task of believing or affirming the incredible. Salvation was by conduct. The question then was: what am I to do?

b. He omitted all the halakha not applicable in his own time. This set a precedent for recognition, even if only implicitly, that aspects of Jewish religious conduct can become obsolete. Examples of the type of material he did not include are the sacrificial cult and the agricultural regulations of Torah and Mishnah that applied to the times when the Temple stood in Jerusalem and Jews resided in Palestine as a sovereign or semi-sovereign people, that is, until 70 A.D. Future halakhic compilers could feel free to omit other segments of halakha which no longer remained viable or to radically change civil law where it was in force in autonomous Jewish communities throughout the middle ages, especially after the French Revolution and the emancipation of Western European Jews.[14]

c. He omitted all the talmudic discussion that led up to decision-making, retaining only the basic halakhic extract. This set a stylistic precedent which served future scholars well. It gave men of initiative and independent learning the courage to extract such bare statements of halakha, by their preferred choice of terminology or opinions, undeniably influencing the future of religious practice.

This work of R. Yehudai had other significant historical implications:

a. He was, in effect, asserting the right to emphasize relevancy by selectivity in halakha.

b. He was practicing what has become a major force for the preservation of Judaism: the updating of previous religious material in an implicit disregard of the tension between divine revelation and human authority.[15]

c. He was furthering the notion of the primacy of contemporary authority in Jewish religious life. This was the accepted doctrine of centuries, that it is to the scholars of each era that one turns for religious validation of practices and norms.[16]

These historical implications of the style of *Halakhot Gedolot* had already been forshadowed in the Mishnah, published around 200. But after many centuries the mystical power of a religious corpus over a people has a tendency to cause forgetfulness of such verities. And so by 750 it was once again a virtual "cultural revolution" which was effected by R. Yehudai. We have no evidence that he was aware of this or claimed it, but it is clear that others saw it in this light from the opposition that arose. The reasons for this opposition characterized by that of R. Paltoi, Gaon of Pumbedita (842-858) were precisely the innovations we have just recounted:

    a. The omissions.

    b. The serious implications of a quick eighth-century response to a question of religious practice unsustained by lengthy and convincing argument based upon prior historic authority.

    c. Like every written text it suffered from an ambivalent advantage. It provided new audiences with an opportunity to peruse the tradition. But like the Torah before it, and then the Mishnah and finally the Talmud, it opened a route to religious independence, to individual exegesis, interpretation and halakhic judgment.

    d. The possibility it would supersede the Talmud.[17]

Books democratize. The revolutionary impact of the invention of printing, like that of the wheel, is well known in cultural history. But even before the invention of the printing press, though to a lesser degree and within more circumscribed geographic limits, the written word inspired religious reinterpretation and innovation. It is true that medieval scholars placed a heavy premium upon *Halakhot Gedolot*. R. Asher of Toledo, of whom we will hear more at a later juncture, wrote that all of it was "words of tradition, upon which one may rely". Nevertheless, they did not always accept its conclusions.[18]

B. *Ambiguities*

In retrospect it can be seen that the work of R. Yehudai is a microcosm of what we spoke of in the first chapter. Here was an attempt to adapt Judaism through creative intellectual activity several centuries after the extant traditions had been formulated. R. Yehudai acted as an individual and his writ of authority ran only as far as the secular power of Islam supported it, within the environs of Sura and its suburbs and as farther afield as Jews voluntarily accepted his views. After all is said, he failed to stem the tide of rising Karaism by espousing an "orthodoxy". Within a century Karaites were branded as "apostates", as we will see in the next chapter. But even then it is a moot point whether the geonim were as successful in cutting loose the Karaites from the tree of Judaism as Judean leaders had been in driving out the Samaritans in post-Biblical times, or as the rabbis were in expelling the Christians during the turn of the first and second centuries.[19]

Herein was part of the ambiguity of the geonic age. Their very sociological reality, the existence of two autonomous centers with each Gaon having equal power sustained by the secular arm of the Islamic state, made for a valid diversity in Judaism. Yet they hoped to establish, each his own view, as the wave of the future. Their use of the talmudic source material as fundamentally authoritative, yet revisable, made for the assertion of contemporary authority. Yet through the issuance of halakhic digests they hoped to curb multiplicity. Their manipulative use of the ban, as will be seen very soon, made for both reactionary imposition of their power as well as the improvement of the rights of the underprivileged. And finally, perhaps the largest ambiguity, is seen in the role of secular power within a pluralistic and voluntaristic religious community. The individual Jew enjoyed his "freedom of religion" within the Jewish community only when and where secular power did not uphold the authority of the rabbi. This became evident during the age of the geonim. Where secular power sustained the halakhic and communal decisions of Gaon or Exil-

arch or lay-council, the individual was not only circumscribed
in the normal affairs of life: civil and criminal law, the
laws of marriage and divorce or inheritance, which require
systematic enforcement for the sake of a rational social structure and civility, but also in matters of ritual which ought to
be a domain preserved for the private relationship between a
person and his God.

Consequently, Judaism has always been restless under circumstances where secular power sustained rabbinic authority and
has sought societies like sixteenth century Holland, Puritan
England, and the New World. And even during the geonic period,
Jews migrated far northward and eastward to escape geonic authority, as we will see. For Jews this effort to establish an
"orthodoxy" was a geonic enterprise modeled after both the
Christian and Islamic religions which had but recently succeeded in the same efforts but was basically un-talmudic. The
geonim sought to disseminate sufficient information to establish uniform practice. And there can be no doubt that this
was in the mind of R. Yehudai, not only in his far-flung correspondence for example with the community of Kairuwan, but
when he wrote *Halakhot Gedolot*.[20]

We have a contemporary example of this accepted diversity
within Judaism during the lifetime of R. Yehudai himself. In
the Fustat community in Egypt there settled Babylonian emigrants as well as emigrants from Palestine. Each group formed
its own synagogue in much the same way as immigrants to the
United States during the nineteenth and twentieth centuries
established synagogues based upon geographic origin and there
perpetuated the customs of the lands from which they came.
Similarly, in eighth-century Fustat, the Babylonians preserved
Babylonian customs and Palestinians preserved their own forms.
And there was a third group, natives, the Al-Cairaha, those of

Cairo and environs who followed yet a third form of religious observance not to speak of Karaites. This was later to be seen in the distinctive differences that arose between the liturgies of Egypt and Babylonia.[21]

Just as the responsa literature provides these insights for us into a positive aspect of Jewish religious development, so too we learn from the responsa literature that the religious trend was reactionary in many respects. Although the earlier rabbinic trends were lenient between the second century B.C. into the period of the Talmud, even after 200 A.D., we find this not to be the case during the geonic period.[22]

From the ninth century, if not earlier, the "ban" was used extensively in order to secure obedience to geonic authority. Under this system the victim was ostracized, sometimes only for thirty days. But if the authorities thought he ought to continue under the ban, a *herem* or .complete excommunication would be issued and then the victim was not only socially ostracized but sacramentally separated from the Jewish community. In that event nobody was to participate in enabling him to discharge his religious obligations, not to circumcize his son, teach his children or even assist in the burial of his dead.[23] On the one hand, the same weapon was used to enforce honest monetary dealings, preserve order in the Jewish community, prevent false testimony in court and protect the interests of women and orphans who had few civil rights.[24] And on the other hand, excessively harsh treatment was meted out in the area of religious and moral supervision in the ongoing battle against Karaism. For minor infractions, against rabbinic regulations, people were severely punished as possible "heretics", Karaites, who opposed rabbinic halakha. One of the most surprising discoveries of the responsa literature might be the information provided by R. Sherira, Gaon at Pumbedita during a good part of the tenth century (968-998), that he and his predecessors used secret police to spy upon citizens to be sure they were meticulously observant of the Passover injunctions against leaven.[25]   R. Natronai, Gaon at Sura (853-856), denounced anyone who merely abbreviated his recital of the Passover Hagadah, the liturgical manual used at the Passover Seder. He regarded this as evidence that the person is a Karaite. R. Natronai was especially harsh toward them, calling them *min*, a term loosely meaning "sectarian" or worse, "schismatic", and applied during earlier centuries to Christians, and pronounced them as unsuitable to be allowed to worship in the synagogues and to be wholly divorced from the community of Judaism.[26]

Even before R. Natronai, Ben Baboi attempted to deny the right of Palestinians to perpetuate their customs and practiced what Salo Baron has called a "pan-Babylonian" program seeking to establish Babylonian hegemony and uniformity over all Jewish communities. In his treatise we have a wide variety of Babylonian liturgical and other ritual practices that Ben Baboi sought to impose upon the Palestinians who defended themselves with the talmudic argument that *minhag*, a newly-arisen custom, nullifies a previously established halakha.[27]   But Ben Baboi was only continuing the work of R. Yehudai who already attacked Palestinians as guilty of religious behavioralism "contrary to halakha" during the first half of the eight century. This was a far cry from the day when a Babylonian rabbi, Rabbah (d. 339), impressed a halakha upon his household by invoking a responsum from "the west", that is, Palestine. But as Louis Ginzberg has pointed out, and is so important for our understanding of the multiplicity of traditions:

> ...what R. Yehudai and Ben Baboi called 'not in accordance with halakha', meant not in accordance

> with the halakha of the Babylonian Talmud, but
> fully correct in the light of the Palestinian
> Talmud.[28]

This then was one of the great ambiguities of geonic history. R. Yehudai sought to establish the hegemony and uniformity of the Babylonian Talmud *as interpreted and transmitted
by Babylonian geonim* in Palestine and other lands of the diaspora. But while they succeeded in making the Babylonian Talmud
the primary source for religious reference and research, they
did not succeed in enforcing uniformity of practice. The text
gained hegemony because of the Islamic cultural realities.
Babylonia was the center of Arabic culture during those centuries and consequently became the center of Jewish culture.
Students came from Spain, Provence, Italy, and other European
and African lands to study in Babylonia and naturally garnered
Babylonian rite and doctrine, but even more so, the text of
the Babylonian Talmud.[29]

The responsa literature, furthermore, bears out that from
the 9th century onward, the geonim of both Sura and Pumbedita
were in frequent communication with Spain despite the fact
that it took a year for a letter to travel the distance. R.
Paltoi sent a whole copy of the Talmud to Spain along with a
commentary. When one considers this in conjunction with the
Seder Rav Amram, the responsum containing the liturgy and the
halakha of prayer sent by Gaon Amram ben Sheshna to Barcelona,
during his gaonate (857-875), it is not difficult to ascertain
how strong was the influence of the entire range of Babylonian
Judaism upon the Jews of Spain. And nevertheless, once again
local autonomy, contemporary authority and scholarly independence asserted itself when Cordova emerged as a great center
of learning during the tenth century under the leadership of
a R. Moses and his son R. Enoch.[30]

We will conclude this segment of our discussion with the
observation that although we have relatively little evidence
of the aggressive thrust of R. Yehudai to bring all of Judaism
under Babylonian hegemony, there can be little doubt that his
reputation had imposed itself upon his and succeeding generations. This is certainly borne out by the 9th century Ben
Baboi who wrote of him:

> 'Mar Rav Yehudai had no equal for many years,
> till this day [a century later]. He was great
> in Scripture, Mishnah, Talmud, Midrash, Toseph-
> ta, in both Agada and practical halakha and
> never said anything he had not heard from a
> teacher. He was great in holiness, purity,
> piety and modesty and was meticulous about all
> the mitzvot, devoting himself to Heaven. He
> brought people close to Torah and Mitzvot, and
> left no successor the equal of himself.'[31]

In the light of this strict conservatism attributed to
R. Yehudai, it becomes ironic that he may be seen to be an
initiator of much innovation and a source for modernist revisionism. Yet there is no other way to evaluate the ultimate
impact of the implications of his work than as early precedent
for the nineteenth century. Furthermore, it would not be
accurate, despite Ben Baboi, to characterize him as so rigidly
conservative. For example, he abolished the halakhic practice
of making possible absolution of vows which were under attack
by the Karaites. And to improve the chances of having his innovation become effective he abolished the study of the tractate of the Talmud, *Nedarim*, "vows".[32]

Another interesting departure in halakha by R. Yehudai is
his prohibition on fasting on Rosh Hashanah. Fasting on Sabbath and festivals had been proscribed for many a century, but
there was no specific prohibition to fast on Rosh Hashanah.

Rosh Hashanah is a solemn holy day, inaugurating "the days of awe", the "ten days of repentance" which are climaxed with Yom Kippur, the day of atonement. It stands to reason that since Yom Kippur is a twenty-four hour fast-day, many people thought that fasting at the beginning, like fasting at the end of the period, is piously meritorious. As a matter of fact, many felt people ought to fast during daytime on all ten days. R. Yehudai, however, sought to extend the nature of the joy of the pilgrim festivals to Rosh Hashanah and thereby minimize dourness and asceticism in the observance of holy days. He based his argument for prohibition on Psalm 81:4, "Sound the horn on the new moon of our festival." His argument is questionable because firstly, this verse is unrelated to Rosh Hashanah. Secondly, when scriptural warrant is sought, halakha is not normally based upon a verse in Writings or Prophets, but upon the Pentateuch. We see, therefore, that other strain operating in R. Yehudai, countering the impression he was burdened with a conservative fixation. Indeed, R. Yehudai displays that same propensity for independent judgment and innovation that was the hallmark of all great halakhists in Judaism.[33] Modernists were later able to argue that customs imposed by historic accidents need not be preserved, that institutions like absolution that begin to defeat their original purpose and become counterproductive to true religion may be abolished, that new directions may be forged by updating the corpus of practice, that one must make peace with historic obsolescence, that despite a quest for unity and similarity, diversity is valid. We will now examine the question of liturgy and synagogue worship in Judaism in the light of these suggestions.

CHAPTER 3

The Geonim: Worship and Theology

I. THE BACKGROUND

There was great liturgical diversity as our period opens. Samaritans, Karaites and other groups had their own liturgies. Probably this diversity would have expanded had not some geonim believed it to be important to man the ramparts against the assortment of sectarians. The Gaon Amram ben Sheshna reflected this growing resistance when, despite his usual leniency in other matters, he became a rigorist in liturgy. He generalized: "We must not deviate..." from the wording of the prayers recorded in the Talmud, and that where a prayer-reader does deviate, "we depose him".[1]

The fifth to the eighth centuries, as the historian Salo Baron has suggested, probably witnessed the liturgical diversity expanded to an irreversible degree. For one thing, there was a Palestinian ritual of which we still know very little. The prayer rites we are familiar with were built by the geonim out of the Babylonian Talmud and its Palestinian mishnaic antecedents. But since the fifth century, Palestinian ritual also grew and changed. The geonim valiantly, but vainly, sought to create at least a semblance of homogeneity, if not uniformity in worship. But the task was formidable. Not only was content, in terms of which prayers were to constitute the liturgy a problem. Even such significant segments of the liturgy as *ábinu malkenu*, "Our Father, Our King" of the Rosh Hashanah

ritual, and Yom Kippur's *Al Het* confessional, were radically
different in the English version from that of the French version, which in turn were different from the versions current
in other countries. Then, too, language was a problem. From
time immemorial prayer was permitted in vernacular even in
ancient Palestine. During the geonic centuries prayer in
Aramaic increased, and when Arabic became widely spoken it was
natural for Jews to want to worship in that language. But
there were also voices to the contrary who opposed prayer in
any language other than Hebrew, and although Aramaic had long
since become acceptable, they now opposed Arabic. This ambivalence has remained part of the prayer picture in Judaism
and became a fiery issue during the nineteenth century. The
classical sources seem to divide themselves into two, however.
The permissive seems to be halakhic, and therefore a more
valid criterion for how to act. The arguments against vernacular seem to be agadic, of the homiletical and folkloristic
variety on the cosmic importance of the Hebrew language or
whether the angels understand any other language. In later
literature, Maimonides probably summed up a substantial body
of halakhic opinion, however, when he argued that not only
were all of the liturgical formulae permitted in vernacular,
but even if the wording was slightly altered from the traditional text, it was acceptable as long as the worshipper
basically followed the rabbinic format acknowledging the Name
of God and his sovereignty.[2] The Tannaites permitted major
portions of the liturgy in any language. The talmudic teachers
maintained that position. The geonim resisted, but as late as
the tenth century, Gaon Sherira still bolstered the case for
vernacular. It was never prohibited. It is instructive to
go beyond the geonic period and see whether the right to
prayer in the vernacular was ever abrogated. The three major

halakhists of the middle ages upon whose massive tomes was based the whole of medieval and modern practice, R. Isaac of Fez, Moses Maimonides, and R. Asher b. Yehiel of Toledo, all reaffirmed the right to pray in the vernacular. During the thirteenth century, R. Asher interestingly informs us, "... the *whole world* follows the custom of women praying in the vernacular..." and since they are as obligated to prayer as men, it is obvious that prayer in vernacular is permitted, "and the individual may recite it in a language other than Hebrew". Ultimately this unanimous viewpoint found its way into what became the decisive authority for what was termed "orthodoxy" in the nineteenth century, R. Joseph Karo's *Shulḥan Arukh*, of which more in a later chapter. Over the centuries halakhic commentators in Spain, France, Germany and Italy were all independently or by mutual agreement, sustaining the concept of vernacular prayer.[3] That it became a matter of acrimonious controversy during the nineteenth century, like so much supposedly "theological" contention, was not inherently theologically necessary, being rather a practical struggle for religious power clothed in theological verbiage. The sources of Judaism required neither Hebrew nor vernacular, both being equally valid. As in so many other aspects of Judaism, this was a combination of flexibility and tradition, a measure of diversity mingled with the quest for homogeneity.

It is not possible here to provide a comprehensive discussion of the growth of the liturgy through the geonic early middle ages, and the struggle that ensued over what may or may not be incorporated into the newly emerging order of worship. Poets frequently composed lengthy new rhymed or unrhymed poems which they attached to different segments of the liturgy.

Among the leading earlier composers of such new elements that set a precedent for expanding rabbinic liturgy were Yose b. Yose, Yannai and Kalir, men whose lives are shrouded in the mists of the fifth, sixth and seventh centuries. But as this genre of literature multiplied, some geonim began to oppose its inclusion in worship. The opposition was relatively universal, culminating in Maimonides and then his son who claimed he "eradicated this error from Egypt". Regardless, the *piyutim*, as they were called, were included in prayerbooks, were even composed by the influential Saadiah of whom we will speak later, found their way into the Ashkenazi prayerbooks as well, and are still in vogue today.[4] With this survey of the background we may turn to the development of worship and then to its theology.

II. BRIEF HISTORY OF WORSHIP[5]

Despite the antiquity of the form of the prayers and the vast number of prayers and blessings, hymns and psalms that were accumulating, there was no prayerbook in Judaism before the ninth century.

Natronai, Gaon of Sura (853-856) probably made one of the major contributions to geonic literature and second in importance to the *Halakhot Gedolot* (previous chapter) when he compiled the blessings used by Jews for all occasions.[6] It is quite possible he did so in order to provide an accessible "official" liturgical manual in order that rabbanite Jews know the distinction between what is valid and what is Karaite "heresy". In his *Seder*, the Gaon Amram (857-874) quoted R. Natronai who, in a denunciation of "These men who modify

the Passover liturgy" called them "heretics and scoffers, and
who are disciples of Anan...."[7] As we will see in our next
chapter, Anan was a founder of the Karaite schism.

R. Natronai had arranged one-hundred *berakhot* (thank-you
offerings, praise to God for a benefit conferred or a great
event experienced), based upon a talmudic allusion to the need
for the faithful to recite such a quantity daily.[8] Along with
this framework he provided simultaneously a basic sketch of
the liturgy of three daily worship periods, morning (*shaḥrit*),
afternoon (*minḥah*) and evening (*màriv*). Assuming what he
listed was the bare outline, the worship format nevertheless
already resembled the synagogue liturgy still in vogue today.[9]

Nevertheless, R. Natronai's responsum was fragmentary.
The first complete *Sidur*, "order of worship", was that of the
Gaon Amram, which he also issued as a responsum to the Jews
of Spain. In it he outlined the entire order of year-round
worship in Judaism. This, the first known manuscript of a
prayerbook in Judaism then became the basis of almost all
future rituals. Additions and omissions were made relevant
to time and place. New compositions were included. Of lesser
significance were the variations that crept into the texts as
manuscripts were copied and endlessly recopied for wide diffusion across North Africa and Europe, and later America. During the middle ages even England had its own prayer rite. The
prayerbook mirrored the trials and hopes of a widespread faith,
and in some cases, it also mirrored varying emphases in theology.[10]

R. Amram's prayerbook, however, was not only a liturgical
text. It also contained a continuous description of the halakhot of worship. This was the format also followed by the Gaon
Saadiah in the tenth century. But perhaps the one next most

important in the development of Jewish liturgy to that of Amram's was the *Maḥzor Vitry*, compiled by R. Simḥah b. Samuel,
eleventh century. Saadiah's actually fell into oblivion after
it was extensively quoted by R. David Avudraham in his master-
piece commentary during the fourteenth century.[11] The liturgies of both Amram and Saadiah ultimately became the basis of
Sephardic worship. *Maḥzor Vitry* became the parent of Ashkenazi
worship, its author having to commend him that he was a disciple of Rashi (R. Solomon b. Isaac of Troyes, France) of whom
we will speak in a later chapter. R. Simḥah lived in Vitry,
France, his prayerbook taking the name of its place of origin.
It became the official liturgy of the Ashkenazi communities
during the thirteenth century. It too contained the full text
of the prayers and a running halakhic commentary. In design
it served the purpose of a full-blown manual of reference for
all of Jewish religious life, containing the halakha of the
festivals along with their respective liturgies, and other aspects of Jewish ritual and ethical conduct. His was the first
prayerbook to contain the Mishnah treatise, *Aḅot*, read during
the six weeks from the end of Passover to Shaḅuot on Saturday
afternoons, and a current version of the Passover Hagadah, the
manual for the Passover Seder.

This, although basically it remains the liturgy of the
orthodox synagogue in the twentieth century, did not by any
means mark the end of *Sidur* compilation. The first prayerbook
of the Italian rite was compiled during the twelfth century by
R. Menahem b. Solomon of Rome, and a wide variety of other
rites arose.[12]

Although during the nineteenth century the liturgy was
radically altered it did not remain unchanged from the eleventh
or even the fourteenth centuries. The prayerbook continued to

be expanded with hymns, dirges, petitional and penitential prayers that were inspired or provoked by the vicissitudes of the middle ages. Kabalah, centered in sixteenth century Safed, Palestine, and again, Hasidism in eighteenth century Eastern Europe, inspired many new elements in worship. The rise of the cantorial mode influenced certain aspects of worship.[13]

Prayerbooks were compiled by medieval mystics, and the leading one was that of R. Hayim Vital, a disciple of the major kabalistic figure, R. Isaac Luria of whom more will be said in a later chapter. It was believed that Luria composed his prayerbook under the direct inspiration of Elijah the Prophet. The composer also assured the worshipper on the title page that praying according to Luria's ritual is a guarantee of salvation. This prayerbook is known as *Siddur ha'Ari*, the name *Ari* standing for *A*shkenazi *R*abbi *I*saac (the name and geographic origin of the composer), also signifying that he was the "lion" (Hebrew: *ari*) of all mystics. This was the prayerbook later adopted by Ḥasidism.[14]

What becomes immediately clear from what has here been discribed is the independence exercised within Judaism by its rabbinic scholars. Such independence was practiced, as in England, even in the face of angry admonition such as that of Judah the Pious (twelfth century) who warned they will have to make reckoning in the hereafter for their liberties with the prayerbook.[15]

III. THEOLOGY OF JEWISH WORSHIP[16]

A. *Theological Freedom*

It is axiomatic that Judaism never developed *a* systematic theology that enjoyed the imprimatur of an ecclesiastical body. Neither scripture nor Talmud produced a comprehensive single-track organized theological edifice sustained by logical arguments, and moving from a starting point to a culmination. Yet, both scripture and Talmud are replete with "theology". Both works contain discussions of the character and function of God, what God expects of man and the eschatological hope of mankind. Both works contain discussions of the creation of the universe by God, His participation in history, and the ultimate hope that He will intrude Himself in the end of days and bring the messianic glory to fruition. No attempt was ever made in the Pentateuch, the Prophets, or the Writings to list a roster of faith, statements of belief to be confessed by every believing Jew. No such attempt was ever made in the Talmud. And the geonim did not attempt this either. As we will see in a later chapter, Moses Maimonides attempted it, and was roundly denounced for it and refuted. And so, Judaism in its many varieties, or *because of* its many varieties, did not issue a manual of dogma incumbent upon the believer. But the literature is replete with theological doctrine, concepts that ought to be believed, ideas recommended for faith; and one can hardly turn a page of substantive Judaic literature without immediately encountering a challenge to believe.

It is true, as one scholar has pointed out, rabbinic literature is more distinguished for its consensus than its dissensions in theology.[17] But it had dissensions. And for the historian of Judaism the dissensions may be the more important aspects to examine. To ascertain what is "Jewish Theology" is still not an easy task even at this late date. The monographs on individual subjects of rabbinic theology Solomon Schechter called for well over half a century ago, in the main, have still not been produced. The many volumes of Talmud and midrash, the medieval halakhic literature and books of ethical and pietistic edification (*musar*) are still largely unploughed fields as far as sophisticated theological scrutiny is concerned. Little has been written on the basis of extensive and intensive examination on the significant subject of Resurrection. Schechter himself in his attempt to survey "some aspects" of rabbinic theology in a book of that name hardly mentioned Resurrection, Immortality, or Eschatology.[18]

Since this book is not exclusively devoted to doctrines of theology, I am not about to rectify the omissions of the past. The footnotes will carry sufficient data and references to help the reader discover other sources that expound those subjects in which each individual has a particular interest. What is of importance here is that the prayerbook was a major witness to what Jews believed. What found its way into the *Sidur's* pages, to be affirmed and confessed in Sabbath and Holy Day worship, undoubtedly provides as accurate an index as any scientific inquiry into precisely what was the theology of Judaism. In another volume I will describe the theology of Judaism as it was inherited from the Religion of Israel and amplified in the talmudic schools of Babylonia and Palestine.[19] Here I will examine that theology as we find it already fully-formed in the middle ages.

There are aspects of the *Sidur* that appear disorganized. But this is due to the manner in which the prayerbook grew. New prayers were added because people liked them. Sometimes they interrupted the pristine order. But as a matter of fact,

the core contents of Jewish prayer happen to be well struc-
tured. Before the original passages of worship, and after
them, have been added a plethora of prayers, psalms, and hymns
and this gives the impression of lack of structure. But even
in these sections there is structure. What happens in a Jewish
morning service is that the worshipper recites psalms and hymns
as an introductory phase. This consists of praises offered to
God, for all that He has conferred, and a variety of prayers
and petitions through which the worshipper expresses his hopes
and fears and seeks his consolations. One might say the opening consists of Appreciation and Gratitude, a recognition that
the material world must be placed in focus. The roster of
daily thank-you offerings made by the worshipper covers almost
all conceivable needs of mankind.[20]

B. *The Concept of Berakha*

The first portion of the prayerbook is highly instructive.
It is called *birkat hashaḥar*, "the morning blessings", and
leads the worshipper, as on the rungs of a ladder, through
many levels of gratitude. But perhaps most important is that
it contains a seemingly strange intrusion, a lesson in ethical
halakha.[21] Yet this is not as strange as it may at first
glance appear, considering the structure of worship. This
structure, begins with Gratitude, moves on through Praise, and
reaches the core of historic worship in Judaism: the affirmation of God as Creator, Revealer, and Redeemer. This includes
the confession of belief in the monotheistic idea which is
made immediately upon affirmation of the Revelation of Torah
and followed by the asseveration of Redemption.[22]

It will be noted when studying the text of the prayerbook
that a recurring element is that formula we call "benediction"

or "blessing", the Hebrew term for which is *berakha*. That
term is best left untranslated and from this point on in this
book will generally appear in the transliterated anglicized
Hebrew: berakha. To call it a "blessing" is misleading because that implies we bless God. This is theologically un-
tenable. God blesses humans. The berakha is the formula
through which the worshipper expresses his gratitude to God
for a blessing conferred. In itself, then, the berakha is
the foundation stone of religion. It affirms the recognition
of the predicament of man as being such that man by himself
is inadequate. In effect, the worshipper attests to the idea
that all of the forces of this universe, whether material,
moral or spiritual, are conferred by God upon man for his
benefit and use, for the purpose of making life viable. Thus
he thanks Him for creation. The worshipper thanks God for his
ability to stand upright but also thanks Him for creating the
sun, the moon and the stars. After affirming Creation he declares the Holiness of God, and then confronts the Revelation.
Before reciting the berakhot, he recites the Mishnah admonish-
ing himself to remember how to live, and what takes priority
in his day's activities: "...the practice of loving deeds
and the study of Torah...honoring parents...visiting the sick
...concentrating in prayer, making peace between people. But
the study of Torah takes priority." Other phrases in that
mishnaic paragraph are obsolete but remain in the prayer text.
For example, the Mishnah reminds the worshipper that he is to
leave the corners of his field for the poor and the stranger
(Lev. 23:22). This is part of the agricultural halakha no
longer operative but it was never excised from the prayerbook,
probably because it continues to have importance for inducing
generosity and concern for the underprivileged. At this juncture it might also be useful to observe that Judaic theology

is a blend of doctrine and morality, ritual and ethics, intermingled. The same paragraph reminds the believer to study
Torah (a ritual) and practice loving deeds (ethics). This is
immediately followed by a declaration of faith that the Creator
of physical life of the present will also grant resurrection in
"a future yet to come", usually translated "hereafter", a word
which hardly carries the thrust of the eschatological time.[23]

The berakha, then, is the humble acknowledgment by the
worshipper of the goodness of his Creator which is unbounded,
even unto resurrection. There is a berakha for everything one
enjoys or encounters, from a drink of water to beholding a
great ocean, from the celebration of great joy to the dark
experience of tragedy (Job 1:21). The berakha has been called
correctly "the basic structural element" of Judaic liturgy.[24]
The berakha, however, harbors a distinct halakhic-theological
truth. It was formulated by ancient sages, and often refers
to rituals introduced by ancient proto-rabbis or rabbis. Yet
such berakhot, referring to religious obligations, read: "We
praise you Lord our God, Eternal Sovereign who has sanctified
us through His mitzvot by commanding us to...", concluding
with whatever the prospective action will be. The *sages* created the ritual: the prayer shawl, lighting Sabbath candles,
kindling Hanukah candles, and so on, and yet they ascribed the
obligation to God. This is a clear assertion that rabbinic
halakha has the authority "as if" it had been divine revelation.[25]

C. *The Shemà Segment of the Liturgy*

Not only does the berakha constitute the preliminary segment of worship, but also dominates the ancient core of the
liturgy. The Shemà and Àmidah consist of a series of berak-

hot.[26] It is with gratitude that the Jew affirms Creation and
Redemption. And by rising to confess the Oneness of God in the
midst of these assertions, he is stressing that it is the *same*
God, the One, that created the universe, that revealed His will
and redeemed His people. With the second blessing before the
Shemà the Election of Israel is affirmed, and is repeated in
the berakha of Redemption. When averring that God created the
Universe, the worshipper also asserts "...with His goodness He
renews each day the work of creation." God constantly recre-
ates the universe. There is much that can be said of the scientific correspondence to this theology, or for scientific
contradiction, but that is not germane to this volume. We are
concerned here only with the theology of worship as found by
the geonim and as transmitted by them and their successors in
the first prayerbooks composed for Jewish worship, and not with
its relationship to science.

   The prayer before the Shemà includes a petition for the
ingathering of the people to the Holy Land.[27] This expresses
a theological unity: God elected Israel to be witness to the
Revelation, and this was the purpose of Redemption. Embedded
within this "core theology" of Judaism are other ideas. Some
might regard them as peripheral but this would be at the risk
of reading modern notions back into talmudic and geonic minds.
One such example is angelology. It is apparent from its presence in the very heart of the liturgy that Judaism contained
belief in the world of angels and that no effort was made to
remove them from the prayerbook. There is mention of "angels"
in the Bible, at least in the form of God's "messengers" who
performed special tasks for Him. Under the impact of Zoroastrianism the angelology of early Judaism was greatly expanded. The representations given in scripture match those

of Mithraism in some cases. Some named angels are identified
with apocalyptic ideas such as Michael or Gabriel. In early
Judaism, Satan was not independent but he soon became so.
During the middle ages, under the influence of early Christianity, he took on new dimensions.[28]

We will not here enter into a careful analysis of the
entire Shemà.[29] But it should be noted that a reminder of a
variety of halakhic items are found in it as well as theological notions. The halakhic guidance, incidentally, is of such
nature as is related intimately to significant theological
concepts. First of all is the confession of Monotheism itself: "Yahweh is our God; Yahweh is One."[30] The first paragraph reminds the worshipper that it is *love* of God which is
asked of him, a love that surpasses all concern with private
interest or property, a love that is therefore both self-
sacrificial and lacking in self-interest (v. 5). This commandment is to be indelibly impressed upon the believer and
taught to his children (vv. 6-7). He is then enjoined to
"bind them as a sign...and write them upon the doorposts..."
(vv. 8-9), from which was derived validation of *tefilin*,
"phylacteries", and *mezuzah*, the encapsulated pentateuchal
passages affixed to the doors of Jewish homes.[31] The *mezuzah*
(literally: "door-post") contains Deut. 6:4-9 and 11:13-21.
As Israel Abrahams has pointed out, Egyptians wrote "lucky
sentences" over the entrance of their homes. The word "phylac-
tery" is an unfortunate rendering of a Greek word which means
an "amulet" or "safeguard". If the phylacteries were originally "safeguards" they certainly no longer were so regarded when
the rabbis called them tefilin, "prayer instruments". There
is nothing in the wording of the texts designed to ward off
bad luck. The content is purely theological, and the worshipper is encouraged to belief through action.

Finally, in the last paragraph of the Shemà (Num. 15:37-41), we have the halakha of *tzitzit*, the fringes to be worn on the corners of one's garments, later relegated to a specific "vestment", the *talit* or prayershawl. Undoubtedly one can trace the *talit* fringes to earlier pagan observances as one can trace the tefilin. But in any religious borrowing the urgent thing is not how a ritual arose in primeval times, but what it comes to mean to a believer. Certain pagan rituals were "Judaized" during the Graeco-Roman period and then in their new form in time became indigenous to Judaism. By the middle ages these rituals were thought to be Jewish from time immemorial. It was in their Jewish format and with their Jewish reinterpretations and spiritualizations that they continued to have a hold upon Jews until modern times. Again, in the *miẓvah* of the fringes (*miẓvah* is how each religious obligation is termed in Judaism) it was not the ritual alone that mattered but the goal: piety (v. 39) leading to holiness (v. 40). And once again we find that perennial idea: God has a right to ask this because He redeemed Israel from Egypt (v. 41). It appears more and more, though both Jewish and Christian scholars might be reluctant to use the terminology, that for the Jew the Exodus (the prototype of Resurrection, in this case a collective resurrection of the crucified body of the Elect) like for the Christian the Resurrection, is the historic proof of God's presence and the basis of God's demand and command.

D. *The Amidah*[32]

Following immediately upon the affirmation of the Exodus, the worshipper or congregation, rises for what is variously termed *Tefilah* ("Prayer" par excellence), Amidah (standing devotion) or incorrectly *Shemoneh Esreh* ("eighteen" berakhot)

since there are nineteen in daily worship and seven on Sabbaths and festivals. It would be utterly impractical to attempt here an analysis of the Tefilah and I will merely com-
ment on certain outstanding characteristics. The Tefilah always, morning, afternoon, or evening, on weekdays, New Moon,
semi-festive days, fasts, Sabbath, festivals and High Holy
Days (Rosh Hashanah and Yom Kippur) contains the first three
berakhot and the concluding three berakhot. The portion between varies according to the occasion. The standard weekday
Tefilah incorporates thirteen paragraphs of petition. The
amidah of Sabbaths, festivals and the High Holy Days include
a segment referring to the occasion itself and the nature of
the celebration. The Tefilot of the High Holy Days, however,
contain in addition long segments related to confession, atonement, forgiveness, the sovereignty of God, human destiny, the
meaning of life, and other relevant theological conceptions.
They contain long medieval poems, designed to elicit piety,
concern, even anxiety, but also hope, confidence and faith.

In view of the sameness of the three berakhot opening and
concluding the Tefilah on all occasions, it may be suggested
that here we have the fundamental theological thrust of prayer
in Judaism. The first berakha of the opening three invokes
God's remembrance of the "fathers" of Judaism, Abraham, Isaac
and Jacob, in order to benefit from their merit. It is interesting how it becomes a microcosm of the whole prayer-thrust
incorporating allusions to Creation, Election, Revelation and
Redemption within itself: "...God of Abraham (First Revelation)...maker of all things (Creation) who remembers the love
of the fathers (Election) and brings a redeemer to their progeny (Redemption)...." The second berakha affirms thrice in
one paragraph faith in the Resurrection as the counterpart to
present life. "...You sustain life with love, restoring the

dead with great compassion; sustaining the fallen, healing the
sick, freeing the bound and fulfilling faith with those who
sleep in the dust...the Sovereign who causes death and restores
life, causing Salvation to sprout." It then adds the berakha
with a fourth reference to the trustworthy nature of God's
promise of Resurrection. It must be conceded that the composers of this passage were taking great care to say something.[33]

The third berakha affirms the Holiness of God thus reaching the climax of the affirmation of the nature of God. The
assertions were triple: He is God and as such the Creator and
Master of life known and unknown, and in His attribute of Holiness is independent and unique before whom the worshipper is
to stand in awe. It reminds the worshipper of his human predicament and places him in better mood for the petitions that
follow or for the celebration of the occasion that follows.
In either case the assertion of God's holiness reminds one of
the dependence and frailty of humanness, as does the remembrance of the "fathers" that man cannot stand alone.

The first of the concluding three berakhot expresses the
hope for the return to Zion of the Shekhinah, the Presence of
God or the Holy Spirit. This was undoubtedly modified from
another form after the destruction of Jerusalem. In a poem
reminiscent of the ámidah in Ben Sira (51:12ff.) the line runs
"Give thanks unto Him who has chosen Zion." After 70, or certainly after 135 it was necessary to pray for a restoration of
the *Aḅodah*, the worship, to the holy center of Zion. Again,
this was a major element of the theology of Judaism for it be-
spoke the messianic hope. The second of the concluding three
was the acknowledgment of God as source of life and salvation,
of reality as well as of the miraculous, whose compassion is
unbounded and permanent. It therefore succinctly affirms the

attributes of the Monotheistic conception which gives hope for the fulfillment of all that came before and for that which is the climax, the three-fold priestly benediction expanded into the "Peace Prayer" with which the Tefilah closes.

The order of worship naturally embodies many other theological concepts. We have here mentioned Monotheism, Creation, God as the Source of all blessings conferred on man, Election, Revelation, Redemption, the Messianic Hope, Resurrection, aspects of the attributes of God and man, and the notion of concretizing the human-divine relationship in such symbols as tefilin. The sixteenth berakha of the amidah establishes faith in the efficacy of prayer. A survey of Sabbath, festival and High Holy Day worship would further highlight the theological doctrines that can be found in the Tefilah which we have not reviewed. Thus the Sabbath liturgy emphasizes the Covenant between God and Israel. High Holy Day liturgy calls attention to such ideas as repentance, atonement and forgiveness, elements in the divine-human encounter which make life possible and turn man from despair. Festival worship further highlights the doctrines related to what is being commemorated. Thus Passover emphasizes the theme of redemption and human freedom, Shabuot (Pentecost, Feast of Weeks) centers on the Revelation at Sinai, Sukkot is oriented to the harvest and is both a festival of thanksgiving and a celebration of divine judgment upon the fecundity of the earth. The liturgy of Hanukah is sparse but emphasizes the rededication of the Jerusalem Temple and the miraculous nature of God's will employed in history rather than the military exploits and national revival. The Purim liturgy adds only the reading of the biblical book Esther to normal liturgy. It both reminds the faithful of the uncertain predicament of the Jewish condition and celebrates the salvation of the community from the satanic plan of Haman. The event becomes a paradigm for the history of Judaism, and the commemoration is also a prototype of constant gratitude for escape from danger. The liturgy of fast-days adds the note of confession of sinfulness and responsibility for adversity in a variety of penitential prayers that emerged out of the middle ages.[34]

E. *Kiddush*

It will be useful here to explore aspects of one prayer which is part of extensive home-family liturgy in Judaism. This is the *Kiddush HaYom* (the sanctification of the day) which precedes the Sabbath and festival opening dinner and inaugurates the holy day.[35] Firstly, it emphasizes how the basic theological thrust of Judaism penetrated the home and was not confined to the public liturgy. The family unit consecrates the Sabbath by proclaiming it holy. The kiddush is that proclamation. That it is celebrated with wine is incidental. Wine was the normal accompaniment of all sacrificial cults in ancient times and was also an integral part of Graeco-Roman banqueting. Considering those facts and that it was used by Christian Jews in the Eucharist it is not surprising that first century rabbis continued it as part of the Sabbath and festival ritual after the sacrificial cult was ended. Secondly, the kiddush provides an excellent example of innovation of ritual to meet changing circumstances and needs.

Studies in the development of the calendar used in Judaism have indicated that there was a shift from the solar year to the lunar, and much controversy. In any case, while this is not germane to fuller consideration here, it should be noted similarly that the counting of days from evening to

evening was not always in vogue. It came about sometime toward
the beginning of the proto-rabbinic period, perhaps in the
first century B.C. It is apparent that if a day began in the
morning, Friday night was not yet part of the Sabbath. But
when the innovation of counting days from sunset to sunset was
introduced, the nature of Friday evening changed and it was
necessary somehow to bring the weekday to a close and open the
Sabbath, to mark a division declaring, "The Sabbath begins."
This was the function of the kiddush: to declare the beginning of "holy time". The evening prayers which could have
served that purpose had not yet originated and in any case for
a long time only morning and afternoon worship was regarded as
obligatory and evening worship as optional, there being no
evening sacrifice in the Temple.[36]

The Sabbath kiddush consisted of Genesis 2:1-3 affirming
Creation, God's cessation from creative activity and His
hallowing of the seventh day, thus setting the premise for
the celebration. It brought theology into the home and made
for weekly repetition of significant doctrines: Creation and
the sanctity of the seventh day. This was followed by the
berakha for the wine and then a paragraph which reaffirmed the
following doctrines: a) The Election of Israel ("who sanctified us with His commandments and has taken delight in us");
b) God ordained the Sabbath for commemoration of the Creation
and c) as remembrance of the Exodus from Egypt. The Election
doctrine is then repeated lucidly in the line, "You have chosen
us and sanctified us from among the nations, and have given us
your holy Sabbath in love and favor as inheritance...." The
festival kiddush, and that of Rosh Hashanah follow a similar
pattern but naturally contain references to the specific occasion being celebrated.[37]

F. *Theology in the Responsa*

Thus far, we have basically surveyed aspects of Jewish theology that are related to liturgy. But it is desirable to indulge at least a brief sketch of some of the problems and views that emerge from the geonic responsa literature that are not liturgy-oriented. Not a great deal of synthesing of that material has been done. But for our purposes, sufficient examples may be garnered.[38]

It has to be recalled that the geonic period spanned the centuries of two major challenges to Judaism. On the one hand, there was Karaism. On the other hand, there was Greek philosophy revived in Arabic that won the intellectual loyalty of thinking Jews.

The responsa inform us of notions held by geonim. For example, the last of the major geonim, Hai, was of the opinion that God's "foreknowledge" does not imply what *will* be. This was in accord with the older view recorded in the Mishnah in the name of R. Akiba, that God's knowledge and man's freedom is basically an unresolved paradox: "All is foreseen, but freedom is given..." (*Abot* 3:19). Akiba and like-minded Jews believed both parts of the paradox although "human wisdom could not intellectually reconcile them".[39] Similarly, Gaon Hai was reaffirming the doctrine expressed by many in both biblical and post-biblical Judaism, that man has free will despite the parallel doctrines that God knows all that occurs in life and history. It is well to understand that religion does have mystery and not every paradox can be resolved.

It appears from the material available that the geonim who busied themselves with halakha nevertheless gave thought to philosophical issues, and when called upon in inquiries, engaged in articulating their opinions. But at the same

time, if Hai is representative, they expressed the historic
caution of a major segment of rabbinic scholars, that one does
not place reliance upon agadah, the non-halakhic lore and literature. It is not binding, and carries no mandate of belief.
Hai used the talmudic saying related to hermeneutics, "the
Torah speaks in the language of men", to insist on the figura-
tive nature of many poetical, anthropomorphic and similar
passages. There are many statements in the Talmud concerning
the supreme significance of agadah and scholars down through
the ages believed it was "revealed" equally with halakha. It
appears to me, nevertheless, that the very fact that no compilation of agadic doctrines or beliefs, no digest of rabbinic
views on the messiah, immortality of the soul, resurrection,
creation, revelation, providence and free will, angels, and
the like, ever arose, parallel with halakhic digests like the
Mishnah and Tosephta, teaches us implicitly that agadah was
not to be considered authoritative.[40] Indeed, it could not
be since the scriptural warrants in some doctrinal issues were
frequently not explicit at all. Maimonides, who often rejected agadah entirely when it was incompatible with his
private brand of rationalism accepted it when it was useful
to press home a point.[41]

But even Hai had already insisted in his responsa that
one cannot dismiss agadic statements as a more rigorous
rationalist like Samuel b. Hofni was doing. He went to great
lengths to attempt to explain the eschatology of Judaism
which, with its complex apocalyptic elements was very confus-
ing for even a learned Jew. There were the elements of the
heralding of the Messiah, the advent of the Messiah, the
Messianic Age, the Resurrection, Judgment, World to Come, the
new heavens and the new earth that were to be created and the

great Armageddon. There was the added complication of the
Messiah, son of Joseph.

Hai seeks to create a sequential scheme. The Messiah son
of Joseph will conquer Jerusalem and declare himself king.
Most Jews will remain unconvinced. But the nations will question Jewish "dual loyalty" and drive them out to go back to
their new state. Jews will be refugees, suffering greatly,
many leaving the faith. The anti-Messiah called Armilus will
kill Messiah son of Joseph and then more apostasy will ensue,
the "pangs of the Messiah" spoken of in rabbinic literature
will now be in progress. Then Elijah will appear and announce
the Messiah son of David whose advent will be marked by his
first miracle, the resurrection of the Messiah son of Joseph.
He will then reign in Jerusalem, prosperity will be experienced and Jews will live in security. Then Gog, determined to
upset the Messianic kingdom will attack Jerusalem and will be
defeated by divine intervention. The nations will then pay
homage to Jerusalem and all Jews will come to Jerusalem to
live. Then a great trumpet will arouse those dead who had
been righteous in life or repented before death, each in the
form which he experienced at the time of his death. After
that each one will be transformed into a healthy and young
person. They will rebuild the Temple, or it will miraculous-
ly come down from heaven. All Jews, and their slaves (*sic*)
will be prophets and all nations will be converted to Judaism.
Those alive at the advent of the Messiah will die at an old
age, as will the resurrected until death will be abolished,
and all the dead will be resurrected to live forever in the
World to Come. This will be marked by the Divine Presence
appearing as a pillar of fire stretching from the heavens to
the earth, thus giving the world the appearance of a new creation. There is a difference of opinion whether this will

last until the year 7000 from Creation or for an indefinite
length of time. In any event, this will come to an end and
the World to Come will replace it where the righteous will
live eternally.[42]

After all is said, however, the theological views thus
embodied in the writings of Hai were not unanimous. Not only
did Samuel b. Hofni differ with him in many instances, the
former being a rigorous rationalist, but also Maimonides ex-
hibits diversity in certain cases. Later on we will see that
the medieval philosophers did not agree on theological issues
nor even on what were the basic doctrines of Judaism. Thus in
theology, touching upon the very heart of what a Jew ought to
believe, or to reject, as much as in halakha, there was a
diversity that left open the possibility of revisionism in the
light of new ideas and under the influences of surrounding culture. As with halakha there was a process of acculturation
parallel with the attempt to preserve and transmit the faith.

G. *Masorites*

There remains only one other area that I select for brief
consideration in this chapter. It is related to worship indirectly insofar as the reading of scripture is a central segment of the liturgy on Sabbaths, New Moons, Holy Days, Fast-
Days and the weekdays of Monday and Thursday. From time immemorial the preservation of an authentic text of the Bible
corrected by specialists and preserved at Jerusalem was a significant task of the priesthood. After the cataclysm of 70
this was part of the anxiety of the rabbis. It is not my intention here to discuss the complex and extensive scholarly
contributions that have been made to the whole subject of the
Masorah, the transmitted text of scripture, nor even to review

how the Masorah, or the present masoretic text, came to be.
Let us only highlight a few landmark items of information and
sketch several conclusions more or less acceptable to a consensus of scholars.[43]

Involved in the problem were the elements of spelling,
vocalization, pronunciation, the use of accents, and the
divisions of words and sentences. Often the meaning of the
Bible could be diametrically altered by the mere use or absence of the *aleph* letter. An extreme example of this is
offered by Rashi in his talmudic commentary where he shows
that if Jeremiah 10:10, "But the Lord God is True", which
reads V'ADONAY ELOHIM EMET, was lacking the aleph of (e)met
and read *met* instead, it could mean "The Lord God is dead".[44]

Between the fifth and the seventh centuries much activity went on apace in both Hebrew and Aramaic textual work.
A major center was Nisibis where there also resided Bible-
oriented Christians who were also making similar efforts to
preserve their traditional Syriac version. Jewish and Christian schools in Nisibis were known for their intensive biblical studies during the sixth century, and whether Christian
Syriac models of punctuation and vocalization developed in
Edessa served the Jews or the Jews influenced the Christians
is still an unresolved historical question. All that can be
said is that they probably mutually inspired one another to
engage in the sacred labors and consulted on occasion. Certainly in an earlier period Jerome and others consulted Jewish
scholars regarding the Hebrew texts.[45] Much of the work of
developing the masoretic text took place during the ninth century in Palestine. There is even reason to believe that
Karaite-sympathizers were among those who brought to fruition
what became the masoretic text of the Bible still used in the

contemporary synagogue. The two major schools of textual research were in Tiberias and were represented historically by
two family traditions, that of the Ben Asher family and that
of the Ben Naphtali family.[46]

Basically, the Masorites did away with both Palestinian
and Babylonian punctuation systems and created their own a-
fresh. The work of Tiberian Masorites was accepted by both
Rabbanites and Karaites, and even the Babylonians, then engaged in seeking to establish Babylonian spiritual hegemony
bowed to Palestinian Masoretic results. Work continued into
the eleventh century. Since that time the variations in manuscripts are slight, and never of such substance as would affect either theology or halakha. The *Biblia Rabbinica* published in Venice in 1524-25 was based upon a text prepared
from numerous manuscripts by Jacob ben Hayyim. These many
manuscripts varied only minutely. Abraham ibn David of Toledo
(1110-1180) already claimed that, "We indeed find today the
Torah written in exactly the same text without the slightest
change, displayed in all Jewish communities from India to the
ends of Spain and Morocco in the civilized world, and from...
Yemen in the south to...the Arctic Ocean to the north." Since
his contemporary, Maimonides, out in Fustat, noted that there
was confusion in the existing scrolls and among the Masorites,
it is apparent ibn David was indulging in poetic hyperbole.
But it may be surmised that although variation continued to
persist the textual differences had no religious significance.[47]

We have previously discussed the question of vernacular
in prayer. It was customary during earlier centuries in the
synagogue to read the weekly portion of Bible in Hebrew and
to have it translated into Aramaic (Targum). During the ninth

century, the Bible, like other classics, was translated into
Arabic for Arabic scholars and patrons of learning as well as
for Jews who understood neither Hebrew nor Aramaic. At that
time, too, Gaon Natronai allowed scripture to be read in Arabic
after the congregation fulfilled its duty to Hebrew and Aramaic. This decision was perpetuated in his *Sidur* by the Gaon
Amram and reaffirmed by Gaon Hai during the eleventh century.
We know nothing about earlier Arabic translations because
Saadiah's tenth century translation became the standard work.
But the custom of Synagogue translation went out of vogue and
the permission was transmuted into what became a private obligation to read scripture at home first in Hebrew and Aramaic and then in other languages if necessary.[48]

A conclusion should be drawn. It would be wrong to overemphasize Judaic concern with halakha and rabbinics in the
geonic period. This brief survey of masoretic and translation
activity is merely the tip of an iceberg. Between 850-1200
biblical learning expanded extensively. Not only the recensions of texts were developed and translations, but also commentaries and interesting foreshadowings of modern biblical
criticism. Rabbanites, Karaites, Christians and Muslims all
joined in recognizing the philological and exegetical efforts
of one another. Biblical research was a major industry. Philology, the composition of grammars and dictionaries, was both
a cause and a by-product. Gaon Natronai during the ninth century complained of the neglect of Bible study and the near-exclusive interest in halakha. He was especially concerned
because of Karaite interest and excellence in biblical research. But by the thirteenth century, Abraham, son of Moses
Maimonides, wrote about one-third of his responsa on biblical
matters.

One might perhaps apply an exegetical statement of a
first-second century tana, R. Ishmael, or at least of his
disciples, to what was happening in biblical research. Jeremiah 23:29 has the prophet saying in the name of God: "Is not
My word like a fire...and like a hammer that shatters rock into pieces?" To this the tanaite scholars commented, that just
as a hammer generates many sparks a verse produces many meanings.[49] Using this freedom, R. Samuel b. Meir (known as *Rashbam*) faulted his grandfather Rashi's predilection for agadah
in his pentateuchal commentary. He, for instance, commented
on Exodus 13:9, "and it shall be for a sign for you upon your
hand", as a metaphor rather than as a source for phylacteries.
Interestingly enough, however, it had no effect upon his view
of phylacteries. Karaites abandoned phylacteries on the basis
of the same exegesis. Perhaps this helps explain the disap-
pearance of Rashbam's commentary which survived only in one
complete manuscript only on the Pentateuch.[50] But it did not
prevent R. Samuel b. Meir from retaining a privileged position
among medieval rabbinic scholars.

It is useful to note that all this indicates that there
was a reasonable degree of realism among those responsible for
the preservation of Judaism. Although they labored at precise
texts, they accepted more than one. Although they were reluctant to see sacred scripture used ritualistically in "profane"
languages, they accepted vernacular. And this once again
points up the perennial truth: there was no authoritative body
or book, no central hierarchy or person who could establish
"the law" or authorize a "code". Halakha was suggested guidance. Diversity was the law of life.

CHAPTER 4

Karaism

I. THE BACKGROUND

In the course of our foregoing discussion I have stressed the thesis of adaptability in Judaism. There was no definition of "heresy" and therefore no way to define an "orthodoxy". What is "orthodox" in an ever-changing spectrum? What is "heresy" when there is no defined dogma? Nevertheless, humans being what they are, and history being the series of contradictions it often is, there were repeated attempts to reject heresy by delineating orthodoxy and cutting off those segments that did not conform. This had occurred twice in the past. During the post-biblical period of the Ezraic reforms the Samaritans were severed from the main body of Judaism. And in the second century the Christian relationship to Judaism was terminated. A third such major attempt was made against Karaism during the ninth and tenth centuries but with less conspicuous success.[1]

The conquest of Persia by Islam led to an expansion of Islam into remote and sparsely populated areas of the north and east of Persia on toward Russia and India. With the conquering armies went immigrant-colonists, and among them were Jews. During the eighth century many Jews migrated into those far-away areas, whether for adventure or for economic reasons, perhaps even to escape the sometimes-heavy hand of the geonim.

Away from the urban centers of Jewish learning and rabbinic authority they enjoyed a degree of independence in their religious life. A number of factors coalesced to lead to a dissenting movement which ultimately emerged as Karaism.[2] Perhaps three factors can be singled out: 1) the migrations; 2) memories of historic conflicts with talmudic Judaism; the Talmud having undergone its latest recension in the hands of the saboraim during the sixth century was but a "recent" imposition in Judaism; furthermore, there were probably remnants of the old factions that were in conflict with proto-rabbinic and rabbinic groups such as the Sadducees and those sects who are known through the Dead Sea Scrolls, as well as Christian Jews, not to speak of the reality of options within talmudic Judaism as between the schools of Hillel and Shammai, and in Babylonia as between the schools of Sura and Pumbedita; 3) the Moslem example in which a major dissenting sect, Shiism, emerged.[3]

The main outlines of Karaism may be described in the following manner: 1) it rejected the Talmud; 2) it rejected the authority of the geonim; 3) it espoused a much more vigorous messianic zeal than other Jews;[4] 4) at times it professed a more rigorous asceticism which was in keeping with the rural background; 5) similarly, in contrast to the urban-metropolitan middle and upper class stratified society it maintained a great sense of social equality.

The origin of the name "Karaites", which may have been used for the first time in the ninth century, is wrapped in mist. The best explanations for it are that the term is derived either from *kara*, scripture, describing the movement's emphasis upon scripture, or from Arabic *karra* (plural: *karra'un*), signifying "scriptural experts". Karaism has to be seen in the context of other dissenting groups within Judaism. Often these dissenting movements were also related to messianic speculation like "millenarians" in Christianity, those who calculated the dates when they expected the Second Coming and the thousand-year reign of the Messiah. Within Judaism not only the apocalyptic speculations appeared, but even in the liturgical poetry of Eleazar Kalir one encounters a sanguinary messianic hope. Solomon ibn Gabirol, a significant eleventh century Spanish poet included the messianic hope frequently in his poems, especially those termed *Geùlah* ("redemption") poems, but cautioned his readers that eschatology is a mystery, and that in contrast with God's giving a date to Abraham and to Jeremiah for the Exodus from Egypt and the return from Babylonia, the third redemption "from every eye is concealed".[5] Like many others, Ibn Gabirol believed that according to the apocalypse, *Sefer Zerubbabel,* the Messiah is to come 990 years after the destruction of Jerusalem, or 1058-60 or by 1068-70 according to the conception that he will come at the end of the first millenium of the destruction. The failure of the Messiah to materialize was among the causes of demoralization of Spanish Jewry, as we will see in a later chapter. And despite that failure the poetry of Yehudah Ha-Levi was suffused with messianism. Messianism also appears as a theme and as a problem in biblical commentaries. The books of Isaiah and Daniel called for special treatment. Ibn Ezra rejected the idea that Daniel was eschatological. But there were numerous other passages such as Genesis 49:10. Rashi's interpretation of some of these passages in both our received Rashi texts and in manuscripts which were conceivably abandoned indicate that not only in Spain and Provence but in the far reaches of France and Germany Jewish scholars were preoccupied with the same problem.[6] We should bear in mind that calculations were constantly being made in order to predict the year of the Messiah's advent on the basis of verses in scripture. Not only were Jews doing this but Christians as well, as we will note when discussing the relationships between Puritanism and Judaism in a subsequent volume. As time progressed, consistently later projections were made. After the circa 1068 date we find 1352 and 1478.[7]

Messianism and sectarianism were often combined. This was especially true in the case of Samaritans who had rejected all the prophetic figures after Joshua and placed almost exclusive emphasis upon Moses. They saw the Messiah as a resurrected Moses and the biblical messianic doctrine as basically a liberation movement. They had none of the concepts of cosmic upheavals that are found in prophetic, psalmist or apocalyptic literature in their scripture. Nevertheless, and despite Judaism's reluctance to grant them full Jewish status, Samaritans were a microcosm of the Jewish predicament. During the sixth and seventh centuries and later they became a diaspora community, many living in Cairo where they had their own synagogues. As late as the time of Maimonides they and Karaites were regarded as part of the Jewish community.[8]

A responsum of Gaon Hai reflects severe criticism of extortionate rabbinic judges who oppressed the poor and granted privilege and profit to the rich. This may be seen as a serious socio-economic problem that would turn people against rabbinic leadership and therefore the Talmud which was presumably the source of their judgments. We must see this as one more significant factor along with the cataclysmic upheavals of the period, the messianic movements and the diffusion of population into new distant areas as conducive to the loosening of geonic control and the rise of widespread diversity in Judaism. Added to this should be the extensive and vigorous missionary activity of Islam, Christianity and Zoroastrianism as well as the gnostic tendencies that permeated all of medieval thought.

Some Jews were ripe for conversion, but others merely for syncretism or dissent. There were large segments of Jews in the Arabian peninsula and in the vastnesses of Iran. These were not living the orderly halakhic Judaism taught in the academies of Babylonia and compiled in systematic treatises of scholars. We find Pirqoi ben Baboi calling one a swine, "who studies the written, but denies the oral Torah...for he understands nothing".[9]

The Islamic conquests shattering the great Persian empire in the east and the Visigothic kingdom in the west escalated messianic hopes. Such hopes persisted for centuries as is seen from Maimonides' *Epistle to Yemen* (1171-72). These hopes were translated into the appearance of false messiahs and increased pilgrimage to, and settlement in Palestine. This in turn stimulated new nationalist-religious attitudes. Although the evidence is sparse and the debates based upon a lack of concrete testimony there is sufficient reason to suspect that these nationalist-religious stirrings went hand in hand with other sectarian teachings that may be traced back to the sectarian divergences of the first century. The tenth century Karaite historians Jacob Kirkisani and Hasan ben Masliah both referred to the writings of Zadok, the supposed founder of the so-called Sadducean movement of the pre-Christian and early Christian era. There were still Christian Jewish groups in existence who undoubtedly preserved other writings that had direct connection with the ancient groups. As one historian correctly suggests, it is simply not plausible to think no traditions at all were preserved even in oral form, if not in writing, by loyal adherents of these sects who persevered through the centuries.[10]

Among the pietistic messianic sects were such that adopted what appeared to be so-called Sadducean halakhic attitudes, but

some of which could have been Christian, and others Islamic.
For example, some prohibited divorce, established seven prayer
periods a day, prohibited meat and intoxicating beverages.
Others abandoned the restrictions on forbidden meats, the diaspora second day of the festivals and the rabbinical marriage
contract. Furthermore, despite all the masoretic efforts there
continued widespread divergence in their reading of scripture.
More importantly a wide disparity persisted in its interpretation. Some insisted Lev. 23:15, to bring the first sheaf of
grain "on the morrow of the Sabbath" signified Sunday, requir-
ing that the Festival of Shabuot always be on Sunday, an
ancient argument of the Sadducees. Others argued that Lev.
23:32 calling the Day of Atonement a *Shabbat Shabbaton*, "a
double sabbath" signified it must always be observed on a
Saturday with the consequence that Passover will always fall
on a Thursday.[11] Whether this had any relationship to the
Last Supper having taken place on Thursday is a matter of
interest, and whether this suggestion came from Christian
Jews is not clear.

After the great Islamic triumphs of the seventh century
that stirred messianic agitation came the Christian stirrings
of the Crusades. The great clash between those two massive
societies led to new Jewish fantasies. We have noted the dis-
appointment of Ibn Gabirol after 1068. Many movements flourished during the twelfth century. In all, for the period of
the geonim from about 600-1300, half-a-dozen sectarian leaders
and over fifteen persons who made messianic pretensions aside
from the Karaite movement, are so far known to modern scholarship. All the factions, sects or movements almost totally
disappeared except for the Karaites. The twelfth century historian of comparative religion, Abu'l Fath Muhammad ash-Shah-
rastani, recorded a summary of Jewish sects, and although some

of those he mentioned had disappeared and he could not name most of the seventy-one he said existed, he indicated the unity that made of all of them adherents of Judaism. He wrote that they: 1) believed in monotheism; 2) believed in the uniqueness of the Torah; 3) observed the seventh-day Sabbath; 4) believed in the coming of the Messiah. Obviously items 2 and 3 separated them from Christianity and Islam.[12]

II. EVOLUTION OF KARAISM

A. *Karaite Dissent*

It was into this milieu of messianic agitation and religious rebellion, a period of imperial clashes and what appeared to be apocalyptic days, similar in many ways to the first century, that Karaism was born. It became both a catalyst bringing together diverse remnants into a major religious movement, and a beneficiary, gaining strength and ideas from these groups. Its reputed founder was Anan ben David.[13] It was he who provided the first manual of non-rabbinic theology and halakha which is the oldest extant Karaite literary remains. Dated 770, it may also be the oldest post-talmudic halakhic-theological work of any Jewish scholar of any denomination. But unlike Rabbanites Anan placed the Prophets and Writings on a par with the Torah. He work was called the *Book of Precepts*. From these humble beginnings Karaism spread through Iraq, Syria, Palestine and Egypt. But in the person of the Gaon Saadiah b. Joseph they met an inveterate enemy who regarded them as apostates. This inaugurated an age of polemics in which Rabbanites and Karaites were locked for centuries. It

made for the emergence of a series of highly articulate Karaite
scholars from 900-1200. Karaism, as a result, gained in momen-
tum and moved on into the Balkans, to Spain and even as far
north as Lithuania.[14]

The chief characteristics of Karaism insofar as its religious interpretations and conclusions were concerned, and which
were perhaps its weakest elements were a rigorous conservatism
and an almost contradictory extreme individualism. The "founding father", Anan, had taught, "Search well in the Torah and do
not rely on my opinion". This individualism remained a constant. Thus during the tenth century a foremost Karaite could
already assert, "You can scarcely meet two Karaites of one and
the same mind in all matters: upon one point or another everyone has an opinion different from that of the rest." The first
element resulted in hardly any basic changes over many centuries
although radical revisions do appear in the fifteenth century,
as we will see. During the 11th century, for example, in Jerusalem, the Karaites accused Rabbanites of "laxity". The
charge, that rabbinic Judaism made religion too convenient
and was too accommodating for its adherents had been made even
in the tenth century and remained a hallmark of the polemics.
It went back to the ninth century when we find Daniel Al-Kumisi
making the same attack. On the other hand, by the sixteenth
century a leading Karaite, Moses Beghi admitted that the early
Karaite scholars were so rigorous in order to establish the
great distinction between the Karaite reliance upon scripture
and Rabbanite reliance upon tradition. To arrive at a consensus even mildly resembling the diversified-yet-homogeneous
rabbinic Judaism was not possible in the light of their as-
sertive individualism. But it is interesting that in matters
of theology, unrelated to halakha, there is little substantial

disagreement between rabbinic Judaism and Karaism although
here and there in our discussion such discrepancies will become evident. Yet their main dissenting agitation was in what
was required of the Jew to do in observance of his faith, and
not in what he is expected to believe. They never wavered in
strict monotheism, a belief in God's omnipotence, man's
personal responsibility for his actions, and the messianic
idea. Even in certain basic halakhic prohibitions which were
related to the theology of the nature of man as created in the
image of God, the Karaites did not depart from basic rabbinic
Judaism because these elements were patently rooted in the
Torah.[15]

The basic teaching of Anan which severed Karaites from
Judaism in Saadiah's opinion was his rejection of talmudic
authority. This opened the sluices to independent halakhic
opinion that left no room for geonic authority which was then
struggling for hegemony. This had ramifications. Anan prohibited levirate marriages. Yet this was an instance in which
he was flying in the face of scripture. Karaism was stricter
than rabbinic Judaism in the Sabbath halakha, but interpreted
"do not boil a kid in its mother's milk" (Ex. 23:19) literally,
as did Philo, and did not apply it to the halakha of kashrut,
thus permitting the mixing of dairy and meat foods. The Karaites reverted to the ancient practice of observing the moon to
set the festivals and the result was (as in the case of Roman
and Orthodox Easter variation) that festivals did not always
occur on the same days in all countries nor were they observed
on the same days as rabbinic festivals, the rabbinic calendar
being a fixed mathematical computation. Furthermore the Karaites did not observe Ḥanukah, this not having been a pentateuchal festival. Such normal Jewish symbols as tefilin and
mezuzah were not adopted by the Karaites. But while this

perception of scripture as not explicitly containing such cere-
monialism led to reducing the complexity of rabbinic ritualism,
the same principle of literalness led to retaining a semi-bar-
baric rule like "eye for an eye" which had been transmuted into
monetary compensation by rabbinic Judaism.[16]

Anan took a curious approach to the food practices and
laid upon Karaites heavier obligations despite his permitting
meat and dairy. He prohibited all fowl except pigeons and
turtledoves based upon an exegesis of Gen. 8:20 and Lev. 1:14.
The former verse said Noah offered clean birds upon the altar
and the only such birds we find ordained for the altar, Anan
argued, were pigeons and turtledoves in Lev. 1:14. That he
evades all of the unlisted birds in Lev. 11 which implied their
appropriateness is not surprising, for what Anan would look for
is explicitness and not inference.[17] Anan also prohibited any
fire from burning on the Sabbath in a Jewish home, even if
kindled before the Sabbath. For this he used a torturous exegesis which considered the continued burning of the fire as
tantamount to the continued performance of work by the one who
kindled it.[18] In the field of divorce the halakha permitting
divorce was based upon Deut. 24:1, in which it is said if a
man finds something unseemly in his wife he shall write for
her a bill of divorce. Unlike some other sectarian groups
referred to above, Anan continued the halakha of divorce. And
even more, he granted the wife the right to initiate the proceedings.[19]

B. *Karaite Maturation*

Anan was followed in leadership by his son Saul, but a
later successor, the ninth century scholar, Benjamin Al-Naha-
wandi, became one of a duumvirate of Karaite "founders".

Islamic literature spoke of "the followers of Anan and Benjamin". It became clear in the works of both Anan and Benjamin that the Torah was not adequate for the middle ages, and that if one is giving up the rabbinic Talmud one must create one's own. And this is precisely what occurred. Undoubtedly Anan's *Book of Precepts* served as a guide for Benjamin's book of the same name and for his *Sefer Dinim* (*Book of Rules*) as well.[20] One could have an interesting exercise comparing the halakhot of marriage summarized by Benjamin with the halakhot covering the same questions in rabbinic Judaism. He does not differ from rabbinic Judaism in such matters as taking another wife after ten years of her failure to bear a child, a husband's obligation to sustain his wife and children, the retention of the *ketuvah* (religious marriage certificate) to protect the wife against destitution in the event of divorce, and so forth. As a matter of fact at the end of his book he says that he has also included rabbanite halakha which has no biblical support "so that you might observe it likewise if you so desire".[21]

This is not the place to review all of the Karaite thinkers and scholars.[22] Certainly a study of Jacob Al-Kirkisani (tenth century), regarded as the greatest Karaite mind of the time, and a prolific scholar, contemporary of Gaon Saadiah, would be rewarding.[23] Of similar interest is Salmon ben Jeroham, a tenth century Karaite scholar who wrote *The Book of the Wars of the Lord* to refute Gaon Saadiah's arguments for the validity of talmudism. He wrote it in rhyme. The poem's content clearly shows that during the tenth century, at the height of the Rabbanite-Karaite polemic, the Karaites regarded themselves as "Israel". They saw the belief in the revelation of the so-called "oral law" as "heresy". They believed God revealed only the Torah to Moses and espoused belief

in the miracle of the splitting of the Sea of Reeds at the time
of the Exodus from Egypt. Salmon also argued that the absence
of the words "God spoke" in the Mishnah, and of any display of
prophecy and miracle shows the six orders of the Mishnah merely
represent "the words of modern men". He then argued concerning
contradictions in the Mishnah, that one sage permits what
another prohibits, showing it cannot be the word of God. Salmon offers a variety of other arguments and clearly indicates
he is attacking Saadiah by naming him.[24]

The important consideration is, as is evident from the
bibliographical study by Samuel Poznanski, that this literature
continued to be produced for almost 1000 years. As far as the
material presently known to us shows, the number of foremost
scholars was not large, and the issues remained more or less
the same. But it attests to the vibrancy and loyalty there
must have been among the adherents of this shunned minority
in Judaism.[25]

As far as the subject matter of Karaite scholarship and
polemics is concerned a good survey of this is seen in the
work of the well-known Russian scholar, Abraham Harkavy, who
made many valuable contributions to modern scholarship in
Judaism.[26] The fourth part of Kirkisani's magnum opus, *The
Book of Lights and High Beacons*, discusses the Karaite halakha. Since it is not a comprehensive review of all of halakha,
he must take up only those areas of the halakha in which there
was serious disagreement between rabbinic Judaism and Karaism.
These included circumcision, the Sabbath, the detailed interpretation of the halakha that flows from the Decalogue, the
establishment of the New Moon, the dating of Shabuot (Pentecost) and matters concerning other festivals, marriage, food
practices, the laws of inheritance, the dress code, the prayershawl fringes and questions of purity and impurity.[27] These

were the questions that remained on the agenda and are found
in the other works through the centuries to a greater or lesser
degree. That this was the case is all the more remarkable considering the above mentioned individualism within Karaism. Although Kirkisani does not elucidate the sources of this radically individualistic approach, it certainly sustains the view
that Anan originally enjoined his disciples, "Search well in
the Torah and do not rely upon my opinion".[28]

III. ASPECTS OF KARAISM

A. *Karaite-Rabbanite Interrelations*

An important contribution made to Judaism by the Karaite
dissent was its compelling the rabbis to take a long, hard
look at aspects of Judaism. Certainly we have no record, if
any ever existed, of a turn to rationalism by post-talmudic
scholars prior to the emergence of Karaism. The Karaite
writers rejected all anthropomorphism and mystical ideas about
heavenly hosts as well as all matters related to demons, evil
spirits and the magical remedies involved in this lore as part
of witchcraft forbidden by the Torah. It is now clear that it
was not only the challenge of Islam that compelled rabbinic
rationalism to emerge, but the internal challenge in Judaism
largely initiated by Karaism. Beginning with Saadiah we find
a rabbinic trend to downgrade agadah, the folklore material of
the Talmud, to explain away anthropomorphism and harmonize
Judaism with Greek and Arabic philosophical thinking.[29]

An interesting sidelight in the Karaite schism is that
for a long time Karaite and Rabbanite Jews intermarried and

protected one another's religious prerogatives in the Ketubah.
Betrothal and marriage documents are frequent among the Genizah
finds. These show that Karaite procedures were protected in
them. One example is that it is stipulated that the bridegroom
will observe the Karaite calendar, another that a Karaite bride
will not have to share with her husband a room on the Sabbath
where lights were kindled, and would not be compelled to dese-
crate the festivals observed in accordance with the Karaite
calendar. Many other examples may be adduced all of which lead
to two conclusions. The first is that marriage between Karaites and Rabbanites was not in the same class as that between
Samaritans and Jews. Secondly, the Karaites had a strong
enough sense of intellectual and spiritual security to impose
their will upon the Rabbanites. Sometimes it was done the
other way and Karaites promised to fulfill Rabbanite requirements. Yet it is surely of more interest to read how a bridegroom promises not to have light in his home on the Sabbath
nor to have sexual relationships with his wife on the Sabbath.
Contrary to the rabbinic view that the joy of sex is an appropriate Sabbath activity, the Karaites regarded it as exhaust-
ing and un-Sabbath-like. And as time progressed the Rabbanite
view became more vigorous in recommending sexual relationships
on the Sabbath.[30]

The use of fire on the Sabbath may not have been of great
moment in the Middle East. But it was of immense consequence
in the frigid weather of Troki, Lithuania, near Vilna, whither
Karaites seem to have emigrated during the thirteenth century.
People had to keep themselves warm or endanger their health.
Consequently we find that by the end of the fifteenth century
there had been an unaccustomed evolution in Karaism. People
were using fire on the Sabbath to heat their homes. It was
vigorously opposed by some scholars and resolutions were

passed in assemblies to prohibit it. But the will of the people had sway in Karaism as it often has in rabbinic Judaism. Thus while a letter of 1483 registers the attempt to permit this, the writer is aghast that anyone would violate the Sabbath. And yet centuries later as documents of the seventeenth century show, they were still enjoining it in public resolutions which means people were using fire to heat their furnaces or stoves.[31] Meanwhile also the communities of Constantinople and Adrianople had adopted the use of Sabbath candles during the fifteenth century, reversing a historic Karaite halakha. There were differences of opinion on this, and some who advocated the innovation as bringing cheer to the home continued to oppose heating homes as too wide a departure from tradition. But when all is said and done, the custom of Sabbath candles moved north from Turkey, as undoubtedly the heating of homes and food moved south. Even where communities continued to object to Sabbath candle-lighting at home, as in Egypt, Syria and Palestine, the individualism of Karaism asserting itself, they often kindled lights in the synagogues.[32]

This new attitude on the part of Karaites to lighting fires on the Sabbath was a far cry from the position taken by Judah Hadassi, twelfth century author of a work called *Eshkol ha'Kofer*, a severely polemical anti-rabbinic volume. In that book Hadassi argued that it is not even appropriate to kindle a fire on the Sabbath for the benefit of a childbearing woman even if her life be jeopardized. He argued from the statistical evidence that "so many women in childbed without a candle or fire who notwithstanding severe labor pains were saved by the grace of God...." Even earlier the thrust of the rabbinic leaders against this germinating insensitivity was to further elaborate ceremonial in order to make a contrary statement.

A special benediction was required for Sabbath candles by the post talmudic scholars and I feel certain this was virtually an anti-Karaite innovation. Since the Karaites were opposed to the kindling of lights altogether and called it a *desecration* of the Sabbath, the Rabbanites went to the opposite extreme and sanctified it with a berakha. They were asserting that not only may a Jew kindle this aid to comfort, but must affirm it to be part of God's gracious hallowing of life.[33]

After the earlier generations of great hostility the two major segments of Judaism began to have reasonable relationships as can be seen from the documents available to us. Marriage between them certainly indicates something. In addition to that Karaites began to study rabbinic literature and not only to obtain grist for their mills. Thus a major fourteenth century Karaite scholar, Aaron ben Elijah, who covers the entire range of Karaite religious thought, including halakha and philosophy, was also well-read in all the major rabbinic writings from the Talmud through Saadiah to Maimonides.[34] In his halakhic work, *Gan Eden,* he portrays the Karaite festivals and provides a reasonable picture of precisely what Karaites observed. He shows that "the first day of the seventh month" (Num. 29:1) is a day of trumpeting and joy (Neh. 8:9) and should be observed as such. But he rejects the rabbinic idea that it is Rosh Hashanah, "New Year's Day", since there is no evidence for that in scripture. And on the basis of Neh. 8:9 that it is a holy day of joy in which there is to be no weeping, he rejects the rabbinic conception of the day as one on which God reviews the deeds of man and writes his destiny in the book of life. On such a day, he argues, the Jew would have to be submissive and penitent and that contradicts scripture.[35] Furthermore he rejects the whole notion that on this first day of the seventh month human beings, in effect, are divided into three groups: the repentant and righteous who are destined for heaven, the wicked destined for hell, and the intermediate. The latter, Aaron points out, in accordance with rabbinic doctrine, are destined for hell if their sins outweigh their merits. This, he argues is a perversion of God's justice for He may be expected to deal with each person precisely according to his deeds. This means a man should be rewarded for his merits, and punished for his sins. With this as the philosophical basis, the Karaites rejected a major segment of Jewish theology: the theology of Rosh Hashanah.[36]

An even more erudite example of the rabinically-learned Karaite who presented Karaitic Judaism to his and following generations was Samuel b. Moses Al-Magribi, a North African who lived in Cairo during the fifteenth century.[37] A younger contemporary who flourished at the same time, Elijah ben Moses Basyatchi (1420-1490) of Adrianople and Constantinople, possessed great erudition which brought him a degree of authority as far away as Poland and Lithuania.[38] Elijah's compilation of Karaite halakha superseded Samuel's and other works and became the standard manual of halakhic reference for Karaism.

Karaism began as a dissent from the halakha of the talmudic schools, but found it necessary to develop its own halakha, its own pattern of observance and norms of conduct. By the fifteenth century this process had become as comprehensive within Karaism as it was in rabbinic Judaism. It is really quite an interesting speculation to consider whether the sixteenth century halakhic compilations of Joseph Karo, Moses Isserles, Joel Sirkes and Mordecai Jaffe, to mention only four of the most prominent, were not prompted by the growing halakhic presence of Karaism. Certainly as early as the

eleventh century attacks by Karaites upon the custom in Rabbanite synagogues to burn many candles and incense in honor of the
Torah on the Festival of Simhat Torah brought a prohibition of
the custom from Gaon Hai. There is also the case of Rabbi
David ibn Zimra (1479-1573).[39] Here we have a clear example
of Karaite impact. He makes many references to them in his
writings including the information that they treated Rabbanite
wine like gentile wine unless the person swore an oath to its
fitness, and would not eat Rabbanite meat unless a Karaite was
present when the animal was slaughtered and was able to testify to its fitness. The strictures against meat and wine were
reciprocated.[40] While, as we have seen, marriage between Karaites and Rabbanites did take place, R. David ibn Zimra forbade
it. He was struck with indignation over the fact that Karaite
women did not practice immersion of the whole body after their
menstrual period but considered a sprinkling to be adequate.
This was a matter of dispute among rabbis and Ibn Zimra took
a vigorous stand. It is, of course, reminiscent of the Christian acceptance of "infusion", sprinkling of water rather than
full baptism, and this perhaps, more than anything else, disturbed Ibn Zimra. In any case he used that as an argument
against marriage with Karaites, declaring their women to be
in a perpetual state of menstruation with whom one is not permitted to have sexual relations.[41]

B. *A Glance at Karaite Religion*

1. *Festivals and Fast Days*

What we see from the above is that one of the most prominent medieval scholars was much preoccupied with the Karaites.
He disputed with them, attacked them, decided halakha stringent-

ly in order to effect a better separation from them, and zealously yearned to convert them.[42] Part of his attack upon them was their mode of observance of festivals and the fact that their dates differed. But there were other matters of concern. The Karaites carefully considered the chemical changes that took place in products and declared it to be permitted to use certain compounds on Passover when they contain grain ingredients that have undergone chemical change.[43] This is basically proper talmudic halakha as well. In theory chemical transformation renders something a wholly new product and thereby frees it from restrictions that were appropriate to the original ingredients. But rabbinic Judaism, in its more stringent forms, has not always adhered to this. Even in modern times this has remained a source of conflict between those who prohibit the use of gelatin unless it is known to be of kosher animal ingredients and those who permit it on the basis of its being a chemically changed product and therefore no longer under the previous restrictions appropriate to a non-kosher animal product.[44]

Certainly if one carefully analyzes Al-Magribi's halakha on the "Kinds of Work Prohibited on Holidays" one must objectively conclude that rabbinic halakhists should have found little to attack. The Karaite treatment of the holy days was indeed conservative. Not only were all those activities that were prohibited in talmudic Judaism also prohibited by the Karaites, but even such activities as were permitted by talmudic Judaism were prohibited by the Karaites.[45] In this as in so many other matters the Karaites were quite pietistically conservative. Yet one great quarrel with them regarding the festivals was that they rejected the second day of the festivals observed by rabbinic Judaism in the diaspora, and followed

their own calendar so that the holy days occurred on different
dates. This meant that from the rabbinic point of view the
Karaites were "desecrating" holy days when they were not observing as holy the days observed by the Rabbanites. Conversely the Karaites deemed the Rabbanites as desecrating holy days
for not observing those considered holy by Karaite decision.[46]

One of the major differences of opinion between Karaites
and Rabbanites, as long ago between so-called Pharisees and
Sadducees, was the question of the offering of the first grain
of the Passover harvest and the counting of the weeks to
Shabuot or Pentecost. Karaites, like the so-called Sadducees
of ancient times took the verse "on the morrow after the Sabbath" (Lev. 23:11) to mean the first Sunday of the Passover
week.[47]

The Fasts of the Karaites also differed from that of the
Rabbanites. They based themselves on scripture to enjoin the
people to fast on the tenth day of the Hebrew month of Tebet,
the ninth day of the month Tamuz, the seventh and tenth days
of the month of Ab and on the twenty-fourth of the month of
Tishri. The Rabbanites fasted on the seventeenth and ninth
days of Tamuz and Ab respectively, on the third day of Tishri
and the tenth of Tebet. The Karaites, as always, were following precise references in scripture.[48] The Rabbanites historically had interpreted the verses differently, taking the
fast of the seventh to mark the assassination of Governor
Gedaliah in 597 B.C. which led to the debacle and complete
ruin of 587 B.C. They fasted on the ninth of Ab as the day
of destruction while the Karaites fasted, probably correctly,
on the tenth. The disparities between Rabbanites and Karaites
were the product of textual inferences and it should not go
unmentioned even at this late date that there were times when
the Karaites may have been correct. Thus in the thirteenth

century the disciples of R. Meir of Rothenburg reported in the
notes that ostensibly represent his teaching that the fast of
Gedaliah was "tradition". Indeed anything non-pentateuchal was
divrai sophrim "sopheric" or *divrai kabalah*, "tradition" from
prophetic or wisdom literature. But in the case of the fast
of Gedaliah it was not even specific. The verses referring
to his assassination did not mention the third of Tishri nor
the fasting. No wonder, therefore, that as late as the third
and fourth centuries some rabbis held it was optional.[49] And
no wonder too that it was one of the practices of rabbinic
Judaism that was abrogated by Karaism.

The same case could be made for abolishing the most important fast-day of the Jewish liturgical calendar (except for
Yom Kippur), the Ninth of Ab, the day that commemorates the
destruction of both the First and Second Temples in Jerusalem
in 587 B.C. and 70 A.D. It might also be suggested that some
of these matters that became basic divergences were relatively
trivial. But that is a value judgment one cannot make when
dealing with the history of religion. When a day is invested
with sanctity it is no longer a trivial matter to the believer
whether that day is today or tomorrow. For the Karaites the
Bible clearly invested the tenth of Ab with a special character. For the Rabbanites "tradition", which was as valid as
scripture, had set the date to be commemorated as the ninth.
For the Karaite the ninth had no significance. For the Rabbanite the tenth had no special character. This same point
applies to other days, festivals and fast days, and when
persons are not observing the same days as sacred they have
a natural tendency to separate for liturgy, and therefore establish separate houses of worship and ultimately form what in
modern times we have customarily referred to as "denominations".
Karaism, therefore, was a denomination within Judaism, and was

never quite rent asunder from the mother faith as was Christianity.

2. *Theology and Ethics*

Elijah Basyatchi, to whom reference was made earlier, provided an excellent summary of the fundamental philosophy of halakha as believed, practiced and applied in Karaism. There can be no question that a cursory examination alone already reveals the profound and extensive kinship between the highly-developed and sophisticated "dissenting" movement and rabbinic Judaism in the fifteenth century. Karaism placed a heavier premium upon scripture but used analogy widely to expand the meaning of scripture and placed a value upon "Karaite tradition". They argued, however, that while Rabbanite tradition abrogates scripture and innovates what is not in, nor derivable from scripture, Karaite tradition never goes "against that which is recorded in the writ of divine truth". And therefore, in summary, Basyatchi said that when a tradition does not contradict scripture, does not create something not derivable from scripture, is accepted by all Israel, and can be supported from scripture, it is to be considered "a genuine tradition, and we must accept it". And this, Basyatchi surprisingly added, applies as well to the Rabbanite Mishnah and Talmud, and that Karaites should study that literature. In addition he refers frequently to Karaite scholars with the title "Rabbi". And thus in four centuries the dissenters had come full cycle. From a rebellion against talmudic Judaism they came to incorporate its elements into their own religious patterns.[50]

Basyatchi also formulated "Ten Principles of Faith" in the style of Maimonides. The ten are literally similar to Maimonides' thirteen. The ten principles include the thirteen

of Maimonides who called them the "thirteen *yesodot*" ("fundamentals" or "foundations"). In order to make this comparison
I offer here those of Maimonides rather than to wait for the
later chapter in which we will discuss him at greater length.

In the following arrangement the number in the left margin
represents the item as given by Maimonides in his series. The
number in parenthesis following the "fundamental" stated by Maimonides represents the item in the sequence given by Basyatchi.

Maimonides	*Basyatchi*
1. The Existence of a Creator. (1)	All has been created.
2. The Oneness of God. (3)	The Creator is eternal.
3. The Incorporeality of God. (3)	The Creator has no likeness and is unique in every respect.
4. The Pre-Existence (Eternity) of God. (2)	The Creator sent Moses.
5. God alone is worthy of worship.	The Creator sent scripture with Moses.
6. Prophecy is true. (7)	The believer must know scripture.
7. The prophecy of Moses is supreme. (4)	God inspired the other prophets.
8. Revelation included both scripture and tradition. (5)	God will resurrect all mankind on the Day of Judgment.
9. The Dual-Torah is complete.	God requites each person according to his deeds.
10. God knows man's actions.	A Messiah of Davidic descent will come.
11. God rewards and punishes. (9)	
12. A Messiah will come. (10)	
13. There will be resurrection of the dead. (8)[51]	

Maimonides' series does not contain no. 6 of Basyatchi's sequence. That was not considered a "fundamental" of the faith in Judaism although the mizvah of religious study was considered of highest priority. It is an *act* of religion, not a matter of "faith" or belief. Maimonides listed only doctrines, not "action". Basyatchi apparently thought that act is so all-important that it must be given the priority of a fundamental doctrine. On the other hand Basyatchi did not list God's exclusive right to worship by His faithful, item 5 in Maimonides' series. Possibly Basyatchi thought this should be taken for granted in Monotheism. Basyatchi probably also considered that Maimonides' tenth fundamental, that God knows man's deeds, need not be specified, since it is implied in the doctrine of reward and punishment. As for Maimonides' ninth, that was the fundamental divergence of Karaism: the rejection of a Dual-Torah concept, a "revealed supplement" (the so-called "Oral Law") alongside Torah. Maimonides' second and third principles were combined into one forming the third doctrine of Basyatchi. Possibly Basyatchi wanted to create a "decalogue" parallel to the decalogue of scripture. In any case this fifteenth century summation of the theology of Karaite Judaism bears out the point that theologically there was hardly a substantial difference between the two denominations. The ethical imperatives summarized by Basyatchi are also quite in keeping with rabbinic ethics, as are his strictures on parent-child relationships, the honoring of the aged and the scholars.[52]

3. *Karaite Liturgy*[53]

Every religious movement must, from the outset, provide its adherents with a liturgy. As noted earlier the worship of Judaism reflects its theology. This holds true for every version of Judaism both in medieval times and in modern times.

The Karaite scholars were bound to remove from their liturgy all those elements of the standard order of worship that they believed to be erroneous accretions from the rejected talmudic literature, as well as such elements or even whole worship periods that are not sustained by scripture. They nevertheless began with the basic proposition of rabbinic Judaism, that ten persons constitute a quorum for public worship. And they insisted that the men don the prayershawls with the fringes for worship.[54] They developed various prayerbooks and there existed among them the same kind of diversity as among Rabbanites.[55]

Anan returned to two daily prayer periods to commemorate the two daily offerings, the *Shaḥrit* and *Minḥah*, morning and afternoon burnt offerings, of the ancient Jerusalem cult. He thereby rejected the third service found in the rabbinic ritual, the *Màriv* (evening worship). He also restored priestly and levitical prerogatives in worship such as the reading of sacrificial passages and the daily Psalm respectively. Later Karaites, however, did not continue these prerogatives, nor were they satisfied with only two worship periods in the five-period Moslem culture. Similarly while Karaites insisted that prayer should consist of biblical verses, in time they allowed the validity of compositions by latter-day Karaites and even non-Karaite poets. For example, the hymn that is chanted to accompany a bridegroom from his home to the place where the wedding is to take place, was composed by a Rabbanite.[56]

In his liturgy Anan provided that it begin with the Torah reading that ordains the daily sacrifice (Num. 28:1-8).[57] Appropriate berakhot were said but here too he followed scriptural models instead of rabbinic examples.[58] He also introduced the customary *Musaph* ("Additional") worship order on those days that had scripturally prescribed additional sacrifices: the Sabbath, New Moons and festivals.[59] According to later authorities, Karaites re-introduced the regular rabbinic annual cycle of Torah readings and called up seven persons each week to read a passage.[60] Anan also had berakhot before and after meals and for a variety of other occasions. But his berakhot varied from the rabbinic in that they were closely related to actual quotations in scripture.[61] The liturgy of the Feast of Weeks was entirely devoid of any of the relationship with the revelation at Sinai ascribed to it by rabbinic Judaism. That significant occasion, despite the Torah being the fundamental cornerstone of the faith, was apparently not commemorated in a sacred festival by Karaites since the Torah had provided for none. Yom Kippur seems to have had four worship periods in contrast to the five of rabbinic Judaism.[62] Since the rabbinic festival Simhat Torah was not scriptural the Karaites did not observe it. In order to celebrate the Torah cycle the Karaites did so on the Sabbath of renewal of the cycle when Genesis was read again.[63]

4. *Summation*

The Karaites were no more monolithic than the Rabbanites. Both denominations enjoyed and indulged a high degree of diversity. At any specific time within both circles it was the power of the majority that governed a given community, not an "orthodoxy". And frequently that majority was backed by secular power.

The theology of Karaism was relatively parallel to rabbinic Judaism with very few substantive differences. The greatest divergence was on the question of rabbinic authority as manifested by the geonim or embodied in the Talmud. For their part the Karaites placed greater emphasis upon scripture.

The Karaites multiplied in some areas during some periods.
But they never became a mass movement and never outnumbered
Rabbanites in any of the great centers. On the other hand,
outside of the major centers where Karaite synagogues established themselves, Karaites may have worshipped in the regular
synagogues and participated fully in the life of the Jewish
community without separate communal identity. This is no
different from modern Jews who in mind and at home may be
"reformist" but attend what may be the only synagogue in town,
which may be more traditional than their private inclinations.
The reverse may also be true, of the more traditional Jew who
is compelled to attend a less traditional synagogue.[64]

There is always a danger of exaggerating the influences
of one religious manifestation upon another. Similarly it
is possible to attribute too great an impact by Karaism upon
Judaism. Yet one must not be guilty of excessive understate-
ment. In every period of history Judaism has evolved in a
variety of expressions. These diverse manifestations of the
same religion have in part been due to internal changes and
in part to external influences. Challenges arise from new
ideas, new environments, new movements. Responses must be
made. And the manner of the response determines the future
course of the religious tradition. As the survey in this
chapter indicates, there can be no question that Karaism had
some impact upon the future course of Judaism. In some instances it compelled rabbis to harden lines and become reactionary. In some instances it influenced flexibility. It
probably had some role in the rise of many efforts to compile
the recommended halakha. In any event, one fact emerges clearly: the authorities in Judaism never terminated the status of
Karaites as Jews, and they remained a denomination within

Judaism. They were perhaps a major precedent coming down from
ancient times right into the nineteenth century that served as
example first for Reform Judaism and later for Conservative
Judaism in modern times.

Historians believe the first reaction to Karaism came from
Gaon Natronai in the ninth century. According to R. Amram who
reported it in his prayerbook, Natronai suggested they be banished from the synagogues and not be allowed to pray with other
Jews until they promise to mend their ways.[65] This was obviously an attempt to duplicate what the rabbis of the first
century had done regarding Christian Jews. But basically the
relationship was ambivalent, having its positive and its negative moments. Not even the ban pronounced on each festival of
Tabernacles for a period of years against the violators of the
prohibition on eating dairy and meat together (namely, the
Karaites) provoked the Karaites more than may be expected.[66]
That excommunication, interestingly enough, was for what would
seem a relatively trivial matter in modern times when most
Jews are such "violaters". But although that soon ceased, as
regards the dietary practices, Maimonides banned meat slaughtered by Karaites and suggested that the Jewish community,
even in the absence of the old constitutional Sanhedrin, had
the power to inflict capital punishment upon "heretics, Sadducees and Boethoseans". Obviously the reference is to Karaites.
His reason: "...that they may not corrupt Israel and cause it
to lose its faith." But as spiritual leader of Fustat Maimonides was leader of *all* the Jews, including the active Karaite
community, and his son and successor, R. Abraham, officiated
similarly. As a matter of record Maimonides in Fustat contradicted himself, denying that the Karaites were technically
minim ("sectarians" or "heretics" depending upon the context

and century) and urged that they be treated with respect as
long as they do not slight the present or past rabbinic
sages.[67]

We have seen above how Karaites and Rabbanites may have
influenced the religious practices of one another. There was
a tendency on the part of Karaites to outdo the pietism of
Rabbanites and this would lead to Rabbanite imitation. For
example, the Karaites had a custom of remaining in a standing
posture all through Yom Kippur in prayer, meditation and pen-
ance. This became a custom among some Rabbanite circles and
is even practiced today in pietistic circles.[68] The polemics,
even if sometimes acrimonious and vituperative, had the positive effect of compelling both denominations to enrich the
corpus of Judaica. A massive religious literature resulted.

Undoubtedly the raw political power of the majority "Establishment" in community after community throughout the lands
of Jewish dispersion had a large role in the decline of Karaism. But I tend to think the causes of decline were also inherent in Karaism, so that even if the absence of communal or
political power had been less of a factor the movement would
nevertheless not have gained permanent mass adherence. There
was the ascetic strain which was not attractive in Karaism.
The problem is also status quo religion versus dynamic religion. The religion which has shown historic adaptability and
has been able to acculturate successfully and yet preserve its
tenets and a perennial stream of identifiable tradition within
radical change has had greater promise than one which has bowed
to conservative doctrine striving to remain anchored in the
past without a vision for the future. Leniency in the halakha
was a hallmark of rabbinic Judaism which Karaism never quite
grasped or emulated. Karaism made out of joyous festivals

days of self-denial while in rabbinic Judaism they were re storative. Karaism deprived synagogue liturgy of the same degree of warmth and variety that was enjoyed in Rabbanite synagogues. It is this principle of life, the survival of the organism that adjusts and undergoes metamorphosis, that brought rabbinic Judaism into the modern world in its wide variety of expressions while Karaism decreasingly played a vital role in Judaism.[69]

CHAPTER 5

Iberia: Glory and Tragedy

I. THE PARAMETERS

This is not a "history of the Jews" and consequently this
chapter will not undertake a survey of Jewish life in Spain.
We will omit discussion of the Jewish "political" status in the
plethora of medieval Spanish states; how Jewish communal "autonomy" functioned; and the social political and economic life
of Jews. It is not how Jews constituted a "state within a
state" that concerns us in this volume. We will not survey
their achievements in astronomy, mathematics, map-making and
navigation in which many medieval Spanish Jews excelled.
Trade, guilds, and finance will not occupy us, nor will their
role in administration and diplomacy in the several Spanish
states, both Islamic and Christian, in which they frequently
enjoyed a large role.[1]

Rather, this chapter will survey the state of Judaism in
Spain. We will examine the acculturation of Spanish Jews to
the cultural milieu and their simultaneous preservation of
Judaism. We will consider the rise of the halakhic literature
and the special spheres of domestic relations (marriage and
divorce). The acculturation will be sketched out briefly in
a discussion of the "golden age" of Spanish Jewish history for
what it teaches about Jewish history as a whole in terms of
the challenge by environment and response by acculturation

plus preservation of faith-values. Spain represents the same
ambivalence seen in the history of Judaism at other times and
in other places. The "golden age" is a time of acculturation
when Jews are deeply immersed in the culture of their environment. They are absorbing from it and contributing to it.
This Jewish experience in its confrontation with the medieval
Islamic world has been justly called a "symbiosis". But then
again we will see retrenchment, the Jewish sage and rabbi pro-
moting separatism, combating secular education, turning his
back on the scientific revolution and the expansive philosophical and literary phenomena of the twelfth to the fifteenth
centuries.

Judaism in Spain was not radically different from that of
Babylonia. But it had its variations. Within Spain there
were variations from Castile to Andulusia, from Aragon to Cat-
alonia, and frequently from one city to another. What we have
surveyed as the theology of Jewish worship in the third chapter applied as well in Spain as in Babylonia. It was to Spain
that the first Babylonian prayerbook was sent. Halakhic practice in the field of ritual and domestic relations which we
will survey was also more or less similar to that of Babylonia.
But it must not be overlooked that similarity is not uniformity. And we will see that the rabbis of Spain were insistent
upon their independence and the preservation of local *minhag*.
Perhaps it is in the area that we will not survey: the civil
law, that Spanish halakha was most directly transformed from
that of Babylonia. That we do not survey it is not to imply
that the vast and significant material that falls under the
category of civil law is not to be considered "Judaism". By
no means. Exodus 21:1-23:19, the Covenant Code, or Leviticus
19, the Holiness Code, certainly point up the reality for
Judaism that there is no separation between the Holy and the

Profane, there is no "secular" and "sacred". All is encompassed by the spiritual values of Judaism. But in contemporary Judaism the ancient or medieval civil law does not function. Not even in the State of Israel is the category of torts and damages, and such specifics as laws of embezzlement, or partnership, trade and commerce, or banking and finance, more than casually or remotely rooted in the halakha. We only survey those aspects of the Judaic faith that have remained part of the religious scene. This means we consider when pertinent in the respective chapters, theological doctrine, liturgy, religious literary output, scholarship and scholars, the ritual of festivals and Sabbath, the institution of the synagogue, domestic relations and moral principles.

That there is a weightier portion that tells of halakha is because halakha was the foremost product of the rabbinic scholars. We will see that frequently Jewish interest in theology led to speculative philosophy that was regarded as dangerous by some of the leading scholars. This caused them to oppose philosophy strenuously. Kabalah, Greek philosophy, science, the challenge of Islamic theology were all very important factors for the medieval Jew in Spain. And as in Babylonia, Egypt, Palestine and North Africa, the rabbis of Spain faced the Karaite challenge.

II. THE "GOLDEN AGE" IN SPAIN

A. *Beginnings*

During the long centuries in which the geonic interpretation of talmudic Judaism evolved in interplay with Karaism, the scene was set largely in the Eastern Mediterranean from

Egypt to Persia. Meanwhile new communities flourished in the Western Mediterranean, notably Kairuwan, Fez and the provinces of Spain. The tenth and eleventh centuries witnessed the appearance of great scholars of Judaism in those areas. They effectively asserted their religious independence from the Babylonian geonim and became authorities in the halakha in their own right. When Islam moved across the Straits of Gibralter to conquer Spain, the Jews of Spain, frequently disadvantaged over the centuries by the Christian powers on the continent, gained freedom and ease and were enabled to participate in the life of society as well as to further the internal enrichment of Judaism. In the wake of the Islamic conquest one of the most notable rabbis of the eleventh century, Isaac of Fez (1013-1103) moved to Lucena in Southern Spain and helped make Spain into an illustrious center of Jewish learning. At that time both the Rhineland and Southern Italy were emerging as unusually well-developed areas of Judaic studies.

But of all these developments in Spain, North Africa, Southern Italy, Northern France and Germany as well as Provence in the south of France, perhaps the most notable phenomenon for several centuries, and the most intriguing from a historical standpoint, is what has come to be called "the Golden Age in Spain".[2] This period may be dated about 950-1150 and saw the rise of great Jewish centers of religion and learning in Seville, Granada, Cordova, Barcelona, Toledo and Malaga. From India to the Atlantic Jews were now becoming immersed in the sophisticated Arabic renaissance. In a way unknown to the Jews of geonic Babylonia, however, the Jews of Spain were acculturating to all aspects of Arabic culture except for the religion of Islam.

When, in 711, Tarik the Great crossed the Straits of Gibralter he and Islam were welcomed by Jews as liberators from the native Visigothic population. This new freedom was an incentive to participate in the science, poetry, linguistics and philosophy of the Arabic renaissance. There are over thirteen-hundred written volumes of responsa that reflect the customs of the home and synagogue, the social manners and dress, the government of Jewish communities, the economics, occupations and institutions of Jews from Babylonia to the Atlantic, from Africa to the North Sea.[3]

One of the advantages the Jews of Islamic Spain enjoyed over previous generations was the new technology of bookmaking. Less expensive paper replaced the ancient parchment and papyrus which kept books out of the possession of the average man and made it expensive for a budding literary genius to find something to which he might transpose his creations. This certainly had an impact upon literary output. But the extent of distribution and availability was still limited by the need to make hand-written copies. For example, the *Introduction to the Talmud* by one of Spain's earliest poet-scholars, Samuel ibn Nagrela, one of the most significant post-geonic scholarly discussions of the history and methodology of the Talmud, has survived only in excerpts.[4] No wonder, therefore, that culture had to be supported by wealthy and influential patrons. And such was the case in Spain. It is owing to that fortunate circumstance that poetry flourished there. A measure of its significance is that even in the North European liturgical work of R. Simḥah of Vitry the bulk of liturgical compositions are by the Spaniards Solomon ibn Gabirol, Abraham ibn Ezra and Yehudah Halevi.[5] Even the liturgical compositions of one of Northern Europe's most illustrious rabbinic scholars,

R. Gershom of Mayence, were not included in the Vitry prayerbook. And this, despite the fact that his responsum on the
status of a reconverted apostate was quoted extensively. It
is evident that R. Simḥah valued the halakha of R. Gershom
more than his poetry.[6]

Poetic composition was often a requisite for a good
career in public life and certainly for standing among the
intellectual elite. Some of the greatest Jewish poets in
those earlier centuries were also among the well-known rabbinic scholars and philosophers. For out of the excitement
of the Arabic renaissance there came a whole series of Spanish
Jews who gave the period its "golden age" reputation. Among
them were Samuel ibn Nagrela, Solomon ibn Gabirol (ca. 1022-
1070), Moses ibn Ezra (ca. 1060-1138) and Yehudah Halevi (ca.
1075-1141).[7]

The twelfth century and Yehudah Halevi, however, represent the summit of the phenomenon. After that the spirit
changed, the rabbis seem to have changed, and ideas changed.
But first we have to move backward in time to examine the roots
from which the Hebraic renaissance sprang. We are not too
familiar with the intellectual and spiritual scene in the
early centuries of Jewish residence in Spain. They came there
in or before the first century or the Apostle Paul would not
have contemplated a mission to Spain.[8] But the first document-
able date is that of Severus, Bishop of Majorica who, in a
letter dated 418, tells of his triumph in converting the Jews
of Minorca to Christianity. Some of those Jews had previously
fled from before the Visigoths who were conquering the peninsula at that time.[9]

B. Ḥasdai ibn Shaprut

Our knowledge of religious life in Spain only begins to take shape in the ninth century with correspondence between the geonim of Babylonia and Lucena and Barcelona in Spain. But it remains meager until the emergence of Abu Yusuf Ḥasdai ibn Shaprut, 915-970. He was a physician and a scholar, knowledgable in Latin. He served as a diplomatic trouble-shooter between Christian and Moslem rulers. We find he both received embassies such as that of Emperor Otto I of the Holy Roman Empire in 956, and went to foreign courts on other diplomatic missions.[10]

For the history of Judaism, however, far more important than his role as a Spanish diplomat was Ḥasdai's role as a patron of culture and virtual initiator of the so-called "golden age". He really serves as a "prototype". For what he achieved in Cordova was repeated in many of the great cities of Islamic Spain. He was a forerunner of a modern "Foundation", offering grants, stipends and fellowships to scholars, poets and scribes. His concern made it possible for at least two significant grammarian-poets to make their contributions to Judaism. Ḥasdai financed the careers of the notable poet Dunash ibn Labrat and Menaḥem ibn Saruk of Tortosa who compiled the first dictionary of Biblical Hebrew. Ḥasdai played an additional significant role merely by setting the example, for others emulated him.[11]

C. Samuel ibn Nagrela (ha'Nagid)

The most important, and perhaps the most colorful of this "golden age" type of personality was Rabbi Samuel ha'Levi, better known as Samuel ibn Nagrela (or Nagdela or ha'Nagid), 993-1063, of Granada. He was the patron of the poet-philoso-

pher Solomon ibn Gabirol. But Samuel was not only a patron of
culture and diplomat like Ḥasdai. He was himself a poet and
halakkic scholar, a composer of liturgy, a master of elegent
language and compiler of a Hebrew dictionary. And yet, perhaps his most important contribution was the establishment of
an academy at Granada, and a library. There he maintained
numerous scribes constantly at work copying manuscripts. It
was not a monastery in the Christian sense where monks cease-
lessly did similar vital work, but the result was the same.
Out of his academy corps of copyists came a steady stream of
Mishnah and Talmud editions that were made available to Spanish students in Granada and elsewhere. But these editions
were also shipped abroad to academies in North Africa, Egypt,
Sicily, and even to the heartland of Judaism, the Holy City,
and to Babylonia.[12]

Ibn Nagrela was a refugee from Cordova in 1013 before he
settled at Granada. This fact too is a "prototype" event of
medieval Jewish history. A great center comes upon leaner
times as a result of persecution. But a brand is plucked from
the fire and kindles a new flame elsewhere, initiating a new
and greater center. There can be no doubt that Samuel played
a significant role in establishing Spanish Jewish religious
independence from Babylonia. Even if his boast that "Spain
had been a seat of Jewish learning...since the days of the
[First] Exile from Jerusalem" was an overstatement, the claim
in itself was a validation for independent authority. This
was identical to the claim made by the geonim to validate
Babylonian independence from Palestinian authority hundreds of
years earlier. This independence was asserted despite the in-
direct communication Samuel carried on with the Gaon Hai of
Babylon through the mediation of the famous scholar of Kairuwan, R. Nissim b. Jacob.[13]

This highlights an interesting aspect of the history of Judaism. There was perhaps never a time when there was not a direct line of spiritual-scholarly communication from one great center shedding its glory upon another until the new one assumed the mantle of historic leadership destined in time to shed of its glory upon yet another. The Babylonian community justly claimed antiquity. But its great talmudic scholars of the third century who inaugurated the Babylonian era of ascendancy had been disciples of the Palestinian R. Judah the Nasi who was editor of the Mishnah. They returned to Babylonia. Similarly the Spanish centers received their initial learning through geonic responsa. And even more important talmudic-halakhic learning in Spain was established by a Babylonian scholar, R. Moses b. Ḥanokh in 972 at Cordova. Furthermore, while scholars now grew in Spain and academies were established in other cities, Samuel ibn Nagrela was also in constant contact with the Kairuwan community and through its rabbi with the Gaon Hai. The Spanish Jews supported the Babylonian academies. Nevertheless Samuel ha'Nagid lived at a time when Spanish Jews were ready for local autonomy in matters halakhic. The son of R. Moses, R. Ḥanokh in Cordova had already begun to assert this. And Samuel further projected the image and the reality.[14]

Aside from his *Introduction to the Talmud*, Samuel also wrote what was probably a major work in the halakha which has not survived. It was, according to his own testimony, a very ambitious work, but is known to us only in fragments. It was called *Hilkhata Gavrata* (Mighty Halakha). An interesting aspect of this compilation is that it proves beyond a shadow of a doubt the thesis that at times, certainly around 1050, and in the case of Samuel, halakhic works were composed in reaction to Karaites, and not only to satisfy an internal communal need for

systematization and summation of complex and extensive material.
Samuel wrote a poem in which he tells of his project and specifically attributes its purpose to polemics with the ever-increasing Karaite presence. It is most interesting that he charges
them with "making lenient the stringent", for as we have noted
in the previous chapter this was a line of attack they made
upon Rabbanites. He also alludes to the fact that "the *minim*
have strengthened the arm", that is, grown in power, and the
only conceivable group that could be termed *minim* ("sectarians",
"heretics") in eleventh century Spain were Karaites.[15] The influence of the Babylonian geonim on Spanish halakha is here
once again evident. In a very small fragment of Samuel's work
we find the names of Amram and Hai, but especially what appears
to be a heavy reliance upon Hai's views.[16] It might therefore
be argued that Samuel was dependent upon Hai and not at all
independent. But we must remember his own declaration of independent authority cited previously. In the *Hilkhata*, of
which albeit we possess insufficient excerpts to state with
any certainty what the case may be, Samuel may have been referring to Hai as a point of view, now agreeing with him and
then again perhaps calling upon Spanish custom or his own
views as an alternative option.

As the newly self-conscious Jewish communities of the west
turned their talents to religious study and research they con-
sciously reaffirmed the historic principles that had always
been operative in Judaism. They developed their own approach
to the study and compilation of halakha to meet their own
Spanish needs. Not only did Samuel ibn Nagrela pursue that
course, but others whose works have been better known also did.
Samuel's contemporary Isaac ben Yehudah ibn Gayyat compiled a
halakhic work with an impressive title, *Halakhot Kelulot* (Com-

prehensive Halakha). This was a book devoted almost entirely
to the ritual of Judaism, encompassing festival observance and
liturgy. And around the same time, at the turn of the eleventh-
twelfth centuries, Yehudah bar Barzillai of Barcelona put together a near-encyclopedia of all the halakha that was of contemporary relevance. Only parts of his massive work survive,
the main section *Sefer Ha'Ittim* (Book of Seasons) is another
collection of halakha covering the festivals.[17]

Some claim Karaism was not strong in Spain. On the other
hand it seems to have been strong enough to be noticed. It
appears that rabbis in Spain did not have sufficient confidence
in merely compiling halakhic guidance-books for their followers.
They engaged as well in severe purges of Karaites. While the
Spanish scholars were asserting their independence from Babylonia and reaffirming their right to Spanish relevance and the
authority of their own contemporary scholars, they adopted
something of the Moslem thrust toward orthodoxy then prevalent
among North African Berbers who had their eyes on Spain. The
Almoravides and Almorhades were religious reactionaries who,
toward the end of the eleventh century and early in the
twelfth century, cast their gloomy reflections over Spain.
Judaism underwent internal crises at such times. Both Arab
incursions coincide with a spate of halakhic writings. And
it may be fair to surmise that both crises inspired the Rabbanites to further action against Karaites. The purges and
the halakhic writing may have been two sides of the same coin.
Certainly Samuel ibn Nagrela shows one side of the coin.
Crisis alone would have been sufficient incentive to cause
scholars to put into writing what they believed to be an appropriate summary of religious practice for this day. But
both factors were manifestly present. There was internal

challenge to the "establishment" and external crisis, in the
compilation of the Mishnah at the end of the third century;
in the editing of the Talmud in the sixth; and in the halakhic
work inaugurated by Yehudai Gaon in Babylonia in the eighth
century. This was again true in Spain during the eleventh
century.[18]

In any event, the appearance of Yehudah bar Barzillai's
work in the twelfth century undoubtedly served a dual purpose.
It provided guidance in rabbinic Judaism and furthered the rejection of Karaite ideas. On the one hand he provided some
evidence for the argument of Karaites that Rabbanites were
superstitious and that they violated the Torah's pronounce-
ments against magic. People, for example, would want to post-
pone weddings because of unfavorable omens in the stars. R.
Yehudah argued against this, as Karaites did, as a violation
of the Torah's injunctions against magic, divination and
astrology. On the other hand the fact that this attitude did
exist within the Jewish community compelled him to defend Rabbanites against the Karaite charges that Rabbanites were guilty
of such violations. He also had to defend Rabbanites against
Karaite charges that Rabbanites were guilty of anthropomorphism. For this reason too he opposed adding the *piyutim* to
worship, for these poems tended to increase the incidence of
anthropomorphism.[19]

D. *The "Golden Age" Ends*

Perhaps the climax of this particular period in Spain was
reached with Yehudah Halevi (1075-1141), a sponge of three
cultures, who lived on both sides of the line of Islamic and
Christian Spain at different times of his life, and rejected
both. The "golden age" in Spain may be said to have come to

a close in the golden verses of Halevi, of whom we will speak
in the next chapter. After the middle of the twelfth century
the major literary activity was in rabbinics. The humanism
engendered in the *belles lettres* of the Arab renaissance came
to a close and the rabbinic scholars seem to have drawn into
themselves as into a shell. Strong voices of conservatism
held sway in the thirteenth and fourteenth centuries. Obviously when surveying five or six centuries within a brief
space it is necessary to generalize. The student should always
be aware, and beware, of overgeneralization. Not all the religious views in Barcelona would necessarily hold true for
Toledo. And the religious practices of Toledo may not have
been upheld in Saragossa.

III. SPANISH RESPONSA

We have seen in our discussion of the Babylonian geonim
that the responsa literature was an important medium for trans-
mission of their opinion abroad. For the historian, whether
of social or religious history, the responsa are vital as
primary sources. This holds true for Spain as well. We can
note historically that there is a coincidence between the
cessation of the flow of geonic responsa from Babylonia and
the beginning of a flow from Spain, France and Germany.[20]
This marks the beginning of western Jewish religious "independence". The notable tenth century R. Moses b. Ḥanokh of Cordova possibly began the Spanish stream, but we have relatively
few items prior to R. Isaac of Fez. Following him we have the
collections of responsa of R. Joseph ha'Levi ibn Migash. There
are many that belong to Moses Maimonides which some historians

include among the Spanish responsa, but it would seem that Maimonides should be clearly identified as an Egyptian scholar
where he did his major work and gained his reputation in
Fustat.[21]

The thirteenth and fourteenth centuries, however, provide
a great yield for us. Most especially are valuable the more
than 3000 responsa of R. Solomon ben Abraham ibn Aderet (1235-
1310) of Barcelona, one of medieval Judaism's leading scholars,
and the 1000 of R. Asher b. Yehiel of Toledo (1250-1328).[22]
These two men spanned a century in which Judaism probably
reached a peak in its Spanish eminence. For along with them
there was a galaxy of scholars, many of whom placed their stamp
upon the Judaism which ultimately emerged as the contemporary
Judaism we know. As a matter of record it may justly be said
that through the disciples he established in accordance with
the old pre-rabbinic dictum of the pre-Christian era "raise up
many disciples" (M. Abot 1:1), R. Asher became in a very real
sense a "father" of contemporary Judaism.

It has been stated that the study of Judaism was being
conducted in so prolific a number of academies under so many
eminent scholars that it had actually reached its fullest
flowering at the time of the expulsion of the Jews in 1492.
A writer in 1486 described Castile as "a land of academies and
students".[23] Indeed, in my estimation the term "golden age"
of Spain, if to be used at all, should be redated as 1250-1490
rather than being accorded to the earlier period of *belles
lettres*. The responsa literature give clear evidence of the
eminence and authority of the Spanish rabbis. One might say
that the condition of which we speak surely stretches from R.
Moses of Cordova through the last major responsa of R. Isaac
ben Sheshet Perfet (1326-1408) and R. Simon ben Zemah Duran
(1361-1444).[24]

There were numerous major scholars of Judaism who left
their imprint upon Judaism teaching in, and writing from their
schools in Spain and Provence. It would require several volumes to review their work and do a minimum of justice to their
lasting contributions. Here we confine ourselves to a few
highlights of only several aspects of Judaism in Spain. This
will center mainly in the area of domestic relations and the
function of the rabbinate in Spain. What those men did in
Spain through their responsa, commentaries and digests of
halakha helped determine the course of Judaism for some five
hundred years. Most especially was this true in the field of
marriage and divorce which remains a major issue for twentieth-
century Judaism in its quest for modernity and the equaliza-
tion of the status of men and women.

IV. THE THEOLOGY OF MARRIAGE IN MEDIEVAL SPAIN

A. *Premises*

The theology of marriage in Judaism for Jews of Spain was
without doubt the same as that which had prevailed in Palestine
and Babylonia, which then prevailed in Provence, France and
Germany and wherever Jews dwelt. Thus it should be borne in
mind that though we expound the notion of diversity in Judaism,
the theology of marriage transcends time and place, even when
details of custom do not.

It may be said that the theology of marriage begins with
Genesis 2:18, "And the Lord God said, it is not good that the
man is alone; I will make for him an appropriate mate."[25]
After the man encounters the woman and goes into ecstasy (2:23)
the Bible tells us: "Therefore a man leaves his father and his

mother and clings to his wife so that they become one flesh"
(v. 24).[26] The attitude of the husband toward the wife is
henceforth to be one of graciousness and gratitude. He is to
understand that without a wife he would enjoy no blessing or
joy and that he is not really a complete man.[27] On the other
hand the woman is to recognize her subordination to man. This
we read in Genesis 3:16. "To the woman He said, I will indeed
increase your labor pains, with distress you will bear children
and to your husband will be your longing; he will dominate
you." Now it should be recognized that while these passages
express a Jewish view of marriage they by no means constitute
a "doctrine", and much less a mandatory "dogma". If a Jew
believes marriage is a mistake in which he is trapped and that
his wife is a bore, he is not violating any serious theological position. Furthermore in the massive incohesive folklore
of a wide variety of midrashic works and the ágadah of the
Talmud there can be found contradictory sayings and dicta of
less inspiring nature. But how to judge the theology is by
examining the halakha. What the scholars required be practiced expressed what ought to be believed. What became the
consensus of life lived was what was really believed.

The premise of the halakha is clearly the love, appreciation and intimacy, but also the woman's subordination, as
exemplified in the examples given above. Thus Maimonides has
summed up for us that "...a man is to honor his wife more than
himself and to love her as himself. If he has monetary means
he is to increase her material benefits commensurately. He
should never cast upon her any excess dread, his words with
her should be tranquil and he should not be angry. Similarly
the sages commanded that the woman honor her husband more than
sufficiently and that she should fear him and carry out all her

tasks on the basis of his commands. He should be in her eyes
as a prince or king, fulfilling every desire of his heart and
keeping distant what he despises...."[28]

The halakhists naturally sought from time to time to summarize the relevant practice. This was, as we have seen,
either in response to the challenge of the environment (Islam,
Christian, Karaite) or simply to fill an internal need. As
the centuries moved forward the understanding of the marriage
theology expanded and deepened. What developed in Spain is
properly evaluated by examining the work of the sixteenth century scholar R. Joseph Karo of Safed because of two circumstances. Firstly he was born in Spain during the fifteenth
century and was of the refugee exodus of 1492. His education
and tradition was that of the Spanish scholars. Secondly,
when he compiled his own Shulhan Arukh around 1565 he based
his halakhic decisions on those of three other Spanish scholars, as well as having relied upon a fourth. In his volume
Even Ha'Ezer Karo summarizes the halakha of domestic relations,
obligations and rights, in every sphere of the husband-wife
relationship. His premise is that "every man is duty-bound
to marry a wife in order to reproduce and whoever does not...
contributes to the Shekhinah [Divine Indwelling Presence]
leaving Israel."[29] Thus Karo equates theologically the man's
perpetuation of the community with his contribution to making
God's Presence felt. And he goes on to say that while one may
not sell a scroll of the Torah--the Pentateuch in its sacred
synagogue form--for any other reason, he may do so for acquir-
ing funds for the study of Judaism or for marrying. And so he
places the obligation of a man to marry on the level of study
of Judaism--than which there is no greater mizvah--and in order
to acquire funds for it exempts one from so stringent an ordinance as not to sell Judaism's holiest ritual symbol.[30]

In the received texts of the Mishnah Aḅot we read in the
name of R. Yehudah ben Tema, whose identity is unclear, that a
man ought to marry at age eighteen. Whether this was meant as
halakha or not in its context is difficult to determine. Actually as it stands the paragraph contains a medley of pedagogical and social advice as well as several observations regarding
the reality of human existence. Be that as it may, this recom-
mendation was embodied in the halakha and emerges here in Karo
as a primary requirement: "It is a miẓvah placed upon every
man that he marry a woman at eighteen years of age, and whoever marries earlier, at thirteen, has the choicest miẓvah,
but he should not marry before thirteen...in any case he should
not delay beyond twenty without a wife, and whoever delays beyond twenty, the court is to compel him to marry in order to
fulfill 'be fruitful and multiply' (Gen. 1:28)...." Karo goes
on, however, to make one exception: the scholar who must delay in order to polish himself up as a scholar. Thus study
still has an edge. But in the supremacy of early marriage,
and the duty to procreate, the value system is clearly evident.
This is further evident from the amount of space accorded it
by Maimonides. [31]

We find then that the theology of marriage for medieval
Spanish scholars emphasized the priority and the centrality in
its purpose of procreation. Furthermore, the whole area of
"family purity" was brought to a complex and comprehensive
fullsomeness in medieval thought. This is a subject which
properly belongs to a survey of biblical and talmudic religious development. But it must be noted that the biblical and
talmudic sources were expanded immensely in the medieval literature and tremendous importance was placed upon the separation of the sexes as related to the enforced separation during
menstrual periods of the female. All intimacy is barred from

the time the woman expects her menses (even before the flow
has actually begun) until seven days after the last blood was
seen, or approximately twelve days at a minimum. She is then
to immerse herself in a ritualarium (a pool designated for
the purpose of ritual purification) after which all forms of
intimacy including marital relations may be resumed.[32]

As a final word it should be noted that the term describing the marriage relationship is *kiddushin* which means
"sanctification" and refers to the act of betrothal and
marriage. The word is used as the Roman legal term *con-
nubium* was used, to denote a legal capacity to enter into
marriage.[33] Thus the term signifies the legal appropriateness of the relationship. Yet the rabbis chose this theological word related to the root for "holy", rather than a
legal term. Undoubtedly this choice of term puzzled scholars
everywhere for a long time. And so man's fancy may roam and
seek explication. Out of Castile in Spain where, as we will
see in a later chapter, medieval *Kabalah* (mysticism) received
a major impetus, came one such attempt to relate man's sexual
life to the ultimate of the holy. In the Zohar (Book of
Splendor), in a discussion of the verse, "You shall be holy
for I the Lord am holy" (Lev. 19:2), the author wrote that
at midnight "the Holy One, blessed be He, is in the Garden of
Eden and greater holiness is abroad". At that time when holiness is diffused throughout creation it is proper for man to
sanctify his life by uniting with his wife. Even more pref-
erable is the hour of midnight of the Sabbath, for then grace
abounds. The author adds, "Therefore, a man should rejoice
with his wife at that hour to bind her in affection to him....
When they are thus united they form one soul and one body....
Then God rests upon 'one' and lodges a holy spirit in it...."[34]

There was more to marriage than meets the eye. It was governed by a rational socially-oriented halakha designed to preserve conservative views of sexuality and morality. But there ran through this corpus of halakha a sense of theological mystery and awe about the human relationship and its predicament before God. The halakha was therefore designed to preserve what the sages innately and instinctively divined to be a sacramental act. We will therefore turn to a brief consideration of the question of sacrament in Judaism.

B. *Marriage as Sacrament*

Marriage is a sacrament. The terminology used for Jewish marriage is a sacramental term. It is true that the Mishnah says "a woman may be *acquired* in three ways". But it also says "a man consecrates" a woman. The "acquisition" provision merely delineates the civil law status that inheres in a marriage. Since she is technically legally his wife once he has given her a minimum coin of currency, an official document, or has had sexual consummation with her, either one of these three actions attested to by eligible witnesses, all of the laws become operative for both.[35]

But in the act of marriage is "consecration", as the Hebrew term *ķiddushin*, "sanctification", is understood. This is borne out by the very formula: "You are hereby consecrated unto me." In the Talmud we read that once a man has consecrated a woman he has in effect made her like holy objects consecrated to the Sanctuary. Just as they are forbidden to anyone other than a priest, so a wife is forbidden to anyone other than her husband. The relationship is covenantal and cultic and therefore is a sacrament.[36] Jews are not accustomed to referring to their religious events or practices as sacraments and often reject the notion. But I believe that it is because there is a fundamental misunderstanding of the term. Furthermore it is measured automatically against the Christian or Roman Catholic notion of sacraments as inherently mandatory for salvation. This, of course, is not the case in Judaism. But that does not alter the fact that Judaism has sacred events, sacraments, that are essential to the proper relationship between the Jew and his faith. Marriage is such a sacrament.[37]

An anonymous Tosafist of the twelfth or thirteenth century on the talmudic text under discussion remarks precisely what I have here intimated. He says that when a groom says to his bride, "'You are hereby consecrated unto me', this means to say, 'to be consecrated to me forever, for me alone', as one says in the case of holy objects 'they are hereby sanctified for God'."[38] Martin Buber has pointed out that to understand, for example, certain facets of the eighteenth century Hasidic movement, "...it is necessary to know, what has been all too little acknowledged, that a tendency towards sacramental life has always been powerful in Judaism."[39]

Since marriage was "a holy thing", a sacrament in a non-salvational Jewish sense, it was necessary to see that all steps leading to it, and later the relationship, would be in accordance with the values of the marital halakha, the guidance that is the will of God or that leads one to the fulfillment of the will of God. Toward this end the medieval Spanish rabbis further developed the already extant talmudic halakha, shaping it to meet the particular needs of Spain.

C. *Monogamy*

Some scholars articulate a thesis that Judaism evolved monogamy, the taking of one wife only, in ancient times, that

despite the halakha allowing for more than one wife, custom
triumphed. But this is a questionable thesis. For if custom
had made of monogamy the regular practice R. Gershom (960-
1028) in France would not have had to issue his ban on polygamy
under pain of excommunication.[40] In any case, that does not
speak to Spain, where bigamy was common.

One cannot place the blame on the Islamic custom, for
this is not satisfactory for a history of religion. For one
thing the Islamic authorities were not necessarily in favor of
Jewish bigamy for Jews had to obtain royal permission in each
individual case. This requirement and permission to practice
bigamy was prevalent also in Christian Spain. Abraham Ibn
Ezra would not have sighed that "one wife was enough for any
man" if he had not himself had polygamous experience or knew
others who had. R. Solomon, the son of R. Simon Duran, serving as successor to his father in Algiers during the fifteenth
century, permitted polygamy at that late date. Without true
historic objectivity, there are scholars who claim Judaism
originated monogamous practice without Christian influence but
lapsed under baneful Islamic influence. Either way Judaism is
purported to be innocent. Such apologetics do not serve the
interest either of history or of religion. There is contrary
evidence where rabbis permitted bigamous marriages. The important question is not whether rabbis favored polygamy but
whether they permitted it. And the evidence shows that it was
practiced and permitted all through the Spanish period and continued in Islamic countries right into the modern age.[41]

Others have accurately seen that there is clear talmudic
recognition of the principle that a man can marry as many
wives as he wishes providing he can support them. The people
of the famous Qumran scrolls deplored polygamy, but Jews practiced it, as the historian Josephus did himself. When Justin

Martyr taunted the Jew Trypho about the Jewish practice of
polygamy he was stating what the facts were. Economics often
made it unsuitable. Often the shortage of women made it impractical. Roman society tended to monogamy and after 212
when all Jews were declared Roman citizens polygamy was a
crime. This was much more so when Diocletian reaffirmed the
legislation in 285 for all inhabitants of the Empire, and
again when the Empire was already Christian and the legislation was renewed in 393. Although Baron says Jews were "little
inclined to obey Roman legislation when it differed from their
own" it is more likely that the principle of *dinà d'malkhutà
dinà* ("the sovereign law is binding") impelled them to obedience in addition to the fear of punishment. In any event in
Babylonia Jews were under no such compunctions, the Persians
being polygamous. The Babylonian Talmud, which was the primary source of guidance for the Spaniards, was not averse to
polygamy.[42]

The talmudic authorities were split on the subject. R.
Ami held that monogamy should be observed but his view did not
prevail. As late as the tenth century the well-known Gaon
Sherira continued to countenance polygamy. The Karaites too
were split with some favoring monogamy and others, such as
Jacob Al-Kirkisani expounding the right to polygamy.[43] Alfasi
in Spain during the early part of the eleventh century, in his
halakhic abridgment of the Talmud, says very simply, "We act
in accordance with Raba", that is, to permit polygamy.[44] I
will not proceed any further with an in-depth analysis of the
halakha of monogamy. What this brief sketch shows, and which
could be vastly amplified from the sources from 400-1600, is
that polygamy was not looked down upon by the most eminent
scholars in Judaism. It was permitted; and despite the statistical question of how many Jews indulged in it, it was

practiced consistently where state law did not forbid it. And
it was practiced even where state law prohibited it until the
rabbinic authorities also banned it on pain of excommunication.
Even after that some Jews rationalized its practice. And where
they were wary of practicing polygamy they practiced concubin-
age, which was a perfectly acceptable relationship in some
parts of Spain and even at times for clergy.[45]

R. Solomon Ibn Aderet, one of the outstanding scholars of
medieval Spain, was not happy with polygamy. He normally discountenanced it, but admitted that the ban of R. Gershom had
not prevailed in Spain nor even in Provence which was "contiguous to France", and the fact is "that scholars and important
people marry more than one wife". Polygamy was practiced in
Castile during the fourteenth century.[46] As late as 1393,
bordering on the fifteenth century, Hasdai Crescas, philosopher
and noted rabbi in Saragossa received royal permission to take
a second wife. This being the case it points in the direction
of establishing the reality of polygamy right into fifteenth
century Spain. The conclusion to be drawn is that modern
scholars have overreacted with anachronistic value-judgments
and unnecessary apologetics.

D. *Child-Marriage*

The status of women as we speak of it with the urgency of
our times requires a separate chapter.[47] But it may be fitting
to indicate here that women were yearning for something other
than subordination and the flesh pots in Spain. Thus R. Asher,
speaking at least of the situation in Toledo ejaculates, "Woe
to our sins! The daughters of Israel have become bold in our
days." And again he argued that "the daughters of Israel in
this generation are not to be trusted". He opposed granting

women divorces upon their demand because, if this was done, he reasoned, "the women would soon set their hearts upon strangers and rebel against their husbands". His son, R. Judah, added, "The women have cursed the land. They invent lies to free themselves from their husbands." But R. Solomon Ibn Aderet did not have the same experience. He wrote: "...The daughters of Israel are chaste." Yet he already saw drastic changes on the horizon.[48]

We see then that women yearned for romance and a degree of freedom, at least in Toledo. But this was not to be. The daughter was under total control of the father. She had few rights in the matter of love, courtship, betrothal and marriage, or for that matter in its aftermath, family life and divorce or the levirate practices. As far as the actual right of whom to marry and when, it is only fair to say that the son had no more prerogative to make a choice than the daughter of the household. Parents, and not the children, decided whom the son or daughter is to marry and when, and what type of marriage settlement there will be, where the young couple will reside, and all the other facets of the marital arrangement. Not even the mother had more than vocal participation, lacking any concrete authority. The father possessed full power over his household. He could order his son into a marriage before the age of thirteen contrary to talmudic halakha, and could marry off his minor daughter without her consent.[49] As one scholar correctly indicates, this marital halakha shows a reaction to the more liberal outlook of the Talmud "and more rigorous conception of the relation between parents and children".[50] But this does not go far enough. The new rigor was true in general. The tendency to leniency in halakha as a whole that prevailed in the classical sources was at an end. Medieval retrenchment was reminiscent of Ezraic post-exilic retrenchment with a bias toward stringency. It is this that ultimately seeps through the centuries and becomes a trickle that grows into a stream and then a rushing torrent in East European Judaism after the sixteenth century.[51] It is that heritage from the thirteenth century which the twentieth century had to confront.

Having placed in perspective the authority of the father and indicated that child marriages were imposed upon the Jewish youngsters of Spain, we should at least look at the remark of one scholar as the possible acceptable rationale of the practice in the light of socio-political conditions of the time. Though not made by a Spanish scholar the remark is certainly applicable during various generations of the thirteenth, fourteenth and fifteenth centuries in Spain. At times conditions were peaceful. At other times unendurable. At any time Jews could be heavily taxed or their property confiscated.[52] This is frequently an important consideration in evaluating some of the less desirable aspects of the halakha that emerge in the medieval period. Thus we find that an anonymous French or German scholar writing in the twelfth or thirteenth century says: "Now we are accustomed to marry off our daughters even when they are minors, because day by day the exile overpowers us, and even if a man has sufficient today to provide a dowry for his daughter, in a little while he'll not have enough and his daughter will remain permanently unmarried."[53] The rabbis obviously were troubled about going counter to a more reasonable position in the Talmud, but they felt they were able to exercise freedom in religious decision. No book, no person, no synod, no dogma, had ultimate authority. Events, as interpreted by scholarly personalities who relied upon research and intellectual judgment, determined the course of religious practice, and even, at times, of belief. Child marriage is a microcosm of this for all facets of the halakha.

V. DIVORCE IN MEDIEVAL SPAIN

The customs leading to betrothal and then on to marriage,
and the nature of the marriage ceremony itself is undoubtedly
of interest to many readers. Yet I am limiting our discussion
of marriage to the foregoing in the interests of conservation.[54]
It seems more important to deal with those questions that involve significant halakhic controversy and border on questions
of social values and philosophical concerns. Monogamy was one
such. Divorce is another.[55]

What has never changed in the halakha of divorce in Judaism is the exclusive right of the husband to issue the writ of
divorce. In modern times, it goes without saying, that regardless of the practices of Judaism, one is not married without a
state license. And one cannot be considered divorced without
civil court procedures. But for those Jews who still wish to
remarry within the parameters of tradition it is necessary to
acquire, in addition to the civil divorce, a document of divorce called a *Get*, which is obtained under the auspices of
the religious authorities.[56]

This document frees both the man and his wife to remarry.
The Reform Movement in modern Judaism no longer recognizes the
requirement. Rabbis of that persuasion will officiate at the
remarriage of those men or women who have obtained a civil divorce. But for most other Jews the *Get* remains a desideratum.
And down through the ages, based upon the biblical text (Deut.
24:1), "When a man takes a woman and espouses her, if it comes
about that she no longer finds favor in his eyes, for he has
found some unchaste matter regarding her, then shall he write
for her a severance document and deliver it to her and send
her from his home." The right was granted exclusively to the
husband to execute the divorce. No change in this occurred

during the centuries and no revision of this halakha ever
appeared in later biblical literature, in the talmudic literature or in the post-talmudic responsa, compilations or commentaries. As a matter of fact I am not even aware of a rabbi
who ever recommended that revision, to allow a woman to execute the *Get*, before modern times. Obviously for a religious
tradition which has witnessed innumerable radical changes in
its halakha over the centuries this seems anomalous. The only
explanation is the mind-set which in the twentieth century in
some quarters is termed "male chauvinist". As in so many other
areas of the halakha related to the granting of prerogatives
to women, as distinct from singing to them paeans of praise
and treating them with tenderness, the male guardians of the
tradition practiced a definite reserve about revision for the
benefit of women.[57]

In medieval Spain, therefore, the inherited halakha gave
the husband inordinate power over his wife. The Mishnah had
allowed the husband to throw the document into her house or at
herself in the street. The Tanaite scholars recognized that
the husband's power in divorce was absolute. But they did
nothing except to use the courts to enforce the rule of *Ketubah* as a civil document as well as a religious one through
which the husband was committed to pay her a marriage settlement.[58] There is no question that the establishment of the
Ketubah during the first century B.C. represents for women's
status what the invention of the wheel meant for technology.
But just as technology was slow to move from the wheel to the
mechanical machine of the eighteenth century industrial revolution, halakha languished in its progress from the *Ketubah*
to full equality in women's rights and prerogatives.

Some changes took place in Spain in terms of reducing the husband's arbitrary and absolute power in divorce. Sometimes they required the wife's consent to being divorced. Sometimes it was only a half-measure in liberating women and merely placed a fine upon the man who divorced his wife without the permission of the communal officials. This was not adequate, however. And yet the tradition had means whereby new approaches could be effected. There were grounds for a wife's request for a divorce. She could demand divorce if her husband denied her conjugal rights, if he treated her cruelly, or made excessive denials to her in matters of personal liberty such as her rights of relationship with her family, and if she was simply unable to accept him personally as a result of his occupation and obnoxious smell.[59] But even these are either mere tokenism or not really concessions to her equality. These are all extreme cases, and speak of compelling him to grant the divorce. But that is still a far cry from her being able to acquire one from a court or execute one herself. But even then R. Asher exacerbated inequality by opposing penalties for a man who refuses a divorce to his wife at her request unless it was specified in the Mishnah. Thus, whatever precedent or machinery existed in the tradition for progress was rejected. This was a typical move by R. Asher, a conservative defender of the status quo and one of the main factors in maintaining the thirteenth century posture into the nineteenth century. One writer considers his efforts "crowned with success" because the wife no longer enjoyed that advantage. There is concern neither in R. Asher of the thirteenth century, nor in that twentieth century scholar, for the injustice meted out to a woman unable to really sue for divorce and unable to execute one while the

118

husband was circumscribed in only a very limited way.[60] In
sum, then, Spanish Judaism remained bound to tradition in
which the woman's status left much to be desired. It is true
that there was some alleviation of the man's absolute and
arbitrary right, but no corresponding rights accorded to the
woman. The best that can be said, probably, at least from
the point of view of those who expound the right to divorce,
is that this right granted by the Bible and continued by the
Talmud was furthered by the sages in Spain. They regarded
divorce as a tragedy but conceded its validity. They rejected
the man's arbitrary, unilateral power, but did not concede the
right of initiating or executing a divorce to the woman.
Furthermore, the harshness of the penalty when a woman committed
adultery was another aspect of her subordination. When she
was found guilty of infidelity she was summarily divorced, by
order of the court, without her marriage settlement. If the
husband was found guilty of adultery he was only flagellated.[61]

VI. THE RABBINATE

A. *Matters Intellectual*

The rabbinate of Spain was perhaps more nearly like the
contemporary rabbinate than any such group before. In Babylonia the geonim had special status and defined authority within the secular structure. The only rabbis we hear of normally
were geonim. Their literature was preserved. Their views prevailed over that of their colleagues whose names we often do
not know. Yet there must have been hundreds of rabbinic scholars in Palestine and Babylonia between 600-1200 who were not

geonim and whose work did not become part of the mainstream of Jewish halakhic literature. The situation was different in Spain. The rabbinate functioned on a far broader scale. The rabbis may have had authority only within their own jurisdiction and there may only have been one authority within the borders of a given city like Granada or Seville. But Spain had many such authorities enjoying equal authority at any given time, each writing volumes of halakha and fructifying the ever-growing corpus of religious literature.

Another aspect of the Spanish rabbinate was its cultivation of the secular sciences and philosophy in a way that was unusual for most Babylonian geonim and the rabbis of Northern Europe. Yet, as we can see from the criticisms of poets and linguists the heaviest weight was placed on rabbinic-halakhic studies although some attention was given to philology and biblical exegesis. They also studied Arabic and wrote in that language, producing books in science and philosophy in addition to halakha.[62]

Rabbis were physicians as well, and to be a physician in medieval Spain it was necessary to have command of scientific works in Arabic. Although Latin remained a despised language because of its association with the Roman Empire which had destroyed Jerusalem and inaugurated the long night of medieval life, the rabbis studied Latin. They needed it in order to deal with Christian notaries in judicial matters and they needed it for polemical exchanges that they may be familiar with the Vulgate and other literature. Yet they were never at home with Latin as with Arabic because it was also the ritualistic language of the Church.[63] Thus we do not find a rabbinic scholar composing Latin works of Judaica before R. Menasseh ben Israel at the dawn of the modern age.

The rabbis were not deeply into the work of translating classical culture into Latin and thereby set the stage for the great developments of humanism and the renaissance. But other Jews were, and sometimes the work of specific rabbis significantly affected specific medieval scholastics. For example Albertus Magnus (1193-1280), a Dominican, reputed to be one of the most learned of the thirteenth century scholastics, relied heavily upon the Spanish-Egyptian rabbi, Moses Maimonides, for arguments to counter Aristotle's theories where they contradicted the Bible. The most serious one was Aristotle's doctrine of the eternity of matter which conflicted with the Judaeo-Christian creation theory. Albertus Magnus used and repeated the arguments of Maimonides. After him, the greatest of all the scholastics, St. Thomas Aquinas (1225-1274), was deeply indebted to the thought of Moses Maimonides. Again the theory of creation influenced St. Thomas, but so did other aspects of Maimonides' philosophical teaching. For example it has been said that the very basis of St. Thomas' systematic development of the relation of reason to revelation, one of the great philosophical enigmas, was taken from Maimonides. The basic idea there is that man needed revelation because although reason could enable him to think his way to great truths only a few men could do so, a thought already put forward by the Gaon Saadiah in the tenth century. And even to those few intellectual giants, Maimonides added, some levels of thought would be inaccessible. Thus revelation was needed to lead man to a knowledge of God which he could never attain through reason.[64]

Through the reading of Maimonides by leading scholastics as well as the use of biblical exegesis of Jewish rabbinic scholars, Jewish thought entered scholastic thought and through that medium it entered the intellectual currents of Roman

Catholic theology. From a theological standpoint, if not by scientific historical judgment, it might be surmised that it was only proper for Judaism once again to fertilize Christianity a millenium after the separation. This made for real interchange, for as noted previously, Judaism was acculturating to certain Christian values, among them the monogamous family structure.

The high point was the thirteenth century as far as this type of Jewish influence in Christian thought is concerned. Not until the reformation and the renaissance was it once more revived and reached new heights in the sixteenth and seventeenth centuries. But although the rabbis themselves, like R. Solomon Ibn Aderet were not directly involved in this process they were in constant dialogue. They were forced into religious disputations and for these they had to be armored with a full arsenal of arguments on the same grounds as their disputants. Ibn Aderet, for instance, frequently discussed matters with a well-known thirteenth century Christian theologian Raymund Martini. He often refutes Martini's arguments in his responsa. [65]

Raymund Martini was charged with fabricating a whole Midrash which he called *Bereshit Rabba of R. Moshe HaDarshan* and published in his *Pugio Fidei* (Dagger of Faith). Professor Saul Lieberman, an eminent Talmudist, however argues forcefully that "there are no serious obstacles in the way of accepting the Midrash as genuine on the whole". It seems to me that the problem of Raymund Martini is a microcosm. The medieval Spanish rabbis were compelled to confront Christian theologians like Martini at disputations. Too frequently, if the Jews put up a successful struggle they would be banished for their efforts. They probably therefore developed a cynicism about it. They exaggerated their refutations of the Christian arguments

to the point where they departed from accuracy by accusing
their Christian disputants of fabrications. A rabbi like R.
Solomon Ibn Aderet would be at a loss to know how else to
handle the great assortment of ágadah that had piled up over
the centuries and which included many statements that were
quite parallel to Christian theology. They did not know how
to argue that what it said meant one thing to the Jew even if
it meant something else to the Christian.[66] Perhaps more than
anything else the Martini incident and other disputations point
up the tragedy of wasted centuries when fruitful dialogue could
have had progressive results. The medieval tragedy was that
Christian polemicists accorded no validity to Judaism. Jewish
respondents were in such fearful defense that they deemed any
concession to Christian thought to be the last nail in the
coffin of Judaism.

The Spanish rabbis studied or furthered the study of the
major sciences of their time, because of their importance for
halakha. They took an interest in astronomy, geometry and
mathematics, as well as hygiene, but above all astronomy.
All of these sciences in various ways related to the halakha,
either because of the calendar that governed holy days, or
for the dietary practices. Not only philosophers like Levi
ben Gershon or scientists, but also rabbis like Abraham ibn
Ezra or R. Isaac b. Baruk Albalia contributed to these sciences, not to speak of Moses Maimonides.[67]

A great debate raged over the study and practice of
astrology. Great personalities ranged themselves on both
sides of the question, again pointing up that perennial historic truth that Judaism was never monolithic and it was impossible to prescribe "orthodoxy" and thereby delineate
"heresy". No less a personage than R. Nahman ben Moses,

Nahmanides (thirteenth century) defended astrology and confessed to his own belief in the efficacy of the role of the
stars in human life.[68]

A characteristic of the Spanish rabbinate was its rationalism. There were exceptions as there always are to any
generalization. But basically they opposed flights of fancy
into messianic speculation even when they occasionally advocated pseudo-scientific cures in medicine which bordered on
the superstitious. They allowed the use of amulets in medical
cures because, for instance, Ibn Aderet was reluctant to prohibit what sages of the Talmud believed efficacious.[69] False
prophets and pseudo-messiahs appeared from time to time and
the Spanish rabbis were more successful in resisting them and
undoing their harm than the rabbis had been in the second century when Bar Kokhba appeared as redeemer, or in the seventeenth century when Shabbatai Zvi incredibly won the alle-
giance of hosts of European rabbis.[70]

The Spanish rabbis also resisted the rise of Kabalah.
This became a moving force toward the end of the thirteenth
century.[71] But the rationalist halakhists rejected the mystic
notions of the occult. Thus R. Isaac Perfet compared the
kabalistic belief in ten gradations of emanations from deity
in the creation of the material world to be only quantitative-
ly different from the belief in a trinity and thereby sought
to place Kabalah into the same category as the Christology in
terms of its validity within Judaism.[72] Yet is has to be
understood that the rabbis encountered crosscurrents of mysticism and sophisticated rationalism. There was Maimonides and
there was the Zohar, the extreme rationalist and the prototype
of Kabalah respectively, both attracting Jewish adherents.
The masses did not participate in scientific philosophy anymore than today. For the average man the rationalist argument

against anthropomorphism was destructive of faith. He had to
envision God as some kind of elderly benevolent grandfather on
a grand throne in the heavens surrounded by his saints. On the
other hand this same average man, while he could not understand
the mysteries and the numbers of kabalistic jargon, was en-
thralled by its anthropomorphisms, its use of angels and demons. The spiritual world thereby became real for him.[73]

The result of years of controversy was a dramatic reading
of a proclamation of excommunication before the Jewish community of Barcelona in 1305. This declared:

> ...for fifty years henceforth, no member of our
> community under the age of twenty-five years
> shall study the works of the Greeks on natural
> science or metaphysics, either in the original
> language or in translation. And no one in our
> community shall teach these branches to the
> children of Israel under the prescribed age....
> We exempt, however, from our decree the study
> of medicine....[74]

Along with the problem of rationalism there was the problem
of allegorization and symbolism. Many preachers and teachers
were looking upon the biblical narratives as allegory or seeing
certain biblical commandments as symbols or metaphors and
thereby reducing the need for observance of certain rituals.
To counter this another proclamation stated:

> ...we declare these transgressors and men of
> presumption accursed and under the ban....
> Their books are works of heresy and should be
> consigned to the flames, or the owners there-
> of will be liable to excommunication. But
> those that shall turn back and repent, Heaven
> will be merciful unto them, the Court on High
> and the court on earth will absolve them....[75]

This was a new turn in Judaism. It set a precedent for
future thrusts for an "orthodoxy" and a "heresy" much more so
than anything that ever occurred in the past. For this was
not at all a counterthrust against a dissenting movement, an
argument with which one might have justified the actions
against Samaritans, Christians or Karaites, if at all justi-
fiable. This was an unprecedented imposition of thought-
control within Judaism unknown since the statement in the
Mishnah given in the name of R. Aķiba to prohibit the study
of extra-canonical scripture. But even there it was not so
much "thought-control" as part of the war against Christianity
in the first century, seeking to eliminate all those books,
whether Apocrypha or New Testament which were supportive of
the developing Christology. This action by rabbis in Spain,
led by so illustrious a talmudist as R. Solomon Ibn Aderet
became a model for future thrusts at heterodoxy and still is
the pattern within certain segments of Judaism which seek to
protect its young from philosophic rationalism, scientific
skepticism and similar areas of human intellectual effort
which, from their standpoint, endanger faith and ritual observance.[76] A fair judgment may be made, however, that the
thought-control effort did not really succeed. Although there
have been periods in some areas, perhaps notably Eastern
Europe in modern times, when those who professed to be the
guardians of "orthodox" Judaism, have eschewed secular studies,
and especially science and philosophy, this has not been a
general condition nor has vigorous rabbinic weight been brought
to bear upon efforts to curtail freedom of thought. It is inevitable that freedom of thought--and religious behaviour pat-
terns--will extend into other areas. And because Judaism has
been zealous in its effort to deny a definition of "heresy"

the "orthodoxy" and the "heterodoxy" remain quite relative and subjective.

B. *Matters Practical*

Rabbis were not salaried in those days. They were compelled to earn a living from means other than religious leadership. Half of the well-known rabbis in Spain were physicians. They served as judges in ecclesiastical courts and as consultants to the government's courts and legislative arm. The rabbi often supervised all divorce cases and served as an appeals judge. In general he was the advisor on all matters that required any connection at all with law, whether domestic relations or civil, even having the power to confirm or reject the regulations of guilds and other societies within the Jewish community.[77] Whether or not to renumerate him was a highly controversial issue. The negative view was very ancient and frequently expressed in rabbinic literature. And for that reason we find so many rabbis were traders or artisans. Many rabbis were wealthy investors, others endured lifelong penury. R. Solomon Ibn Aderet succeeded in his financial enterprises. While R. Jacob b. Asher supported himself by money-lending, his brother R. Judah, less fortunate, records in his will what a constant struggle life was for him and all the reverses he sustained, finally reluctantly being compelled to accept a community stipend. By the end of the fourteenth century, the concept of a fixed salary for the rabbi became widespread. This has remained the practice since, with the rabbinate emerging as a regular profession. With fixed salaries and the expectation that the rabbi can now serve the community on a full-time basis came the expansion of his functions into the pastoral and administrative role.[78]

VII. ASPECTS OF SPANISH JUDAISM'S INFLUENCE

In the foregoing we have attempted to survey some of the highlights of medieval Judaism as they were reflected in Spain. We have concentrated on the eleventh-thirteenth centuries and have not fully traversed all the roads and byways. But at least what was characteristic of Spain has been glimpsed. The responsa literature and the forms of acculturation engaged in by Jews, and conversely, elements of resistance to it, an ambiguity that stalks the history of Judaism, were outlined. We saw the development of both rationalism and Kabalah, subjects yet to be futher adumbrated, constituted a major event in Judaism and brought into focus the perennial ambivalence which has made it almost an anomaly to speak of a genuine "orthodoxy" or a real "heterodoxy". We have examined the theology of marriage in Spain, but will yet see that twentieth century American practice is more indebted to that of Northern Europe. And finally we have cursorily examined the office of rabbi.

In the next chapters we will survey philosophic thought in Spain and take a closer look at the great debates and the dramas that ranged far and wide over rationalism, Kabalah and messianism. We will see the emergence of folk-Judaism in Northern Europe which often reflected medieval folk-superstition as well as Judaism. Because we cannot examine all themes worthy of examination we must be content with a brief selection of vignettes.

One final word must be said. Ritual observance of certain practices such as the tefilin, the washing of hands before eating, the saying of certain berakhot, even certain practices related to the dietary halakha, were in a state of neglect during the early medieval period. The testimony for this is given by

scholars ranging from the geonim of Babylonia through the thirteenth century. In an article on this neglect one scholar has
suggested that the result was the development of *public* ritual
as an alternative to private ritual.[79] Should this suggestion
be accurate, it would mean that many of the public ritualistic
and liturgical practices of the twentieth century American
synagogue, largely peopled by descendants of Ashkenaz Jews,
are rooted in the practices of the Sephardic Jews of medieval
Spain. Among these are unison prayers, Ḥanukah lights kindled
in the synagogue, a congregational sukkah and a congregational
Passover Seder. The Gaon Natronai, as early as the ninth century, was not happy about congregational sukkot he heard about
in Spain. He wrote that although scripture in Nehemiah 5:16
seems to indicate there was a sukkah in the Jerusalem Temple,
Jerusalem was different, since Jews came from everywhere on
pilgrimage during the festival, "and shall Spain become Jerusalem to which we will go in pilgrimage?"[80] This tart reply
by Natronai may already show that the geonim as early as the
ninth century felt Spain slipping from their grasp. In the
eleventh century Gaon Hai reluctantly conceded that a congregational sukkah was permitted and cited that it was done in
Bagdad.[81] The custom of Spain, at least in Aragon, was that
the congregation joined for the *ḳiddush* after worship in the
public sukkah in the synagogue courtyard, and then went home
to eat, a custom almost universal in twentieth century North
America.

This development of public ritual as an alternative to,
or a pedagogical instrument aimed toward revitalizing private
observance, is a characteristic of the twentieth century. It
is possible that certain of the conditions that led to casual-
ness in ritualistic behaviour in Spain are also present here,
chief among them independence from even the kind of semi-cen-

tralization represented by the geonim of Babylonia, acculturation to the majority milieu and a high degree of secular education.

VIII. LEAVING SPAIN

A. *Marranism*

The Spanish experience came to a violent end in July, 1492. The most unusual aspect of it was the development of mass crypto-Judaism, a process in which the Jew conceals his Judaism, but does not abandon it.[82] The subjects frequently reverted to open Judaism at an early opportunity. It is difficult to know how many Jews were involved in the series of mass conversions at Minorca (418), Clermont (576), Spain and Lombardy (629), or how many of these or their descendants rejoined Judaism. In Judaic religious terminology these people were called *anusim*, "the compelled ones". They were looked upon more kindly in halakhic literature than voluntary apostates.[83]

Marranism in Spain, however, was different from all other cases of forced baptism because it was a condition of life that became a hereditary culture, and in some instances endured into the twentieth century.[84] The need to conceal his Judaism affected the Jew in both Islamic and Christian Spain, but the mass problem which has garnered widest historical fame followed the outbreak of widespread violence throughout Spain in the summer of 1391 inspired by Ferrand Martinez, Archdeacon of Ecija. The great community of Barcelona was decimated and never restored. Statistics are not reliable and therefore the

fifty thousand dead reported, and the two-hundred thousand
forced baptisms in Aragon and Castile, may be pardonable ex-
aggerations for an age of doubtful records. But it is safe
to assume that tens of thousands accepted Christianity, with
thousands upon thousands following them in the first decades
of the fifteenth century. A similar widespread outburst took
place in 1473.[85]

The Church opposed conversion by force and discountenanced
the activities of churchmen like Martinez or secular princes
that brought about such mass conversion of Jews. Nevertheless,
once these people were children of the Church, if they lapsed
they were "heretics". The Church, on its formal level, had to
take certain prescribed action. But more dangerous to the
Marrano was the hostility of the masses as well as of political
and ecclesiastical leaders. For the phenomenon of Marranism
not only resulted in a mass of people diffused throughout
Christian society that were in contempt of Christian doctrine
while pretending to follow it, they were also gaining positions
of great wealth and prominence in both the state and the Church
as "Christians".[86]

The only solution to the dual problem of hypocritical
Christianity practiced by Marranos and mass popular resentment,
seemed to be a formal campaign against heresy by the Inquisition. It was clear that these people were proper subjects for
the Inquisition by Church law. They took their children to
church for baptism and then "washed off" the baptism at home;
they received the sacrament of marriage from the priest and
then another private "Jewish" one at home; they observed the
Judaic Sabbath, ate kosher meat, sometimes even practiced circumcision, and secretly sent donations to the synagogue. They
often formed Catholic societies under the patronage of a saint
in order to have a religious fellowship in which to observe

Judaism, and frequently openly expressed disbelief in the doctrines of Roman Catholicism.[87]

The Inquisition began its work in 1480, and although it
acted diligently, condemning many, and in time enlisting the
population to help expose Marranos, it failed to resolve the
Spanish problem. The kind of religion the Marranos practiced
is depicted in an "Edict of Faith" of the Inquisition which
summoned the faithful to denounce the heretics. Among the
signs to look for on Fridays, and expose, were, "...putting
on clean or festive clothes...in the evening lighting new
candles...." At other times they were to see whether the new
Christians were "keeping Jewish fasts...keeping the feasts and
festivals of the Jews, in particular the feast of unleavened
bread, which falls in Holy Week...." The "Edict" lists many
other Judaic religious practices and evidences that the Marranos were quite observant of a large segment of Judaism.
The sentence of the Inquisition against a convicted victim
was announced at an "Act of Faith" or *auto de fé* (*auto-da-fé*
in Portugal) and he was burned at the stake. But it should
be made clear that the Inquisition, contrary to the popular
misconception was not directed against Jews. It was directed
against heretics, among whom a very large number were those who
were seeking to straddle the fence: to escape the disabilities
of being Jewish and yet not totally giving of themselves to the
Christian faith.[88]

The traditional view here stated that Marranos were quite
loyal to Judaism and therefore subject to the punishment of the
Church as heretics and lapsed Christians, is rejected in some
quarters. It is argued they were "detached from Judaism", and
that the Inquisition operated with a fiction, driven to what it
did "by racial hatred and political considerations".[89] Although I do not accept these views, this is not the place to

analyze them. That is a task which requires a monograph in
itself in order to cover the responsa, homiletical and exegetical writings that impinge upon the question. At least
three conclusions are clear, however, from a cursory survey of
the sources. One is that there was much ambivalence among
Judaic scholars on the right of a Jew to save his life by accepting another faith, or on the extent of the requirement for
martyrdom. A second is that the medieval theory of the Church
correctly did not look upon Jews from a racial perspective.
The third is that competent scholars seriously diverge in their
interpretation of the same sources. But two points should be
borne in mind: 1) the formal policy of the Church was to regard the label "Jew" as one of religion, so that if a Jew became a Christian he was no longer a Jew, and therefore was
subject to the rules that affected all other Christians in
matters of heresy; 2) the rabbis in Spain, France and Germany
all generally took a lenient position toward *ànusim* and this
could exacerbate Christian suspicion. Even if Marranos appeared as "gentiles" to some Jews at the end of the fifteenth
century, they might still be "heretics" in the eyes of the
Church and subject to the Inquisition.[90] On the other hand
it does appear clear that after the Spanish monarchs Ferdinand
and Isabella totally dominated Spain they allowed the Inquisition General, Thomas de Torquenada, free reign. His objectives
seemed to go beyond the purification of Spanish Christianity
to the total expulsion of Jews. The confiscation of their
property certainly had attraction to the royal pair.

B. *The Demise of Spanish Judaism*

   While the Inquisition ferreted out Marranos as heretics,
reaching up into the highest circles of Spanish government and

public life, the Jews of Spain remained secure from its activity.[91] But after Islam was driven from the Spanish peninsula and a purely Christian Spain was possible, the expulsion of the Jews was inevitable. This expulsion was ordered on March 30, 1492, and was to take place by July 30. Christopher Columbus opened his diary with the words, "In the same month in which their Majesties issued the edict that all Jews should be driven out...they gave me the order to undertake... my expedition of discovery...." The relationship between the two events still remains a historical enigma shielded by the unknowable canons of Providence.[92]

Judaism, however, was already in crises in Spain by then. The physical expulsion settled the problem, but for some decades it was going through a phase which I can only interpret as being a prefiguring of the Dutch and Italian vanguard of modern Judaism, which will be explored in the next volume. R. Isaac Arama of that period accused Averroeists, followers of the thirteenth century Arab philosopher, Ibn Rushd, of "spreading the gall of heresy throughout the world". Averroeists argued that the soul ceased to exist at death, that Aristotelian natural morality and law were sufficient and superior to the Torah, and urged the young to study philosophy rather than Talmud. Arama condemns them for explaining away the great events of Jewish history by astrology, and the miẓvot of the Torah as allegory.[93] Between the challenge of Averrolism and the defection of conversos Judaism suffered much weakness. But as in all such periods retrenchment and consolidation usually regenerated the community. The expulsion from Spain, however, brought Judaism to its total expiration in the Iberian lands in 1492.

The Edict of Expulsion gives as the reason for the order the prevention of Jews from further damaging genuine Christianity in Spain through their continued influence upon the Marranos. That the Expulsion was not a "racial" act is evident from the fact that parallel laws were enacted affording protection for Jews who convert, and even exempting them for a period from the processes of the Inquisition. Furthermore, the Marranos were not expelled. The Edict certainly provides only a theological concern: "...According to the report presented to us by the Inquisitors, there is no doubt that intercourse of Christians with Jews...causes the greatest harm.... It has led to the undermining and debasement of our holy Catholic faith...."[94] As in all events of history there are antecedents to antecedents. The Edict was a Christian climax to centuries of hostility between Averroeism and the Church. Since the twelfth century when the Islamic philosopher, Ibn Rushd, lived (1126-1198), the Inquisition was used against Christians who adopted his thinking, most especially for espousing his concept of double truth, that what is not theologically true may be philosophically true. In essence Averroeism denied Creation, Providence and Immortality. Jews had translated his Arabic writings into Latin, and his doctrines had acquired a significant following that perservered for centuries despite the Inquisition. It is said that by the beginning of the sixteenth century it was "almost the official philosophy of Italy".[95]

We must consider several points. Many conversos still lived among Jews. Averroeism was a strong heresy in Spanish Judaism. The Inquisition, which dealt with Christian Averroeists, since the thirteenth century, ironically not being competent legally to investigate or punish any kind of Jews, whether Averroeist or otherwise, could not extirpate the heresy in Spain. Considering how the faith of conversos was undermined by both the Jewish Averroeists and believing Jews, and

the wide influential diffusion of conversos in the Christian
body politic, it is quite likely that pious Ferdinand and
Isabella, driven by a passionate Torquemada, saw no other
solution than expulsion.

CHAPTER 6

Philosophy in the Medieval Mode:
Theological Judaism

I. LIMITATIONS

This is not a "history of Jewish philosophy" nor an attempt to elucidate the thought of Jewish philosophers in the middle ages.[1] In this chapter we will attempt only to take note of one aspect of Judaism during the middle ages, the cultivation of the philosophy of religion or theology. We will not distinguish between these two terms as those of special technical concern might wish to. For our purpose, one who is a scholar of ideas, doctrines and practices that relate to God is a "theologian". And we will use that term synonymously with "philosopher of religion".

The limitations I set here by discussing only the Gaon Saadiah b. Joseph, Yehudah Halevi, Rabbi Moses ben Maimon, and touching only lightly on several others in passing, are of necessity personal choices. The basis of the selection, however, is the conviction that the three named men represent the highlights of the subject and that they also mirror the characteristics of the problems and the attempted solutions. Furthermore, in the case of Yehudah Halevi, for instance, he became a forerunner of several modern positions in Judaism. He foreshadowed the emotionalism of Ḥasidism, the yearning for national liberation of the religious Zionist movement, and the rejection

of rationalism alone as the avenue to deity and as a method of
exposition of Judaism. Moses Maimonides became the "patron
saint" of what is called "modern orthodoxy" embodying for that
segment of Judaism the synthesis of rationalism and faith, of
scientific learning, and theology along with observance of
tradition to its fullest. Saadiah merits attention for three
basic reasons. Firstly, he was an exception among geonim in
being a philosopher. Secondly, aside from several lesser
significant known and unknown predecessors, such as the Egyptian Isaac Israeli who flourished in Kairuwan during the ninth
and tenth centuries, Saadiah was the first of medieval rationalist Jewish theologian-philosophers. Thirdly, it was Saadiah's thought-system that had its influence in the centuries
after him in variegated forms.

There will be no attempt here to trace the interrelationships between these three Jewish theologians and the systems
of thought which influenced them. Saadiah was eclectic. He
relied on the Mutazilite Islamic Kalam, which had deep affinity with Judaism in its emphasis upon strict monism in the
nature of God, and man's free will; and he worked freely within both the Platonist and Aristotelian systems. On the other
hand, Yehudah Halevi was an independent philosopher unidenti-
fied with any school. He did not attempt to harmonize his
faith with reason as Saadiah before him or Maimonides after
him. He argued that Judaism is above reason and is in full
possession of truth. But Maimonides accepted the challenge of
Aristotelianism and sought a synthesis of that system with
biblical theology. His reliance upon Arabic Aristotelians
like Avicenna was heavy, as he in turn became a source for
Catholic theologians.[2]

Finally the sphere of discussion will only encompass
several of the great issues that agitated the age. As I in-

dicated earlier, what Jews generally believed entered the
prayerbook. The theology of the liturgy includes such themes
as Creation, Revelation, and Redemption. Under this last heading, taking poetic license to define it quite broadly, I will
include the eschatological themes such as the messianic idea,
reward and punishment, hell and heaven, immortality or life
after death, the last judgment, and resurrection. I also am
selecting the doctrine of freedom of will because upon it rests
much of the discussion related to human responsibility, sin,
and atonement, in turn related to reward and punishment and the
afterlife. The concept of Revelation includes the doctrine of
the Election of Israel and the Covenant.

II. SAADIAH

A. *The Man and His Work*

Saadiah b. Joseph (882-942) came from Fayyum in Egypt and
after residing in Palestine and Syria he was selected as Gaon
of Sura in Babylonia. He was in the vanguard of the new medieval studies in philology, philosophy, Bible, commentaries,
liturgy, and rabbinic literature. In 933 he wrote his main
treatise in Jewish philosophy-theology in Bagdad, in Arabic,
the title of which is *Kitat al-Amanat w'al I'tiqadat*. In Hebrew translation this came out as *Sefer Ha-Emunot ve Ha-Deot*,
and in English as *The Book of Beliefs and Opinions*. Saadiah
wrote an "Introduction to the Talmud" and a compendium of halakha; he composed a prayerbook with commentary and a compendium of liturgical halakha. History fated him to be a leading
antagonist of Karaism. He was the first to translate the Bible

into Arabic and was the first real philologist in biblical study using cognate Arabic to determine the meanings of Hebrew terms.

The Arabic title of his philosophical treatise explains what Saadiah was seeking to convey. Arabists indicate *Amanah* means "affirmation of faith" and *itaqad* denotes "belief based upon reason". Thus *Beliefs and Opinions* is not preceded by the definite article, signifying that these are not *the* beliefs and opinions, excluding all others. They are not "dogmas" that are mandatory and not the only beliefs. They are a "selection" of the principle ideas of Judaism. Others may delineate other significant concepts as being fundamental in Judaism. And others did.[3]

Although Saadiah was an Egyptian gaon in Babylonia, new research into the ever-accumulating literature on or by Saadiah indicates that he provided the initial input for the direction later taken by the scholars and poets of Spain and had a hitherto unsuspected influence upon North European pietism.[4]

The major problems Saadiah faced were the apparent conflict between Revelation and Reason, the problem of how and whether God created the universe, and the nature of God. Saadiah emphasized the need to believe out of knowledge rather than mere acceptance on faith, arguing that belief based upon reason will be a better form of belief and will lead to improved character which is the purpose of all belief. Saadiah wrote of three sources of truth common to all: 1) Direct Observation or Sensation, that which is based upon the human senses of touch, taste, sight, smell and hearing; 2) Intuition of the Intellect, which leads to instinctive value judgments; 3) Logical Inference, the process of reason. He then added that Judaism has a fourth source of truth, Revelation, which

is the parallel or synonym for "Authentic Tradition". The
thrust of his argument after that is that reason can validate,
confirm, or explicate what is already known by revelation.[5]

B. *Highlights in Saadiah's Thought*

1. *Creation*

Saadiah's argument that the world had a beginning in time
and therefore a Creator, follows the Islamic Kalam. The argument basically is that matter is finite and finite matter will
have an end. It therefore had a beginning. Matter is generally a composition of various structures. Such finite compositions go through a steady process of generation and decay.
This material process of generation and all the celestial
bodies going through perpetual motion point to the reality
that none are infinite, all are subject to time, and therefore were created by a Creator. God is a Creator-God, and by
rational inference creation implies the unity of God, the pure
monotheism of Judaism. The dualism of Zoroastrianism, surely
a factor in Babylonian thinking, he opposes as unlikely. He
argues that the opposition of two forces with contradictory
wills would render a stable universe impossible. As far as
what was in "space" before the act of creation or how could
"time" be measured without existing things, Saadiah responds
that prior to the act of creation by God there was no time or
space. But Saadiah had no sense of the geological ages and
such remote distances in time as science later uncovered or
Greek philosopher-scientists were prone to think about. He
believed strongly in the validity of the Hebrew liturgical
calendar and so when he wrote his doctrine of Creation in 933
he said the world is 4693 years old! Inherent in Saadiah's

argument is the notion that creation by God was *ex nihilo*, from
nothing whatsoever that was pre-existent. This was how he and
all generations of Jewish theologians, with rare exceptions before modern times, understood the testimony of Genesis 1:1.[6]

Saadiah proceeds to draw a variety of conclusions attendant upon the notion that God is the Creator. We are not entering into an exposition of these ideas but will merely summarize his discussion of the nature of God. God is a unity.
He is incorporeal, possessing no material aspect at all, for
only thereby can He be eternal. As Creator, eternal, and the
only One in the universe, He also possesses unlimited power
and knowledge which are the attributes styled "omnipotent" and
"omniscient". The latter alone makes it possible for Him to
known the deeds of man.

How can one speak of this Creator who is timeless and im-
material so as not to be subject to the ravages of the finite,
as "seeing" or "speaking" or "stretching out his arm" and so
forth, as scripture consistently speaks of him? Saadiah sees
these aspects of scripture in a metaphorical way, rejecting
the literal reading of the verses. His argument is quite
rabbinically traditional in line with the statement, "scripture speaks in the language of men" which had emanated from
the school of R. Ishmael.[7]

In this way Saadiah affirmed the traditional doctrines of
God and Creation rooted in the Revelation, but brought to bear
all the canons of Greek logic and Arabic philosophy to prove
that the faith of Judaism is in consonance with the highest
reaches of human reason.

2. *Revelation*

Saadiah argues that the religious truth of Judaism origi-
nates in revelation, that it is the only religion that origi-

nated in an authentic divine revelation and is therefore the only true and valid religion. While the generosity of this argument toward other faiths may seem questionable to some modern minds, the reality of course is that the other religions argued similarly throughout medieval times, and some continue to do so.

Nevertheless, Saadiah also argues that the content of the revelation forever embodied in scripture and in its divinely revealed interpretation, the Talmud, is consonant with human reason. This signifies that reason is capable of reaching the content of a truth revealed by God. If so, what need was there for a revelation? Saadiah's reply is that revelation is evidence of God's compassion. God had made it possible for man to grasp divine truth and live the moral life sooner than he would have groped toward it by reason alone, unaided by revelation. This idea took root in medieval thought, and as noted in the previous chapter, through Maimonides it entered Roman Catholic theology. Saadiah gave the notion a dual thrust. On the one hand revelation was designed to enable those who cannot reason to these ends, to acquire instant truth. And on the other hand, revelation remains a check on the philosophers themselves from succumbing to error. Whatever they reason out must be measured against revelation as the ultimate criterion of truth.[8] Saadiah writes: "...this type of knowledge (I mean that which is furnished by authentic tradition and the books of prophetic revelation) corroborates for us the validity of the first three sources of knowledge." And again, the thinker needs revelation because until he hits upon truth through reason, "...he would be without religious faith, and even when he has hit upon the teaching of religion and has it firmly in hand, he is not secure against being deprived of it again by some uncertainty

that might arise in his mind and corrupt his belief." Finally
one might consider that the central notion of Saadiah's doctrine of Revelation is his summation as to why God had to reveal and support with miracle what man could ratiocinate for
himself; "...God, exalted and magnified be He, afforded us
quick relief from all these burdens by sending us His messengers through whom He transmitted messages to us, and by letting
us see with our own eyes the signs and proofs supporting them
about which no doubt could prevail and which we could not possibly reject. Thus He said: 'You yourselves have seen that I
have talked with you from heaven' (Ex. 20:19)...." And so,
Saadiah argues, all of the truth of scripture is to be believed
"because its authenticity had been proven by the testimony of
the senses". This concept of a divine revelation publicly made
and witnessed ruled out the possibility of deception. In the
eyes of Saadiah it implies that other claims, such as that of
Christianity and Islam are not valid. This notion became the
formal position of historical Jewish religious philosophy until
the modern era.[9]

3. *Eschatology*

The word "eschatology" is here being used as a rubric to
include all phases of "the end things": immortality or life
after death, the messiah idea, what is commonly referred to as
heaven and hell, reward and punishment, last judgment, resurrection. That this overall subject is extremely significant
for the thought-system of Gaon Saadiah is evident from the
sheer space he accords it in his philosophical work. We cannot possibly do more than slide around the periphery.[10]

a. *Free Will*

Saadiah believes that the goal of all creation is man.
He infers that from the order of creation delineated in scripture (Gen. 1), and believes reason proves it. He argues that
nature places "whatever is most highly prized in the center of
things". From the seed of fruit he moves on to the phenomena
of the universe; and since in the scheme of science in the
tenth century Saadiah sees the earth as the center of all, the
objective of creation must be on earth. This objective has to
be man. Since earth and water are inanimate, and beasts are
irrational, they cannot be the goal. The only creature which
embodies the highest qualities, being both animate and rational
is man, and so man must be the goal of all the processes of
nature.[11] Furthermore, scripture teaches that man has free
will (Deut. 30:15, 19): "...I have set before you this day
life and good, death and evil...choose life...." Saadiah
could have cited Genesis 4:7 where God tells Cain he can
master sin, but for some reason did not. He adds, however,
that scripture teaches that man has the capacity to acquire
knowledge and therefore know the past, how to choose his be-
havior pattern and how to build for the future. Saadiah uses
Ps. 94:10, "He that teaches man knowledge", as the source for
a very comprehensive attitude toward man's capacity to attain
the highest of scientific knowledge, to invent technology, de-
vise the amenities of civilization and practice the art of
government both in its military and diplomatic facets.[12]

With this Saadiah rejects the Islamic idea of predestination. He places into the human realm the capacity to choose,
the divine will that man choose, and man's obligation to choose
the right way. This then makes it just for man to have to
suffer the consequences of his bad choices. There is no

morality where there are no options. And there should be no
responsibility where there is no freedom of choice: "...man
cannot be considered as the agent of an act unless he exercises
freedom of choice in performing it, for no one can be held ac-
countable for an act who does not possess freedom of choice and
does not exercise this choice."[13]

b. *Reward and Punishment*

Saadiah is troubled by the fact that God has "prepared
for man painful torment and perpetual sojourn in hell-fire".
But he accepts it by balancing it with "the promise of perennial delight and perpetual reward". He believes that this
prospect of spending eternity in hell is a deterrent from evil,
and eternity in heaven is a good incentive for man to be good.
He finds the source for this belief in Daniel 12:2, that the
dead will arise "some to everlasting life, and some to re-
proaches and everlasting abhorrence". Yet Saadiah realizes
that the concept of punishment for sin is not adequate to
justify the broad range of adversity and suffering in the
world either such as overtake children or natural calamities
that sweep away the innocent as well. And so Saadiah adds what
one scholar has called "the notion of purification". This
means that part of human suffering in this world is to purify
the righteous of whatever sin he does possess in order that
he might enjoy total bliss in the hereafter. And conversely
some of the good fortune enjoyed by the unrighteous in this
world enables God to sentence him to perpetual suffering in
the next.[14]

The place of perpetual reward and punishment, for Saadiah,
is what is called "the world to come". Again basing himself
upon tradition, he refers to the place of reward as *Gan Eden*,
"the garden of Eden", for that term sums up the most magnifi-

cent of God's creations. The place of perpetual punishment
is called *Gehinnom*, "the valley of Hinnom" which was a place
of desolation and perpetual burning of refuse. These are also
called "heaven" and "earth". Interestingly, Saadiah does not
seem to have a word for "hell". The "world to come" will have
no physical attributes at all. And since there will be no
need to work for a livelihood by day and relax or enjoy other
pastimes such as solitude and sex at night, the "world to
come" will have only perpetual light and no alternation of day
and night, no divisions into "time", no need for weeks, months,
or years.[15]

This view of reward and punishment was closely tied to
the belief in resurrection. The "world to come" followed
resurrection. The two questions that remain are: what
occurred after death in the here and now? and when would
resurrection and the "world to come" occur?

c. *Resurrection*

It appears that in Saadiah's reading of tradition that
when a human being dies in this world and his soul departs,
nothing really happens to the body or the soul relevant to the
question of sin or reward and punishment. A "non-existence"
seems to ensue until the ultimate resurrection and judgment.
The body decomposes in the grave and the soul awaits resurrection. According to Saadiah the resurrection will be preceded
by the advent of the Messiah.[16] Briefly it may be stated that
Saadiah's view is that the soul is created to join the body,
and the two remain united in this world. When the person dies
the soul and body are temporarily separated. When God decides
to do so, He will bring the Messiah and then inaugurate resurrection. Then the body and soul will be reunited. The united

person will then be judged for his deeds during his earthly existence. He argues that the soul is created at the time the bodily form of man is completed and is of the same substance as the heavenly spheres, but even finer, and the soul provides the sense organs with their faculties. In other words, the soul constitutes man's ability to function.[17] What occurs at death? God sends an angel for the purpose of separating the soul and the body, but human beings never see the soul leaving because it resembles air. The soul is then stored up until the time of retribution. This notion Saadiah bases upon Proverbs 24:12, "and He that keeps your soul, does He not know it? Shall He not render to every man according to his work?" For Saadiah this verse signifies that God knows each individual soul and stores it up, ultimately to treat each one as required on the Day of Judgment. But good souls are stored with God, evil ones either wander about or are kept in confinement. One source even says angels fling it about like a ball. Saadiah adds that the souls are first in a state of suspension for twelve months after leaving the body until the body decomposes; during this period, he says, the soul suffers misery over the knowledge of what is occurring to the body. As in Zoroastrianism, he believes the first three days are what is known in certain sources difficult to trace, as "the chastisement of the grave". These souls then are stored until God's will brings the end of time to the world and resurrection is inaugurated.[18]

Saadiah confidently then asserts that every Jew believes in the ultimate resurrection.[19] He takes it for granted that in the light of the doctrine of *creatio ex nihilo*, that God created the universe from no pre-existent matter whatever, it is not difficult to believe He can restore disintegrated bodies. In addition he avers there is scriptural support to prove there will be a resurrection of the dead at the time of the redemption, the Messiah's advent. Saadiah grants that there is some ambiguity in the verses concerning whether resurrection is a national restoration or a revival of individual bodies. He takes the position that redemption and resurrection will take place at the same time, the opposite of Maimonides' posture.[20] And here we may pause to note that Saadiah reflects one view in a historic ambivalence in Judaism about several matters: a) the nature of, and the relationship between the Messianic Era and "the world to come"; b) the relationship between both of those terms and "resurrection"; c) the nature of immortality or life after the death of the body in this world, and of resurrection; d) the relationship between reward and punishment and "life after death" as distinct from the period after the final judgment.

Saadiah sees no conflict between resurrection and redemption despite the first being a futuristic existence and the other being primarily a this-worldly national regeneration. He posits that the Messiah will come and resurrection will occur *in this world*.[21] The Messianic Era will then remain in progress for an indefinite time until God wills to bring this world to an end and usher in "the world to come". At that time there will be resurrection of all the dead of mankind for retribution in the Final Judgment.[22] In closing this section then we note that for Saadiah the ultimate bodily resurrection of the dead to stand in final judgment follows the Messianic Era.[23]

d. *Messiah*

Saadiah is the first of Jewish theologians to introduce certain new elements into the messianic idea although he builds

from talmudic foundations.[24] At least two talmudic alterna-
tives can be noted. One is that the Messiah will come when
Jews repent, the other that they will have to suffer through
a long era of diaspora darkness until God will bring the Messiah. In the final period they will be under great persecution, and in despair many will leave the faith. Those who
remain faithful through this suffering will be redeemed.
Saadiah introduces the figure of Armilus (some read Armilius),
probably a personification of Rome, standing for the name of
the founder of Rome, Romulus, and possibly symbolically for
the Church. The Talmud has a story which Saadiah adopts, of
a Messiah of the tribe of Joseph who will appear in Galilee
as a preliminary Messiah and will conquer Jerusalem. King
Armilus will seize it from him and kill him, ushering in a
time of great persecution. Elijah will appear to the faithful; the real Messiah, the Davidic Messiah, will follow, will
take vengeance and effect the redemption. After the Jews are
again gathered in the Holy Land and are at peace with all the
nations, the resurrection will take place. Then will the
Sanctuary in Jerusalem be restored as described in Ezekiel 40.
The world will be a happy place, prosperity and wealth widespread.[25]

4. *Summary*

In the light of the varied and complex elements and some
of the ambiguities in the broad spectrum of eschatological
ideas it is well now to summarize the views of Saadiah as he
read scripture and Talmud.

Saadiah taught that the goal of all creation is the human
being. The human being has freedom of will and therefore is
personally responsible for his actions. He will be punished
or rewarded according to his conduct in life. Man possesses

a soul which enters his body at birth and leaves it at death. The soul is deposited either at the throne of God or suffers confinement, depending upon whether the person was good or bad, until resurrection. During the period after death there is no special existence, merely storage. When God brings the Messiah to effect the redemption of the adherents of Judaism there will be a preliminary resurrection of righteous Jews. The messianic period will endure for as long as God wills it, and during this time the prophetic utopian promises will be in effect. Finally God will bring this world to an end by inaugurating universal resurrection in which all humans will stand in divine judgment. At that time the righteous monotheists will be consigned to eternal bliss, the wicked, including atheists and polytheists, to eternal damnation. The "world to come", a purely spiritual existence, will then be inaugurated in a "timeless" and "spaceless" universe.

That Saadiah's views were only one strand in Judaism will be seen in discussing Maimonides. As a matter of fact, his view of the "suspension" of souls after death, a virtual "no-life-after-death" theory, did not enter what was later termed "orthodox" Judaism. This segment adopted the Maimonidian view that the soul is rewarded or punished in a "life after death" in what is popularly called "hell" and "heaven". And this has no relationship to the ultimate resurrection and eternal bliss or perpetual damnation.

One final word may be added concerning the views of Saadiah on Christianity. He dealt with the Trinity and with the question of the termination of the Torah and the rest of the halakhic corpus.[26] Saadiah denies that abrogation of Torah will take place, using a combination of scriptural verses and reason. His position is that the people of Israel will exist as long as the heavens and the earth (based on Jer. 31:35f.),

and they are a people only by virtue of their religion. Therefore that religion can never be terminated. And finally he
sees in Malachi 3:22f. verification that the Mosaic Torah
shall continue until the coming of Elijah. For Saadiah the
coming of Elijah heralds the day of resurrection, and will follow the messianic era. And so for Saadiah the Torah's function, indeed the function of all Judaism, will not cease with
the messianic era. In this way he obliquely or directly refutes the Pauline thesis that with the manifestation of Jesus
the Torah was no longer operative, even from the Christian
perspective that Jesus was the Messiah.[27]

III. YEHUDAH HALEVI

A. *The Man and His Work*

The scene shifts from Bagdad to Toledo, from the eastern
Babylonia-Persia area to the west, to Spain. There is a decline in process in the east, a "golden age" flourishing in
the west. There is also an incipient struggle between the
Cross (Christianity) and the Crescent (Islam) for control of
Spain. The Jew stands between them, buffeted by both, in a
quandary as to whom to support. Jews were in the armies of
both the opposing forces.

It was into this tumult that Yehudah Halevi was born
around 1080.[28] A physician-poet, he lived on both sides of
the border of Christian and Islamic Spain and witnessed the
decimation of Jewish communities on either side of the line.
He not only studied Talmud in the great schools of the south
but acquired the many-faceted Arabic culture of science,

philosophy, and poetry. The heaviness of tragedy in the air
during the twelfth century, however, turned Halevi to more
serious efforts than his earlier love poems or compositions
designed to flatter his patrons. He became imbued with the
problem of Jewish destiny. He took up many of the messianic
currents of his day and concretized them into a proto-Zionism
over eight-hundred years before the birth of Theodore Herzl
and twentieth-century political Zionism. Like the Zionists
of the late nineteenth and early twentieth century Halevi rejected acculturation. He rejected the philosophical rationalism of his time in which people like Saadiah strive to "prove"
Judaism, often unable to compete with the reality of the
blandishments of Christianity and Islam.

Halevi represents a different type, the emergence not
only of the nineteenth century Religious Zionist in the
twelfth century, but also of the nineteenth century "neo-
orthodox" Jew, and possibly of the eighteenth century Hasidic
Jew. Halevi, as I see him, is the proto-type of several
modern movements, a foreshadowing and a prophetic prefiguring
of modern orthodoxy, Zionism, and Hasidism.

Halevi is rooted in the events of Jewish history: the
Election of Abraham and Israel, Exodus from Egypt, the Revelation of Torah. In Revelation and Election he sets up the twin
pillars of Judaism upon which all had to rest. While he
writes his philosophical magnum opus, *An Argument for the
Faith of Israel*, better known in English as *The Kuzari,* in
the style of a Platonic dialogue, his philosophy is not in
the mood of rational inquiry and speculation that one finds in
Saadiah and Maimonides. Halevi begins with the premise that
God's will is unknowable by human reason. Religion is as much
metarational as metaphysical. The divine will can only be
discovered through revelation. Philosophical reasoning can

sustain two sides of a question. Divine revelation provides instant truth. In a very real sense Halevi took what twentieth century existentialists came to call a "leap of faith". The drama of Sinai is for him what verifies the truth of Judaism, not feeble human argument. But while he particularistically stresses the religious superiority of Judaism and of God's having chosen Israel to transmit it to the world, the very framework of the dialogue, the conversion of a gentile kingdom to Judaism, points the way to a non-racial, non-ethnic conception of "who is a Jew?" He who adopts the faith is a Jew, and all humans are welcome. This was, of course, a bold offensive on the part of Halevi in an age when Judaism, as he himself indicated in the title of one of his manuscripts, was a "despised faith".

In scanning the views of Halevi we will devote our attention to what was of greatest consequence to him: that the experience in history, of Election and Revelation, is what validated Judaism. But before we enter into that, a word about the Khazar motif in the dialogue is in order.

B. *The Khazars*

According to the legend King Bulan reigned over the Khazars around 740. They were a people who inhabited what is a section of the contemporary Soviet Union north and east of the Black Sea extending as far as the Caspian Sea. He had a persistent dream. In this dream an angel tells him that his intentions are good but his deeds are not acceptable. The king therefore began a search for a true faith and way of life. *The Kuzari* offers a fictional record of the king's conversations with a philosopher and representatives of Islam, Christianity and Judaism. The Jew is Halevi's main protagonist, and as in all

Platonic dialogues, the protagonist triumphs and the king converts himself and his kingdom to Judaism.

Historically, the following is a summary of the background.[29] A tenth-century Arab author remarked that in
Khazaria "sheep, honey and Jews exist in large quantities".
For a variety of reasons Jews who had been transported or fled
there from the times of Assyrian, Babylonian, and Roman wars
were reinforced by migrants from the Byzantine and Sassanian
Empires to the south. Khazaria apparently served the same
function in the east as Charles Martel fulfilled in the west.
In 732 his victory over the Arabs in Spain checked their on-
slaught on Europe, and it appears that Khazaria stemmed that
advance in the east in the eighth century, thus assuring that
Europe would remain Christian.

There was current a legend that Turks and Mongols were
descendants of Abraham from his sons by his third wife,
Keturah. Bulan, therefore, felt great affinity for the
Abrahamite monotheism which he heard about from Christians,
and Islamic sages as well as Jews. Ultimately, according to
a tenth-century letter by King Joseph to Ḥasdai Ibn Shaprut
in Spain, a certain King Obadiah brought Khazaria into a fuller
traditional form of Judaism. In some respects, however, their
Judaism appeared Karaitic, for Khazars used no light on the
Sabbath, did not leave their homes, used only psalms in their
prayers, and denied knowledge of the Talmud. The Gaon Petah-
iah describes them in this fashion. But it is also possible
that they were not necessarily Karaitic, only "biblical", for
they also offered up animal sacrifices as late as the eleventh
century, rites not practiced by the Karaites. In any event
the Russian kingdom of Kiev conquered them and they did not
remain a factor of significance after the tenth and eleventh
centuries.

Yet the Khazar Kingdom had inspired much romantic legend among Jews. It presented a large and powerful European nation as having voluntarily accepted Judaism over Islam and Christianity and reawakened the immemorial dreams of the triumph of Judaism as the world's faith. This motif was seized upon by Yehudah Halevi as his way of giving Judaism an ego build-up at a time when it was at low ebb in both Christian and Islamic Spain.

C. *Yehudah Halevi's Philosophy*

Yehudah Halevi is more poet than philosopher. He does not place the same importance upon reason as Saadiah did, and is not captivated by the technical terminology of philosophers. While other philosophers sought to harmonize Judaism with Paltonism or Aristotelianism, as the case may be, Halevi maintains Judaism is the truth and requires no validation by philosophic reasoning. To Halevi the most significant verification of a religion is historical experience. And for Halevi God's selection of Abraham is a historical fact. That this same God of Abraham, Isaac, and Jacob revealed Himself to Moses and gave him the Torah is another fact of history. Reason is guesswork, history is the genuine source of truth, and miracles are to be believed as historical evidence. For Halevi the source of all religious truth is the revelation found in the Bible. That it is true is verified by its having taken place in public to those people whom God had especially chosen because they were especially prepared. He traces the descent from Adam to Abraham and through Isaac and Jacob to Moses, through a line, all of whom "represented the essence and purity of Adam on account of their intimacy with God".[30] When God decided to reveal the Torah to Moses, however, He did not

do this in private but in the sight of all Israel so that
there might be no question of its occurrence. Furthermore,
Halevi argues that only this genuine form of supernatural
revelation provides true religion. And only when this kind
of revelation is attested to by indubitable historical experience can one claim he has a genuine revelation and therefore is in possession of true religion.[31]

Halevi also argues that God gave Moses all that was
needed for observance of the faith, revealing all the halakha
for the dietary, cultic and other observances.[32] These miẓvot
are what is required for man to come close to God and to merit
the world to come. All Jews can attain prophecy, but prose-
lytes who join the Jewish faith cannot. Halevi thereby ex-
hibits a notion of Jewish superiority although he concedes it
is only a spiritual one and does not signify rights to political or economic domination. Yet, it is perhaps the least
palatable of his notions for moderns. He writes, "Those, however, who become Jews do not take equal rank with born Israelites, who are specially privileged to attain to prophecy,
whilst the former can only achieve something by learning from
them, and can only become pious and learned, but never prophets."[33] Halevi adds to this the notion that even Jews can
only achieve prophecy in the Holy Land. And he then enters
into much exposition about the sanctity and significance of
the land. In these pages he virtually expresses a twelfth
century proto-Zionism.[34]

In this way, and in a variety of allusions throughout the
book, Halevi binds up into a neat package the belief that God
chose the Jewish People from the beginning, personally revealed
the Torah and its full explanation to Moses at Sinai in the
sight of all Israel which therefore witnessed it and was able
to attest to its historic factualness. He extols the virtue

of Israel in that it is observant of the commandments. And he
explains the nature and significance of the whole berakha system in Judaism as well as the liturgy. He sees the requirements God has placed upon the Jew as a source of enhancement.
Halevi waxes eloquently, "...he is glad and rejoices, and his
soul exults whenever he has done a good action...." And for
Halevi a "good action" is as much one of the ceremonial or
ritualistic practices as it is a social or ethical obligation.[35]

Unlike Saadiah, Halevi does not expatiate upon eschatology. Just as the Bible does not dwell at length upon these
ideas Halevi also merely affirms them briefly. He believes
in immortality of the soul, in reward and punishment after
death. He affirms thereby man's personal responsibility for
his actions and labors at defending its corollary, man's free
will. Resurrection does not play a role in Halevi's exposition of Judaism.[36] Halevi explains that God's foreknowledge
of man's actions does not restrict man. Man does not have to
choose what God knows. God knows what man will choose! The
unusual point in Halevi's exposition is that God's knowledge
of the future is like our human knowledge of the past. Our
knowing the past does not change it. So too God's knowing
future history will not affect the shape of things to come
which are determined by man's freedom of action. Halevi
writes: "For the knowledge of events to come is not the
cause of their existence, just as is the case with knowledge
of the things which have been."[37] There is an exception to
this in matters that are directly affected by God's miraculous
interventions. He also rather contradicts himself by allowing that actions can be the product of a chain of causes related to God and yet claims they are uncontrolled.[38]

159

To recapitulate: Halevi is very conscious of the need
for a national regeneration of Israel. He believes Jews
originated both philosophy and science. He believes that only
Jews, by birth and tradition, belonged to a group with a
special religious aptitude. Only in Palestine, he believes,
can this nation flourish at its best. He sounds like the
twentieth century Ahad Ha'am as he argues that in Palestine
alone prophecy can flourish. But Halevi, the profound nationalist, was at the same time a deeply pietistic person.[39] This
is what points to his being a prefiguration of a Religious
Zionist with a Hasidic emphasis upon pietism over reason, a
love of song and poetry as religious expression. He may also
have been the first person to formulate a real "credo" during
the middle ages when he had his rabbi in the dialogue begin
his discourse with the Khazar king by saying,

> I believe in the God of Abraham, Isaac, and
> Israel, who led the Israelites out of Egypt
> with signs and miracles; who fed them in the
> desert and gave them the holy land, after
> having made them traverse the sea and the
> Jordan in a miraculous way; who sent Moses
> with His Torah, and subsequently the prophets
> who confirmed His Torah by promises to those
> who observed, and threats to the disobedient.
> We believe in what is contained in the
> Torah....[40]

This "credo" also reflects his basic religious teaching: that
God is the God of history; the miracles are factual historical
experiences, and because they were publicly witnessed are all
that is needed to validate Judaism; Moses was the key personality and through him was the Torah given; there is reward and
punishment related to one's degree of obedience; Jews must believe and live the Torah. Just as history validated Judaism

so history is the main process through which all pass to the
ultimate goal. That ultimate goal of history is the messianic
redemption. But he believes that that moment can only come
when Israel yearns for the land so deeply that the people love
even its stones and its dust, and he cites Ps. 112:14f.,

> You shall arise and have mercy on Zion
> For it is time to favor her,
>   the moment has come,
> For your servants love her stones
>   and pity her dust.

And in his discussion of agadah the folklore aspect of talmudic
literature, he speaks of a famous passage in which it is said
seven things were created before the physical world: Paradise,
the Torah, the pious, Israel, the Throne of Glory, Jerusalem,
and the Messiah son of David.[41] He says this all ties together, and in his exegesis Halevi is virtually giving us a
capsule theology: Paradise is the ultimate place for the Torah
to lead the pious to; the Torah is the aim of creation for it
is the essence of wisdom; through it the bearers of Torah become the truly pious, and this is Israel, among whom rests the
Throne of Glory. Jerusalem is for them alone; and the best of
men, the Messiah, will guide them there.

Halevi's deep mystical piety is nowhere better expressed
than in certain of his poems. Perhaps it comes through most
clearly in the poem "Lord, Where Shall I Find Thee?":

> Lord, where shall I find Thee?
> High and hidden is Thy place!
> And where shall I not find Thee?
> The world is full of Thy Glory!...
> ...I have sought Thy nearness;
> With all my heart have I called Thee;
> And going out to meet Thee
> I found Thee coming toward me.

When one ponders such lines one clearly perceives why
Yehudah Halevi did not seek proof for the existence of God in
syllogisms or other forms of philosophic proof. For him it
was proven in a direct mystical encounter,

> And going out to meet Thee
> I found Thee coming toward me.[42]

IV. MOSES MAIMONIDES

A. *The Man and His Work*

Moses ben Maimon is said to have been "by far the most
comprehensive mind of medieval Jewry".[43] For some peculiar
reason the exact moment of his birth has been preserved. He
was born in Cordova, Spain, at one o'clock on a Sabbath afternoon, the day before Passover, the 30th of March, 1135. Thus
he had barely become a bar mitzvah when the Almohades, a
zealous Islamic sect from North Africa, took possession of
the city and both Jews and Christians were in peril if they
practiced their faith. Some Jews openly became Islamic,
while preserving Judaism secretly, prefiguring the later Marranos. Others left Spain. The Maimon family departed, some
maintaining they too had become outward Moslems. Certain historians hold that this may be inferred from the fact that Maimonides took great pains to defend this type of behaviour in
an essay entitled *Treatise on Religious Persecution*. He is
vague about his own posture but did argue that confessing a
belief that Mohammed was God's messenger, which was all the
authorities required, was not contrary to remaining a believing Jew.[44] It was in 1165 that he settled in Fostat, Egypt,

where he was physician to the royal court of Sultan Saladin,
and where he attained an immensely prestigious reputation. An
Arabic author wrote of him, "Galen's medicine is only for the
body; that of Abu Imran (Maimonides' Arabic name) is suited
for body and soul....If the moon had resorted to his art, it
certainly would have obtained the perfection it lacks...."[45]
He wrote at least ten medical works in Arabic and it appears
that the last literary effort of his life was a medical work
published in 1200.[46]

But it was in Fostat that he also ultimately emerged as
one of the great Jewish scholars of all history. His acronymic,
RaMBaM ("R" - Rabbi; "M" - Moses; "B" - ben, son of; "M" -
Maimon; the two "a's" merely represent vowels that allow the
RMBM to be read) is perhaps one of the best known household
terms in Judaism. The first of his three greatest religious
works is a *Commentary to the Mishnah* which he began at age
twenty-three and worked on for ten years. It is in this work,
originally written in Arabic, that he outlines his famous thirteen principles of Judaism, not accurately transmitted in the
àni maàmin ("I believe") series in the prayerbook.[47]

Maimonides' next major Judaic effort was his monumental
compilation of the entire halakha as he saw it at the end of
the twelfth century. But he preceded this around 1170 with an
enumeration of the so-called "six-hundred and thirteen commandments" of Judaism. He found all previous efforts to be de-
ficient. He enumerated two-hundred and forty-eight positive
commandments (obligations) and three hundred and sixty-five
negative commandments (actions from which a person should be
restrained). The reader should, however, not be confused concerning this. This enumeration is the maximum possible for
all types of Jews, of all ages and both sexes, in or out of
Palestine, some on the Sabbath or festivals, some daily, some

at prayer and some at dining, all *combined*. No one person at any time, anywhere, is obligated to six hundred and thirteen separate commandments. No Jew can conceivably fulfill six hundred and thirteen *separate* commandments in his lifetime. Each person has a limited number which is his obligation, and by performing this limited number he may in his lifetime fulfill thousands of miẓvot, but they will be the same limited selection fulfilled over and over again. Like his halakhic compilation as a whole, as we will see, Maimonides' enumeration of the so-called six hundred and thirteen commandments was taken to task by rabbinic critics.[48]

Maimonides next turned to the magnum opus of his life, the *Mishneh Torah* or *Yad Haḥazakah*, consisting of an Introduction and fourteen divisions, written in Hebrew in a style imitative of the Mishnah. It was completed around 1180. This work too was not universally accepted. Maimonides' views were rejected for various reasons: a) he did not supply sources for his selection of halakha; b) his views were sometimes suspect because of his philosophical or theological premises and conclusions; c) his halakha was sometimes rejected as not being the adoption of a correct talmudic precedent; d) he gave no reasons for his views.

The last great work of Maimonides was *Dalalat al-hairin* or *The Guide for the Perplexed*. This again was written in Arabic between 1185 and 1190. It is considered by some "the greatest philosophic book produced in Judaism".[49] In its Latin translation it influenced many Christian thinkers. But again, like his previous works, this too came in for much criticism. His discussion of anthropomorphism was attacked, and there was great suspicion concerning his views on resurrection.

A historical judgment of the influence of a significant
thinker cannot be made on the basis of whether or not his views
received unanimous approval. Furthermore, the contrary may be
valid. The greater the negative reaction the greater may be
the evidence that the thinker is feared for his views. This
may signify he propounds error and confusion and is inimical
to a tradition. Or it may merely signify that some fear the
changes his thought will inspire and would rather preserve the
status quo. In any case, one judgment at least is therefore
possible. When a thinker is vigorously opposed it is clear
evidence of one or the other, that he is greatly feared for
the attractiveness of his views, or for the error of his views.
In either event it is clear that he will have a strong influence whether against his views or in favor of them. And
this is probably a fair judgment of Maimonides. Far and above
any individual theologian or halakhist in Judaism, second only
to that collective group of teachers embodied in the corpus of
the Talmud, Moses ben Maimon played an exceedingly influential
role in Judaism. Whether one agrees with his views in philosophy or with his decisions in halakha, he has to be reckoned
with. And yet I am prepared to make the judgment that it is
in the field of halakha primarily that he gained his historic
position in Judaism and that had his reputation been dependent
upon *The Guide for the Perplexed* perhaps he would have had a
greater role than the first century Alexandrian philosopher,
Philo, but no greater than that of Saadiah, and far less
prestige than he actually enjoys. As a matter of fact his
Guide was taken notice of primarily because of his halakhic
importance. It is not generally known that some of the leading anti-Maimonidean scholars of the time were so incensed
with both his *Guide* and the opening division of *Mishneh Torah*,
Sefer Hamàdah (The Book of Knowledge), that they induced the

Dominicans to burn them in 1233-34. It was only out of his
tremendous respect for the halakhic reputation of Moses Maimonides, although he does not specify why, that R. Solomon
Ibn Aderet excluded his works from a general ban on "the books
which the Greeks have written on religious philosophy and the
natural sciences".[50] In the light of this we will be examining the philosophy of Maimonides with relevant cross-references
to his halakha.

B. *The Philosophy of Maimonides*

It is apparent from the paucity of technical philosophical composition within Judaism that this was not a major
thrust of Jewish theologians or scholars of Judaica. And when
such writings were undertaken, as in the case of the rare
ancient writer of philosophy like Philo or the exceptional
case of a philosopher-Gaon like Saadiah, it was primarily to
explain Judaism to intellectually-oriented Jews who were attracted to the majority culture. It was less an effort to explain Judaism to the non-Jew than to retain the "modernist"
of each respective era within the parameters of a viable Judaism. This was the case with Maimonides, and it is significant
that while he wrote in Arabic, he wrote the Arabic in Hebrew
alphabet characters. Obviously that was not designed for the
non-Jewish student.[51]

What Maimonides was anxious to do in the first place was
to save the faith of his pupil, a certain Joseph Ibn Aknin of
Alexandria. And beyond that "to enlighten a religious man who
has been trained to believe in the truth of our holy Torah...
and at the same time has been successful in his philosophical
studies. Human reason has attracted him to abide within its
sphere;...Hence he is lost in perplexity and anxiety."[52]

1. *Anthropomorphism*[53]

One of the significant quarrels that was waged against
Maimonides was on his view that one should read the Bible's
statements concerning God as metaphors. He points out that
idolaters do not believe the idol they worship is God. They
believe the idol is a form which represents the "agent between
God and His creatures". Therefore, he argues, those who believe that the physical allusions to God in the Torah such as
"arm", "mouth", and the possession of emotions like "anger" or
"love" indicate the "form" of God, in other words, if in this
way they believe God is corporeal, they are as bad as idolaters. For Maimonides, though God is not to be represented
with an ear, or as hearing, in a way which could be construed
as having a bodily form or any type of attribute, it remains
a reality that God does "hear" prayer and is "pleased" with
man's fulfilling ritual ceremony. If man cannot understand
that contradiction, it is only because the paradox is beyond
his intellectual capacity.[54]

On the other hand there were scholars who argued that
man's intellectual capacity is not the issue. They opposed
Maimonides for what they believed was his establishment of a
new source of authority alongside revelation, and for depriv-
ing the average man of the comfort of possessing a true faith
if it is not based upon rationalism. Anthropomorphism was not
the only issue between Maimunists, those who admired and supported Maimonides, and the anti-Maimunists, those who opposed
him. The subject of eschatology, most especially that of
resurrection, came in for much criticism. Furthermore, the
process of exegesis which did away with anthropomorphism was
also a process which could be used to explain away the necessity for observing some of the rituals by expounding upon them

as symbolism. As already noted earlier, ritual observance
was notably weak during the thirteenth century.[55] In addition
to this, very serious scholars like the Provencal sage, R.
Abraham ben David of Posquieres (1125-1198) took strong exception to Maimonides' denial of the validity of anthropomorphism. Maimonides had declared that one who believes God has
substance and form is a *min* (a "sectarian" or "dissenter",
perhaps worse, a "heretic") who loses his share in "the world
to come". To this R. Abraham of Posquieres appended a critical note rejecting Maimonides' use of the term *min* with such
harsh ramifications for one who has an anthropomorphic notion
of deity. He wrote, "...many greater and better people than
Maimonides shared this notion according to what they perceived in scriptural verses...."[56]

2. *Eschatology*

The problem of Maimonides' God versus a more Personal
Deity evident in the pages of scripture who walks and talks
with man, was a major cause of anti-Maimonidian sentiment.
But there was a second equally as significant. This was the
question of eschatology. It has already been seen in discussing the theology of the prayerbook, a selection from Gaon
Hai, and most especially the philosophy of Gaon Saadiah, that
the eschatological beliefs in Judaism were tracable to talmudic lore and were embedded in the liturgy. The average unsophisticated Jew believed God rewards and punishes quite
literally and physically, that man can find comfort in the
eventual resurrection that will entitle him to witness and
enjoy the messianic era in this world, after which he will
enjoy eternal life in the world to come. Philosophers might
play variations on the themes, but the pious Jew was not
steeped in the subtle discrepancies.

Maimonides, however, caused a furor among scholars because they either recognized that he did not share the traditional belief or that he was so hopelessly confused about it
that there was a danger that his perplexities will lead the
unsophisticated to anxiety and the sophisticated to disbelief.
For one thing Maimonides did not mention the doctrine of resurrection in either the *Mishneh Torah* or in the *Guide*. The fact
that he had affirmed it in the *Commentary to the Mishnah* was
not enough to overcome the other omissions because he wrote
the latter, as we have seen, relatively early in life. As far
as some of the rabbinical scholars of more conservative bent
were concerned, he could have changed his mind and come to un-
belief or at best to the same state of perplexity that he
seeks to cure in his *Guide*. For that matter it is not totally
beyond possibility that he wrote the *Guide* as much to convince
himself as his disciple Joseph Ibn Aknin. In any event its
absence from a halakhic treatise, even from the philosophic
section at the beginning of the *Mishneh Torah*, "The Book of
Knowledge", would indicate a lesser emphasis upon it in terms
of its being a mandatory belief. Its absence from the *Guide*,
furthermore, would imply he had no rational way to present it
as a valid and intellectually acceptable proposition.[57]

The following is a brief sketch of the probable posture
Maimonides took on the matter of eschatology. In general this
is summed up in his exposition of the last four of the "thirteen fundamentals".[58]

a. *Free Will*

His "tenth fundamental" reads, "The Lord, bless Him,
knows the deeds of man, and does not obscure His eye from them
as the deists think...."[59] In his *Guide* he expounds the idea
that since God's knowledge is of a nature which man cannot

grasp it is not correct to argue that there is a contradiction
between God's knowledge and man's free will. Thus a correct
understanding of Maimonides' conception of God's knowledge
allows for the conviction that he also affirms human freedom
to choose and act although he does not state it. Some philosophers, like Joseph Albo (1380-1444), argue similarly.
Others sought other explanations. Ḥasdai Crescas (1340-1410)
maintains that there is a degree of limitation on both God's
omniscience and human freedom.[60] It is, however, in his
Mishneh Torah that Maimonides gives his clearest attitude on
the question of freedom. Man's freedom is unlimited. He
utterly denies any degree of determinism or predestination.
He points out that prophetic Judaism which admonishes man to
high morality would be a hollow mockery if man did not possess
the freedom to be good, if he had already been destined to be
evil. This is the only basis for divine justice: that man
is free to act and is then rewarded for righteousness and
punished for sin. There Maimonides, however, did not take
up the question of God's knowledge and merely let it rest as
too profound and complex a matter for man to comprehend. It
must be remembered that this was before he wrote the *Guide* and
explained his theory of God's knowledge. Some scholars were
quite upset that he posited human freedom and left God's
knowledge unreconciled, and the aforementioned R. Abraham ben
David of Posquieres was one who was very critical of him for
threatening the simple faith of the pious by raising problems
he did not solve.[61]

In addition to the problem of God's knowledge there is
the problem of whether or not Providence operated in the world
and how this might conflict with the notion of human free will.
Maimonides takes that up more extensively in his *Guide* and responds that there is only general Providence but not special

or individual Providence, along the lines of Aristotle, except for humans. In the case of humans there is individual Providence, and if a person is on a ship which sinks the person drowns because of Providence, for free will is limited to the moral sphere and does not apply to his ability to control events in nature, life and death, hunger and abundance, and the like. These are obviously complex and sometimes irreconcilable conundrums.[62]

b. *Reward and Punishment*

The "eleventh fundamental" is stated by Maimonides as "...the Lord, bless Him, gives reward to the one who fulfills the mizvot of the Torah and punishes the one who violates its admonitions; the greatest reward is the world to come and the strongest punishment is to be cut off from that..."[63] It is clear from this that Maimonides is speaking of the individual and not of biblical collective retribution promised to Israel as a whole. It is not clear that he is referring to a post-death time only, for in connection with the world to come he says it is "the greatest reward", not the *only* reward. This is only one of the ambiguities in Maimonides. On the other hand he is also implying what some modernists would hope to be true, that punishment does not take place in the lurid areas of the netherworld called "hell", but is merely the absence of the bliss available in the world to come, by being "cut off".

Historically, the greatest problem related to this doctrine of reward and punishment has been that which is called "theodicy", the justice of God. Why do righteous people suffer, and wicked ones prosper? The talmudic rabbis discuss this as well and in some instances they apply the biblical promises of reward for righteousness to the afterlife.[64] Certainly the Mishnah earlier had already indicated that

there are certain mizvot for doing which man benefits here and
now, but also stores up for himself a dividend for "the world
to come".[65] Moses ben Maimon scanned the biblical and rabbinic
sources and came to what he undoubtedly believed was a proper
summation.[66]

Maimonides asserts all men have both merits and sins.
The righteous man is the one who possesses more merits. The
wicked man is the one who possesses more sins. The person who
manages to balance his deeds equally is classed neither as
righteous nor wicked. Repentance has been provided as the
means to overcome sin and enter the class of righteousness.
Yom Kippur (Day of Atonement) is the special occasion set aside
for a concerted effort to attain the degree of righteousness.
However, Maimonides points out that one cannot assess this
matter as a statistical one alone. Quality enters the question. Some individual merits may be far greater than many
sins, or at times one sin may outweigh many merits. Thus a
basically wicked man may have fulfilled one great act of merit
that outweighs many long years of sinning. God alone can
assess the relative value of a merit or a sin. And what occurs on Yom Kippur, whether a person is forgiven or will be
punished during the coming year, is known to God alone. Other
medieval thinkers added that what appears to us may not always
seem to bear this out. Therefore we must realize a seemingly
wicked person enjoys benefits here and will endure his suffering in hell, while some righteous people suffer here but will
enjoy only bliss later.[67]

Joseph Albo believes, and is more specific and lucid than
Maimonides, that there is reward and punishment both in this
world and in the afterlife, and that they are both physical
and spiritual. A study of rabbinic sources would certainly
bear out that this is a fair assessment. Judaism does not

express itself in a systematic theology but rather in numerous
sayings and anecdotes of countless teachers over a period of
centuries. Therefore almost every conceivable viewpoint is
represented, and each viewpoint is multi-shaded. Most especially is the problem complicated when trying to sort out the
relationship between reward and punishment with the "three
worlds" sometimes spoken of in Judaism: the here and now,
ólam hazeh, the messianic era, *y'mot hamashiah*, and the world
to come, *ólam habà*.[68] This becomes more complex when "world
to come" has to apply to two worlds: post-Messiah when resurrection occurs, and post-Final Judgment after resurrection!

What should be realized, therefore, is that there is no
monolithic position in Judaism. Some thinkers believed literally in all phases of the doctrine, and asserted both physical
and spiritual aspects to it. Maimonides was not always con-
sistent and this is what created the furor over his views.
On the other hand, because there was so much room for variations on the theme in Judaism, many scholars defended Maimonides. And because of this diversity in Judaism, there was no
possibility for the establishment of "dogma" that would in
turn define "heresy". Indeed Maimonides tried to do that by
stating that there were a number of classifications of people
who would not enjoy "the world to come". We will speak again
of this when considering his doctrine of resurrection, but we
should also note that he allowed for repentance to overcome
any degree of sin and re-admit the erstwhile sinner to candi-
dacy for the world to come.[69]

In the scheme of Maimonides, it should be noted, there
is no emphasis upon heaven and hell in the popular conception
of those terms. For him reward and punishment first take place
physically in this world, as the Torah delineates. But beyond
that there is a spiritual reward and punishment in the world

to come, which will be after the resurrection after the days
of Messiah. Then "reward" constitutes enjoyment of eternal
bliss, "punishment" *the absence of that bliss*. Maimonides
does not describe a hell in the same way as other medieval
thinkers where the sinner undergoes fiery damnation, although
we will note some hesitation on his part. Basically, however,
he treats "hell" or *gehinnom* as a place of deprivation, an
absence of the bliss of the righteous, a total annihilation
of life, contrary to the eternal bliss of those who attain to
the world to come. No matter how many important scholars came
to his defense, the fact stands out as indisputable that Maimonides only feebly describes a "hell" and its torments in his
Commentary and ascribes the notion to "some say", not ranking
it as a doctrine. Punishment for Maimonides was the annihilation of the soul and the deprivation it suffered by never ex-
periencing the ultimate eternal bliss which is stored up for
the righteous.[70]

c. *The Messiah*

The twelfth fundamental enunciated by Maimonides is that
of "the days of the Messiah, to believe faithfully that he
will come...and that he will enjoy power, exaltation, and honor
over all the kings of the past...and a principle of this fundamental is that there can be no king over Israel other than of
the dynasty of David and progeny of Solomon...." It is apparent from this statement that for Maimonides the Messianic
Hope is a very physical and literal one of national regeneration in this world under a Davidic monarch. He connects the
messianic hope with his discussion of the world to come by
enunciating the idea that because the ultimate objective of
human life is to enjoy perpetual bliss it is necessary to have
the Messiah who will liberate the Jews from all oppressors "who

prevent them from proper preoccupation with Torah and mizvot".[71] It is interesting that Maimonides evades the Christian messianic issue by defining the Messiah in terms distant from those ascribed to Jesus. He declares, "that king who will arise of the progeny of David will be wiser than Solomon; and he will be a great prophet, almost like Moses our rabbi...."[72] After that will come "the world to come", which will never end. But "the era of the Messiah is this worldly, when the world will continue in its accustomed manner, except that sovereignty will return to Israel...."[73]

The messianic idea, then, for Maimonides portends a real historical event, but is to be merely the vestibule to the world to come. For some versions of Judaism, especially the kabalistic, the messianic event is a cataclysmic time when the fall of man is to be reversed and all of creation restored to a pristine perfection.[74] It is difficult to determine upon what basis Maimonides makes his brief messianic statement. The fact is that the sources for the nature of the Messiah are so plentiful the concept cannot be defined monolithically. There is abundance of views as to whether the Messiah is to be an ideal person, a paragon of virtue, a redeemer, or only the king of Israel after God redeems them, or whether "the Messiah" is an age of history, or a meta-historical era. The apocalyptic literature adds some items to the idea not expressed by most prophets, and some ideas rarely articulated, and then only ephemerally. The expanded concept was brought to a substantial development in rabbinic literature and resulted in what has been called "messianic speculation". This subsequently became the basis of Christian millenarian movements.[75] The sequence of elements include certain signs that the Messiah is due, tumultuous upheavals called "pangs of the Messiah", the advent of Elijah to announce his coming, a messianic trumpet heralding him, the ingathering of Jews to the holy land, the acquisition of new members of the faith, the cosmic struggle of Gog and Magog, the messianic era, the transformation of the natural order, resurrection of the dead, the Final Judgment, and the world to come.[76]

Maimonides surveyed the eschatological issue in the introductory segment to his thirteen fundamentals in the *Commentary on the Mishnah*. He concluded that the talmudic rabbis were using metaphor and parable when discussing the afterlife, and that all the physcial images should not be taken literally. Human beings will enjoy spiritual bliss only, and the punishment of evil will consist in the fact that the unrighteous will not enjoy that bliss. He therefore identified the Garden of Eden and *Gehinnom* (Hell) in this world. It is in this context that Maimonides once attributed physical punishment to the wicked in the hell of this world, a notion that is not clear and was insufficient to appease his detractors. Primarily Maimonides emphasized the resurrection of the dead. And it was in this *Commentary* context too that he expounded the naturalistic-historical messianic idea which we have already briefly outlined. The messianic age will be precisely as our own historical time except that sovereignty will return to Israel in order that the people may attain the higher aim of life: the spiritual bliss of the world to come. What he said in the halakha of *Repentance* cited earlier, Maimonides repeated in his *Melakhim* (Kings): "King Messiah will arise and restore the kingdom of David....He will rebuild the sanctuary and gather the dispersed of Israel. All the ancient laws will be reinstituted...sacrifices will again be offered ...."[77] Maimonides goes on to declare this doctrine to be a mandatory biblical belief, citing a variety of verses. And

he avers that there need be expected no miracles from the
Messiah, nor will he revive the dead, just as R. Aḳiba asked
for no miracle of Bar Kokhba, the second century messianic
pretender.[78] The sign that the claimant is truly the Messiah,
said Maimonides, is that he can prove his Davidic lineage, is
a pious scholar, wins Jews back to faith, rebuilds the sanctuary on its original site in Jerusalem and gathers the dispersed; in short: success will verify the truth of the claim.
And then he will win the world to God, in accord with Zepha-
niah 3:9, in reference to the peoples of the world, "that they
may all call upon the name of the Lord to serve Him with one
consent".[79]

Maimonides teaches that none of the laws of nature will
be set aside during the messianic era, any verses in scripture
to the contrary to be taken metaphorically. The war of Gog
and Magog will follow the advent of Elijah and both will pre-
cede the Messiah. But Maimonides hedges on all the details
and says, "neither the exact sequence of those events nor the
details thereof constitute religious dogmas. No one should
ever occupy himself with the legendary themes...." And then
Maimonides states the purpose of the messianic era:

> The Sages and Prophets did not long for the
> days of the Messiah that Israel might exer-
> cise dominion over the world, or rule over
> the heathens, or be exalted by the nations,
> or that it might eat and drink and rejoice.
> Their aspiration was that Israel be free
> to devote itself to the Torah and its wis-
> dom, with no one to oppress or disturb it,
> and thus be worthy of life in the world to
> come.[80]

d. *Resurrection*

The "thirteenth fundamental" is stated by Maimonides to
be "the resurrection of the dead, which I have previously
clarified". Where did he "clarify" it? He referred to it
earlier in his prefatory essay to the thirteen fundamentals,
but hardly "clarified" it. He devoted merely a few lines of
incohate remarks in a very lengthy essay, referring to *Gan
Eden* (the Garden of Eden) as a delightful place, *Gehinnom*
"the term that describes suffering and punishment that will
overtake the wicked; and the Talmud did not explain the form
of that punishment". It is rather difficult to follow Maimonides at this juncture. When does that hell-experience
occur? Is it when a wicked man dies that he faces it, or
when the wicked is resurrected and is not awarded the world
to come? Maimonides is not at all clear on this. This is
stated before his next statement, which is that "resurrection
is a fundamental of the Mosaic fundamentals, and there is no
religion and no faithfulness to Jewish religion for anyone
who does not believe it; but it is only for the righteous".
This implies the previous "*eden*-experience" and "*gehinnom*-
experience" were prior to resurrection. But this was not
clarified by Maimonides. Furthermore, at least two talmudic
sources, to which Maimonides seems to allude when he speaks
of the sun that will burn the wicked, do indicate that a
scorching sun is an active force in the world to come, precisely when Maimonides argues only deprivation of bliss is
the fate of the wicked. R. Simon b. Lakish (third century)
is quoted as saying there is no *Gehinnom* in "the time to
come" but the Lord will apply the scorching sun to roast the
wicked and heal the righteous (Malachi 3:19f.).[81]
What I have here indicated is only part of the problem
lucidly seen by Maimonides' opponents concerning his views of

the eschatology. They were not certain of what he believed despite his affirmations. In the *Guide* he did not even mention it. And in the *Mishneh Torah* it appears that "the world to come" is identical with "immortality of the soul".[82] As a matter of fact this was the accusation made by R. Abraham ben David of Posquieres.[83] Finally Maimonides quite cogently argues that "the world to come" is not in some historic future or in some post-historic future, but is in contemporary existence with this world, for it is *post-mortem existence*. In other words he is clearly arguing that the permanent bliss of the righteous begins at death, and is the equivalent of that which is called "immortality of the soul". In this scheme, what happens to resurrection? Again, therefore, in the margin we read a strong critique by R. Abraham who accuses him of denying that in the end of days there will be the cosmic upheaval foreseen by the prophets and the establishment of a new world.

Confronted even during his lifetime by much criticism Maimonides was compelled to reformulate his view in his *Treatise on the Resurrection of the Dead*. Here he introduces a novel note, that the dead will be resurrected in body in this world sometime after the coming of the Messiah, after which they will die again and enjoy eternal spiritual bliss.[84] What need is there for the resurrection of the body if it is to die again? Maimonides replies that the knowledge of such mysteries is beyond man's capacity.

That there was ambiguity, ambivalence, and diversity in medieval Jewish theology is therefore self-evident. As is normal among humans, advocates of each view regarded those who espoused something different as bordering on heresy. But to formulate more than a "consensus" was not possible, for the faithful Jew did not have to subscribe to any particular set of tenets.

All of the elements of eschatology: free will, reward and punishment, a place for the soul (heaven and hell), the messianic era, the resurrection and the world to come, have their roots in biblical literature and were expanded in intertestamental writings. There were undoubtedly both Zoroastrian and Greek influences. The biblical notions, fertilized by Persian and Greek ideas, became vastly expanded in the rabbinic literature and were thus transmitted to medieval Judaism. Medieval thinkers simply had no certain dogma to go by and struggled to define a theology of eschatology out of the raw material they inherited. A variety of eschatological conceptions ensued and these are taken up and transmuted in their own way by modern thinkers.[85] One thing is clear from our brief survey, however, and that is that medieval thinkers in Judaism believed in eternal damnation (Saadiah) or eternal deprivation (Maimonides), and that the abundant apologetics one hears or reads in current writings in Judaism that "Judaism rejects the doctrine of eternal damnation" is simply not in accord with the sources.[86]

It will be recalled from Chapter Three of this book that the resurrection of the dead was part of the liturgy. That sinners could not be resurrected is implicit in the notion that sinners are punished in hell for twelve months and after that the body is consumed and the soul burned. Other classes of severe sinners remain in hell for punishment forever.[87] Thus in early rabbinic theology we have a clear statement of the possibility of eternal damnation for certain sinners such as *minim* (a term difficult to define), *epikorsim* (another indefinable term), those who reject the Torah and those who reject resurrection, amongst others. Maimonides may have been disturbed by the notion of eternal damnation, and as we have seen, did not adopt it in the sense of torment, but did adopt it as deprivation. This was undoubtedly one of the causes of opposition to him. As noted earlier Saadiah argued that eternal damnation is simply part of divine justice, a typical medieval argument. Naḥmanides, in the thirteenth century, was also quite comfortable with the idea that the righteous rejoice as they see the wicked suffer.[88]

Taken as a whole it is not difficult to ascertain why many leading rabbinic authorities opposed Maimonides' theology during the thirteenth century. But it was not only his theology that came under fire. His halakha did as well, and most especially the effort he engaged in to explain the *reasons* for miẓvot.

3. *The Purpose of Precepts*

Maimonides believes that every positive and negative commandment in scripture has a rational, historical and useful purpose. And he sets out to explain these purposes.[89] In general he maintains the purpose of all the observances and precepts of Judaism is to perfect the total man, both body and soul. He points out that this is clear in terms of legal and moral precepts, but not at all clear in ceremonial or ritual observances. Accordingly he hopes to provide a convincing argument for the significant purposes involved in ritualism.

In the process of pursuing his task in his rational way Maimonides arrives at conclusions that are similar to findings of more scientific historians of religion in modern times. Some of his conclusions regarding this aspect of halakha were no more acceptable to some scholars than certain aspects of

his theology. They had within them the seeds of serious ramifications. We cannot do more than touch upon several here.

a. *Sacrifices*

Maimonides argues that the sacrificial cult was appropriate for the level of religious aptitude of ancient Israel.
Maimonides sees clearly that the detailed ritualism of the
cult of Israel was not far different from that of all the
pagan religions. The religion of Israel outlawed human sacrifice. But otherwise it was akin to the heathen forms of wor-'
ship. Maimonides is of the opinion that the decision of God
and Moses to allow it was the result of religious psychology.
It was assumed Israel will outgrow it and it will disappear.
He apparently argues in this fashion oblivious of his self-
contradiction in envisioning the restoration of sacrifices at
the time of the Messiah.

The interesting point made by Maimonides is his comparison of the evolution of religious institutions to the evolution one finds in the processes of nature. There is growth,
change, and adaptation. He argues that it is impossible "according to the nature of man" for him to give up entirely
what he is accustomed to and turn to a new mode. Gradual
development is needed. And so, to ask Israel to give up the
sacrificial system, he writes, "it would in those days have
made the same impression as a prophet would make at present if
he called us to the service of God and told us in His name,
that we should not pray to Him...that we should serve Him in
thought, and not by any action."[90] With this he explains why
the prophets were frequently impatient with the sacrificial
cult. In effect, they saw it, according to Maimonides, as a
concession, and not as a primary objective. God's primary
objective was for the Israelite to live God's will. The cult

was merely one medium through which, by transferring all worship to God, idolatry would be obliterated and Judaism's moral system established upon firm ground.[91]

Although Maimonides does not draw conclusions from his theory of evolution concerning other ritual practices of Judaism and did not call for innovation in his own time, his theory remains a valuable asset for innovators in all periods. When a society outgrows a certain institution, that institution may cease to serve the religious purpose it once did and may be discarded. Contemporary Judaism has often engaged in revisionism by applying Maimonides' evolutionary thesis combined with the thrust to historicism acquired from scientific inquiry since the nineteenth century.

Other purposes Maimonides determines were inherent in the religious practices of Judaism were for people to reject personal desire and to develop temperance in all the sensual pleasures. This reduction of sensuality in turn motivates toward holiness.[92]

b. *Dietary Practices*

Perhaps it is his discussion of dietary practices which had the most serious ramifications. No reason is given in the Torah, nor surmised by the talmudic sages for the forbidden food practices in Judaism. But Maimonides argues that they are forbidden because they are unwholesome. He is the first scholar in Judaism to attribute the dietary practices to hygiene. His argument is novel, and as a physician-scientist often persuasive, but undoubtedly wide of the mark. There is a difference between a reason for a practice, and a by-product of a practice. Hygienic advantages may frequently have been by-products of the dietary practices. But Maimonides argues that they were the underlying reasons.[93]

Thus he avers that pork was banned because its food and habits are loathsome. But chickens are very dirty too. He hints at the danger of high cholesterol when he argues that the fact of the intestines was barred because it interrupts digestion "and produces cold and thick blood; it is more fit for fuel...". But he obviously was not really aware of so many other sources of high cholesterol in permitted cuts of beef and in eggs. Yet if God had designed dietary practices for the health of man, as Maimonides is urging, one might have expected a higher degree of medico-scientific anticipation upon God's part.

Undoubtedly the most interesting of his dietary suggestions was the one he makes on the prohibition of the mingling of meat and dairy. This is taken to be prohibited three times in scripture where we read "do not boil a kid in its mother's milk". From this grew the entire complex of halakha not to cook or eat meat and dairy foods together or to use the same pots, utensils, dishes and tableware for both meat and dairy. Maimonides guesses that "it is somehow connected with idolatry, forming perhaps part of the service, or being used on some festival of the heathen". But he confesses that he had not yet found it mentioned in the books he researched.[94] The ramifications there too are interesting. For it appears that once the real reason is known, and if that reason is no longer operative, the need for the practice may well be obsolete, and the practice dispensable. Thus Maimonides is also correct in pointing out that twice out of the three occurrences of the prohibition not to boil a kid in its mother's milk, the prohibition is in the context of sacrificial cult provisions. The third time it is in a dietary context and I venture to say the two former ones were older, the third, in Deuteronomy, was the latest, and perhaps already recorded at a time when

184

the reason was forgotten. It sounded like a food taboo and was therefore placed in that context. In any event we now know that it was an ancient Canaanite practice and was probably prohibited in the cult of Israel as part of a general pattern not to indulge in Canaanite practices that appeared abhorrent to Israelites.[95]

c. *Circumcision*

In his explanations of religious practices, Maimonides probably strives for objectivity. But his view that the Torah instituted sexual prohibitions "to inculcate the lesson that we ought to limit sexual intercourse altogether, hold it in contempt, and only desire it very rarely" is a rather subjective reading into the Torah of his own presuppositions and explains his rigorous conservatism in the halakha pertaining to sex and women. His rather ascetic view leads him to an odd explanation of circumcision. He argues that one of its objects is to limit sexual intercourse and weaken the organ of generation. He sees the commandment "as a means for perfecting man's moral shortcomings....Circumcision simply counteracts excessive lust; for there is not doubt that circumcision weakens the power of sexual excitement and sometimes lessens the natural enjoyment...."[96]

V. TRANSITION FROM RATIONALISM TO MYSTICISM

The thirteenth century saw the Maimonidean struggle in full force. The fourteenth century saw a decline in the rationalist movement symbolized perhaps in the person of Ḥasdai Crescas. We will therefore close this chapter with a few thoughts on the transition from rationalism to mysticism.[97]

Crescas was born in Barcelona in 1340 and lived through the difficult fourteenth century with its terrible years, especially of 1348 and 1391, both of which had a great impact upon the destiny of Judaism. In his major theological treatise *Or Adonai* ("Light of the Lord") Crescas establishes once again the independence of Judaism from the rationalism of Aristotelianism, allowing it to stand upon its own indigenous ground. He disagrees with Maimonides on almost every philosophical position Maimonides had adopted from the Aristotelian system. Using the same method of logical analysis as Aristotle and Maimonides, Crescas disproves all their positions, and like Yehudah Halevi he shows that philosophical method is uncertain and inadequate for faith. One must fall back upon scripture, he insists, and ultimately one knows there is only one God because Deuteronomy 6:4 says so: "Hear, O Israel, the Lord is our God, the Lord is One."

Crescas sees six fundamentals in Judaism after the existence of God: God's knowledge, Providence, Power, Prophecy, Freedom, and Purpose. Crescas believes God's knowledge of all that exists and occurs is no problem for man's freedom. God knows all the real and all the contingent. Knowledge of the contingent is reconciled with man's freedom. Whatever man will choose God will know, and at all times He knows the possibilities. Man has freedom to act, but can choose and control only in the moral sphere. In all other matters God's providence operates. But His providence does not always provide for direct reward and punishment according to conduct in this world. The balance will be corrected in the next world. Therefore the suffering of the righteous here is not a problem of God's justice. The individual is simply part of a whole. He inherits situations when he is born, becomes involved in circumstances as a member of a given society, and is therefore possibly caught up in the suffering God brought upon that society. But all such adversity in the scheme of providence may, after all, be justice, for whatever is from God is good, though we may not quite see how that operates.

Crescas insists upon God's omnipotence so any miracle can happen, even Bilaam's talking ass in Numbers 22. Crescas totally rejects Maimonides' idea that prophetic power is attained by a person who has a superior intellect and imagination plus divine grace. Crescas argues that since Maimonides is compelled to agree a prophet requires divine grace, why not simply accept the direct scriptural evidence that a prophet is a man of divine charisma because God chose to use him, with no recourse at all to the intellect?

In addition to the doctrines listed previously Crescas believes the following are essentials of Judaism: Creation, Immortality, Reward and Punishment, Resurrection, Eternity of the Torah, the superiority of Moses as Prophet par excellence, the Messiah, and the priest's ability to know the future through the Urim and Tumim.[98]

Unlike Maimonides and the philosophers who stressed the attainment of perfection through the constant development of the mind, Crescas stressed the cultivation of the love of God. And herein probably, more than in any other view, is the bridge that leads from philosophic speculation to romantic mysticism. Although he does not count the Election of Israel as a fundamental dogma of Judaism he takes it for granted. And he argues that Judaism did not require devoted individual missionaries to win souls to God because the entire community of Judaism is a collective missionary, for which purpose Jews were sent by God into a widespread diaspora. Crescas comes

close to the Christian idea of "original sin" and teaches that
"...the entire race of mankind became predisposed to degenera-
tion and oblivion". Circumcision is therefore a continuous
sacrifice of flesh and blood to atone for Adam's sin. He
goes further, and implies he knows of the old tradition that
Abraham actually sacrificed Isaac on the altar contrary to the
denouement in Genesis 22, and that God accepted this sacrifice
as atonement for Adam's sin on behalf of all the future progeny
of Abraham and anyone who enters the covenant.[99] All of the
complex ceremonial halakha in Judaism Crescas sees as leading
Jews to greater love of God and to orientation toward martry-
dom for His sake when the need arises. The latter view, when
he wrote *The Light of the Lord* around 1410, was certainly con-
sistent with the historical realities of the fourteenth century and the loss of his only son in the persecution of 1391.

VI. THE AFTERMATH

The fifteenth century was a time of great hardship for
Jews. The conditions under which Jews lived in Spain, culminating in the mass expulsion of 1492 were not conducive to
creative speculative philosophy or to the very premises of
rationalism. The search for certainty escalated and men like
Simon ben Zemach Duran (1361-1444) and Joseph Albo (1380-1445)
labor once more at establishing dogmas that would define an
orthodoxy and separate heterodoxy out of the community. For
Duran it is absolutely essential that the Jew believe that the
total content of the Torah was divinely revealed and is therefore literally true.[100] And he insisted that there were basic
principles of Torah that a Jew must believe or be considered a

heretic. He found three such dogmas in Judaism: God, Revelation, and Retribution. One must believe there is a God who reveals Himself and Whose revelation is binding at the risk of retribution. This point of view of Simon Duran became better known as that of Joseph Albo, whose work *ikarim* (Basic Principles) is devoted to this question of dogmas in Judaism. Albo, however, is more specific about "derived principles" which must be believed, such as the doctrine of Resurrection and the advent of the Messiah. He rejects the idea that Christianity or Islam were revealed, having been a faithful student of Crescas who wrote a work against Christianity.[101]

Nevertheless, as always, when dealing with many writers and scholars over long periods of time expounding complex questions of philosophy and theology intermingled with halakha, piety and apologetics, one must be cautious. Indeed, Albo is seeking to stabilize dogma. Indeed, Albo and his predecessors have a love-hate relationship with rationalism. Appropriately Albo writes a critique of the doctrines selected by Maimonides, arguing that a talmudic sage denied the idea of a Messiah and therefore Maimonides is wrong to include it as a fundamental.[102] He shows how there are notions that are far more important than some of Maimonides' which he does not include, such as Free Will. But in the final analysis, after his defense of dogma, his critique of extreme rationalism, his thrust for homogeneity of belief, Albo really puts an end to the possibility of defining a heretic in Judaism. Albo argues that only if one deliberately contradicts the Torah is he a heretic, but if one is merely guilty of error because of misinterpretation, he is not a heretic. Obviously there is a fine line between deliberately contradicting and sincerely misinterpreting. Thus Albo himself makes some radical suggestions about possibilities that inhere in Judaism contrary to the thirteen fundamentals of

Maimonides. Contrary to the latter's fifth fundamental: it is appropriate to worship God alone and no other substance or existence beneath Him, Albo argues it is not contrary to Judaism to believe in the efficacy of a mediator.[103] Certainly there is no precise biblical warrant to deny the validity of mediation.

In the final analysis, however, Albo puts together eleven doctrines, for he ascribes "derivative principles" to each fundamental. These are: a) for the fundamental of God: the unity of God, His incorporeality, His independence of time, His freedom from all defect; b) for the fundamental of Revelation: God's knowledge, the possibility of prophecy, the authenticity of God's messenger; c) for the fundamental of Retribution: Providence. This already gives us eleven basic doctrines in Judaism. And then he supplements these with six other dogmas: creation *ex nihilo*, the superiority of Moses over all prophets, the immutability of the Torah, that human perfection can be attained through mizvot, resurrection, and the messianic doctrine.[104]

It was on the basis of his derived principles that he argues against the Christian claim that Jesus performed miracles and therefore was he whom he claimed to be. Albo asserts that miracles are not the test. The test of the prophet is in public witnessing of God actually revealing Himself to the Messenger as in the case of Moses. And for this same reason of invalidating Christianity Albo says one must believe the Torah will not be replaced, and therefore the Christian claim that the New Testament has succeeded to its position of honor invalidates the Christian faith a priori.[105]

And yet the problem remains ever-present in Judaism: can religion change over the course of history? Is there legitimacy in the massive halakhic revision that has occurred within

Judaism in the light of these medieval attempts to formulate
dogma? Is diversity and heterodoxy, after all, valid?

Albo responds that physicians change prescriptions with
the progress of patients. Similarly religion can undergo revision. But so far was Albo willing to go. In entering a
discussion of details he hedges. He says only the first two
statements of the Ten Commandments were heard by the people
and they imply the three fundamentals. Only the three fundamentals, therefore, cannot be changed. But all that was taught
by Moses may be revised by succeeding prophets who can prove
they are superior to Moses.[106] This would tend to put Judaism
in a straightjacket. But it is obviously more designed to
disputing Christianity than in confirming Judaism. For the
entire historic experience was contrary to what Albo is saying. Judaism had been undergoing revision since the beginning,
and much of the Torah was no longer operative. Yet no scholar
or sage had pretended to be a prophet greater than Moses.[107]

With this we will close our examination of medieval theology. What has been sustained from Saadiah to Albo, a period
of five hundred years, is the vast diversity within Judaism.
There were efforts to establish supremacy for certain notions,
but these were usually obliterated in disputations and controversy which tended to preserve freedom of inquiry, decision,
and conduct. It would be totally erronious to regard medieval
Judaism as monolithic whether in practice or in belief. We
have yet to turn to France and Germany and examine how the
process materialized there, and how this multi-colored tapes-
try was then carried to Eastern Europe from which it again
traveled westward and across the seas to North America and
modernity. And we have yet to see how Kabalah entered into
the mainstream and ultimately spinned off a major denomination

within the faith, Ḥasidism, an eighteenth-century product of sixteenth century mysticism and thirteenth century halakha.

CHAPTER 7

France: The Ripening of Talmudism

While Judaism flourished in the Islamic lands, from modern Iran in the east to Spain in the west, another series of communities constituting an even more extensive center of learning and piety was growing in what is today both French and German territory, largely in the Rhineland. This community did not produce the great philosophers brought forth in Spain, nor the superbly talented poets. But it produced unsurpassed talmudic scholars, first-rank halakhists and a plethora of rabbinic commentators. In the final analysis it might be possible to ascertain an interesting internal symbiosis in Judaism. The theology of Spanish thinkers and the halakha of Franco-German rabbis together constitute the belief and practice of the modern era. And in turn, while Spanish scholars like Alfasi, Maimonides and R. Asher formed a major trio of sources for halakha, the theology and pietism of German scholars gained ascendancy in East Europe. Thus it was the mutual interaction of halakha and theology from both areas that became the ground upon which was erected contemporary Judaism. This symbiosis came about because the northern community traveled eastward to become the Judaism of that massive East European resevoir out of which sprang American Judaism, the major segment of all western Judaism in the twentieth century. And yet, when these same East European Jews desired to examine a theological treatise delving into the roots and explanation of doctrine they naturally tended to explore the writings of the Spanish philosophers, the German pietists and those who succeeded them in the kabalistic circles which emanated from Spain and Palestine.

Twentieth century Judaism, therefore, is the meeting ground of both Spanish rationalism and Kabalah, of Spanish and Rhineland halakha and pietism. It is now to the northern, halakha-oriented Judaism that we turn.

I. THE HISTORICAL SETTING[1]

Jews resided in many centers in northern France since the earliest of times. These included places that later became famous as centers of Jewish religious life and learning, among them Paris, Rheims, and Troyes, all of which were diocesan seats. It also appears clearly in the literature of the time that Jews lived in rural settlements in the environs of the larger centers.[2]

The sixth and seventh centuries offer evidence that they were present in sufficient numbers for kings and church councils to take note of them in suppressive decrees. Thus after the Visigothic Sisebut sought to suppress Judaism in Spain in 613, the Frankish king Dagobert attempted the suppression of Judaism in France in 633. How far back the presence of Judaism in France went, is hard to know. There is scant evidence beyond a few tombstone inscriptions, but it appears that Jews lived in Gaul from the Roman period. Certainly church councils such as the Second and Third Councils of Orléans, 533 and 538, point to the presence of enough Jews practicing Judaism as to make it necessary to bar Christians from marriage with Jews, or for Jews to convert their slaves to Judaism.[3]

It was during the reigns of Charlemagne (Charles the Great, 768-814) and his son Louis the Pious (814-840) that the history of Judaism in France really begins.[4] But of spiritual life we have very little information before the eleventh century. It appears that a Jew named Isaac served in an embassy sent by Charlemagne to the eastern Caliph Harun ar-Rashid in 797. According to legend he brought back a Babylonian scholar named Makhir in 802. Makhir established an academy at Narbonne and therewith opened Jewish religious scholarship in France. By the twelfth century Lunel was a great center which welcomed students from all over, providing free education, room and board, scholarships and even clothing.[5]

Jews increasingly settled into communities of France during the ninth and tenth centuries and by the twelfth century Paris too was a major center where, according to Benjamin of Tudela, the twelfth century traveler, there are scholars "unequaled in the whole world, who study the Torah day and night".[6] Possibly French Judaism had reached its highest point of development by that time. In 1182 in an abrupt and unexpected reversal, Philip II Augustus of France, the architect of the future unified French national state, expelled the Jews from his realm. An interesting account of what a devoted son of the church believed to be the valid reasons for the expulsion is given in a Latin history written at the time by a monk, Rigord. The reasons run the gamut from the belief that Jews killed a Christian each Easter as a sacrifice in contempt of Christianity, to their seizure of church vessels as surety for loans and huge real estate holdings in Paris. Rigord attests to a very high Jewish population, that "a great multitude of Jews" had flocked to France because the French were peaceful and liberal and the king merciful. Philip recalled them in 1198 but the thirteenth century saw further decline.[7]

In a great sense this was a microcosm of similar events to follow until the climactic Spanish Expulsion of 1492.

In general the pre-Crusade period of development, the generations prior to 1096, was the most vigorous. It was during the late tenth and early eleventh centuries that there came to fruition that Judaism which was destined to be the father of East European and North American Judaism.[8] This is what is generally called Ashkenazic Judaism, as distinct from the Sephardic Judaism of Spain. As in the case of Babylonia and Spain, the responsa literature of the French rabbis is a valuable source of information. However, we should not over-value the significance of responsa literature as some historians are sometimes prone to do. We must remember that at times responsa are written tendentiously, in the hope of persuading a person or a community to a point of view. They may also sometimes be written as a chore that has to be fulfilled and not necessarily at the leisure of the writer who has the sources and the time for research, and to accurately record his well-reflected-over thoughts.[9] But the presence of responsa from or to a given city at a particular period or even a precise year is evidential for us of religious activity and scholarship at that place and time. And so, for instance, from the fact that R. Kalonymus of Lucca (in Italy), who flourished about 880-960, having moved to Mayence in Germany around 887, wrote a responsum to R. Moses of Arles, indicates that Judaism was flowering in a community other than Narbonne in Southern France during the ninth or tenth century.[10]

We are on more certain ground during the next century with R. Joseph Tob-Elem (960-1030), a native of Narbonne and a disciple of an already well-known scholar who was often called "Rabbana Jacob the Prophet and Gaon".[11] Surprisingly, despite his great reputation during the eleventh and twelfth

centuries Rabbana Jacob is not known to have had a precise
impact upon Judaism other than what may have come through his
disciples. R. Joseph was one of those many "spreaders" of
Judaism who, by moving to a new community and establishing a
new academy, expanded the presence and quality of Judaic
scholarship. He moved to Limoges and the twelfth-century
scholar, R. Jacob Tam, grandson of Rashi, informs us that R.
Joseph shaped the customs of Limoges and Anjou.[12] We see
here that kind of link-chain developing through which northern
Europe's scholarship, emanating in the first instance from
Provence, and as we will see later, coming even more abundant-
ly from Germany, had its influence upon all facets of subsequent Judaism.

One of the disciples of R. Gershom (950-1028), R. Jacob
ben Yakar, settled in Worms during the eleventh century and
there established a major German center of learning, as did
another rabbi, Isaac HaLevi (1000-1070). Both of these men
preserved the teachings of two different German schools, both
of Mayence, that of R. Gershom and that of R. Eliezer the
Great (980-1050). To Worms came Solomon b. Isaac of Troyes
in 1060, a young Frenchman seeking learning as Christian students might have traveled to Bologna or Paris or Oxford and
Cambridge. The German schools held supremacy at the time,
and Solomon, later to be famous as "Rashi" studied under both
R. Isaac HaLevi and R. Jacob b. Yakar. Thus, embodied in
Rashi were the two major traditions of German Judaism brought
from Worms back to Troyes where Rashi established his own
school and became a major link in a very long chain.[13]

II. R. SOLOMON BEN ISAAC OF TROYES (1040-1105). RASHI.

A. *The Man and His Work*

   Prior to the calamity of the summer of 1096 when Jewish
communities in the German Rhineland were decimated, the Jews of
France took their spiritual-halakhic guidance from Mayence and
Worms. Rashi was a vintner without what we today would call
"academic credentials". Consequently nobody turned to him for
guidance in religious practice and he had no great disciples
other than one of his grandsons, R. Samuel ben Meir. But
after 1096 and the destruction of the Rhineland centers along
with much literary treasure, the pupils of Rashi in Troyes incorporated into their notes the scholarly remains of the
eleventh century teachers, along with the teaching of their
own great master.[14]

   As has often been noted, many scholars were more brilliant
than Rashi, and his exegetical commentaries are hardly original.
But his position in the history of Judaism is significant in
that he preserved in his writings a portrait of French Judaism.
Very little is known of his life, much legend having woven itself about him.[15] In addition to having studied under the men
previously mentioned he either studied with R. Isaac ben Judah
(1000-1080) at Mayence before returning to Troyes, or before
having gone to Worms.[16] After returning home he supervised
the family vineyards and, if he functioned as a rabbi in Troyes,
he did it, as the custom still was, at no salary. There are no
great events or triumphs on record to mark stages of his life,
no elaborate career growth of which to tell. He was born the
son of an unknown vinter and died quietly where he was born.
But the monument he left behind, the massive commentary on
scripture and Talmud have made of him one of the most signifi-

cant medieval scholars, and undoubtedly the brightest luminary of France.

Yet R. Solomon b. Isaac probably emerged the luminary he
became because his commentary illuminated texts for the average
student or layman. He was not a creative thinker. He did not
conceptualize or generalize. He wrote no extended excursi or
essays. He did not reflect on the great principles of Torah
or Talmud. He was strictly an exegete who briefly interpreted
terminology, copied out midrashic explanations and elaborations
on verses and provided philological information.[17] He usually
made the most obscure text lucid and this gained him the historic position he enjoyed. He used the previous work of R.
Moses haDarshan of Narbonne (eleventh century) who wrote a
mystic and folkloristic commentary, gathering many agadic
sources together, which in turn were preserved in Rashi's commentary. Rashi makes extensive use of agadic midrash although
he does in some instances confess that a given midrash may not
fit the natural meaning of a text. More important, however, is
the fact that by including so much folkloristic embellishment
in his commentary, Rashi's work achieved two things. First of
all, it was able to serve as devotional literature for the
family, and secondly it preserved a vast number of legends and
traditions in easily accessible form in an age when society
suffered from a paucity of books. We have seen how severe were
the controversies over anthropomorphism in Spain. In northern
France Rashi was unconcerned and even stressed those supernatural elements that the common man readily believed and even
looked for in his faith. Thus he believed that R. Ishmael of
the second century had gone to heaven by use of the divine
name.[18]

Above all, Rashi's work on the Talmud was not a halakhic
compilation in any sense of the word, and Rashi has never

played the role of halakhist in Judaism. He was, perhaps in medieval Christian terms, scholastic, and not a canon lawyer. His contemporary, R. Isaac of Fez (and later, Lucena, Spain), was a halakhist upon whose work all future halakha partly was based. Another contemporary, Nathan ben Yehiel of Rome, composed the Arukh, a talmudic lexicon which became indispensable for the understanding of the text as well as for cross-references of subjects. These three tools, the halakha of Alfasi, the technical apparatus of Nathan of Rome and the lucid exegesis of Rashi became a significant tripod upon which was erected medieval Judaic studies. As others have indicated, later scholars regarded Rashi's commentary so indispensable that they applied exaggerated paeans to him such as "without him the Talmud would have remained a closed book".[19] It is not a denigration of Rashi, however, to encourage a modern student to undertake the exploration of Talmud even if he does not risk the additional burden of reading Rashi. The Talmud in modern times is undoubtedly better understood in large measure because many scholars during the intervening centuries utilized Rashi. But by now the instruments at hand render Rashi no longer indispensable.

As noted, Rashi was not a major halakhist. Yet he did write responsa. In these responsa we see reflected his character and some of his ambivalent views. He was a genial person who pursued good human relations. He was kindly disposed to those who accepted baptism under compulsion. He was very traditional, however, and regarded innovations as dangerous, but was occasionally more liberal than his colleagues.[20]

B. *The Influence of Rashi*

Rashi cannot take a position alongside Saadiah, Maimonides, Alfasi or R. Asher of Toledo, since we have from his hand neither a statement of what he believed to be the doctrine of Judaism, nor an extensive halakhic compilation in which he set forth what he believed religious practice ought to be. On the other hand, he was not a man of controversy like Maimonides, and in slow stages his commentaries brought his influence out of northeast France to Provence and from there to Spain and Italy. Through Germany it went to southern Europe, Africa and Asia, fertilizing the writing of many a scholar and indirectly affecting halakhic decisions and the direction of Judaism. More than this, his influence spread to Christian scholarly circles and through him in the first instance, Christian scholars of Judaica became familiar with rabbinic literature.[21]

Rashi had a major influence upon R. Simḥa of Vitry, author of a liturgical work which also contained much halakhic data as well as responsa. His influence was also strong upon sons-in-law and grandsons. These relations and disciples and their disciples in turn formed a school of commentators in France and Germany that held intellectual hegemony for two centuries. They were known as Tosafists, the commentary compilation being called Tosafot (Supplements).[22] The Tosafists devoted themselves almost exclusively to talmudic studies and created the characteristic later reflective of East European Judaism. Partly this was, as noted earlier, because the Church increasingly caused the segregation of the Jew. In any event these studies were so intensive and the scholars so influential that of R. Jacob Tam it was said, he was unmatched in talmudic knowledge since the days of the Talmud. Among the later

Tosafists were R. Meir of Rothenburg, who, as we will see,
played a major role as a conduit of Judaism to East Europe and
on to comtemporary religious practice, as well as R. Asher who
moved from Germany to Toledo. He too, through his Spanish
disciples was a conduit to R. Joseph Karo, of the sixteenth
century, and therefore to contemporary Judaism as well.[23]
Probably it is accurate to say that because the German schools
so surpassed the French in numbers and in durability the influence of Rashi passed across into the German Rhineland, having even greater thrust there than in France. But before that
happened northern France flowered. Schools flourished in Ile-
de-France and Normandy, Paris becoming a major center. In
Paris resided Judah Sir Leon (1166-1224) who was compelled to
leave after the expulsion of 1181 but returned in 1198. Among
his disciples was the famous Moses of Coucy, author of one of
the earliest attempts to survey the so-called six hundred and
thirteen mizvot to which we have referred earlier.[24] Another
two important disciples of Paris were Isaac ben Moses of Vienna
who was a major conduit of French Judaism to Austria and the
east, and Samuel ben Solomon Sir Morel of Falaise (1175-1253)
who taught R. Meir ben Baruch of Rothenburg (1225-1293). The
latter became the greatest authority of his time and bequeathed
thirteenth century German Judaism to all future centuries.[25]
R. Yehiel of Paris who had to witness the burning of the Talmud
in 1240 was the last leader of note in Paris, but when he left
for Palestine in 1260 French scholarship even penetrated the
ancient seats of learning.[26] His disciple R. Perez of Corbeil
who migrated to Germany was the teacher of Mordecai ben Hillel
whose authoritative commentary-halakhic abridgment combination
became an important source for the teachings of the fourteenth
and fifteenth centuries, ultimately being practically "canonized" in the work of R. Moses Isserles in sixteenth-century

Poland. We here see established the first links of "the chain
of tradition" without which cannot be understood the ultimate
development of late medieval and early modern Judaism which
calls itself "orthodox". Rashi is not the first link, but
rather R. Gershom who will be discussed in our section on
Germany. Many of the links were German. But many significant
masters of talmudics and halakha in Germany who transmitted
this immense intellectual heritage to central Europe, Poland
and Russia, were students of the northern French scholars in
Troyes, Rameru, Dampierre, Paris and elsewhere.

Rashi's influence in talmudics was equaled by his role in
the furtherance of biblical exegesis. Fifty commentaries were
written upon his commentary on the Pentateuch alone. Some of
them, like R. Samuel ben Meir's are superior to Rashi's. He
divested himself of Rashi's method of using agadic folklore
and addressed himself only to exegesis of the text. So too was
the commentary of Simon Kara (1070-1140) who rejected midrash
agada and boldly denied that the prophet Samuel wrote the book
that goes by his name, contrary to tradition.[27] Among others
who used Rashi were the famous Maimonidian philosopher and com-
mentator R. David Kimhi (1160-1235) of Narbonne and R. Moses
ben Nahman (1195-1270) famed as *RMBN* (or Nahmanides) of Gerona,
called Bonastruc da Porta in some literary sources. But Nahmanides far surpassed the folkloristic elements of Rashi, having extensive interest in Kabalah. Rashi became famous not
only in Provence but among the Spanish scholars of note like
R. Solomon Ibn Aderet and R. Nissim of Gerona (fourteenth century) who wrote an extensive, wordier, Rashi-like commentary on
the work of Alfasi. But most of all there was the disciple of
the Tosafists, R. Asher b. Yehiel, born a German, a disciple of
R. Meir of Rothenburg, but a major representative of French

talmudic study, transplanting it from the Rhineland to Toledo,
Spain, and becoming, like R. Meir of Rothenburg and Mordecai
ben Hillel, a significant founder of sixteenth century Judaism
through his Spanish links to Joseph Karo.[28] From this point
forward French and German talmudism gained ascendancy from Spain
to Palestine. R. Isaac b. Sheshet, in a moment of gushing enthusiasm paraphrased Isaiah, "From France goes forth the Torah
and the word of God from Germany." The Turkish scholar Elijah
ben Abraham Mizrahi who gained great fame was an enthusiast of
Rashi and the Frenchmen.[29] That Rashi and French and German
talmudism finally gained hegemony is perhaps best brought out
in one curious circumstance. R. Joseph ben Ephraim Karo (1448-
1575) was born in Spain and lived in Palestine. He was a Sephardic Jew and a kabalist who wrote an encyclopedic talmudic
reference work and commentary to the halakhic compilation of R.
Jacob b. Asher of Toledo (fifteenth century). And in this work,
called *Bet Yoseph* (School of Joseph), the principle talmudic in-
terpreter whom he cites is Rashi.[30] This is the Karo to whose
digest of halakha, the Shulḥan Arukh, were added the supplemen-
tary notes of R. Moses Isserles of Poland whereby the book became the sixteenth century canon of "orthodox" halakha. And
thus the link-chain stretched from Rashi of Troyes to East
European "orthodoxy" and thence to contemporary Judaism.

III. SOME ASPECTS OF FRENCH JUDAISM

A. *Observations*

     As in other periods and other places the Jews were accul-
turated in medieval France other than in actual religious belief

and practice. Historians have shown that sufficient evidence proves a high degree of social interaction between Jews and Christians in France in those centuries, as contrasted with Jews who lived in Poland and Russia in more recent centuries. They used the French language and names, indulged in local fashion in dress and basically had good social relations with their Christian neighbors.[31] Even marriage customs were adapted to the local fashion, and French was used in the liturgy. This is all certainly affirmed when a medieval pietist, disapproving, writes: "As are the customs of the gentiles, so are the customs of the Jews in the majority of places."[32]

Seen in this light the thesis stated earlier is upheld once more. For the most part, unless restrained by state or church, Judaism has not prevented integration of Jews with those of other faiths and has not discouraged a general tendency to acculturation. When we touch upon matters of belief or upon those rituals which express that belief we are getting to the heart of theology and religion at which point the Jew diverges.

What was the religion of the Jew in France 800-1400? In all probability it was basically the same as that of the Jew of Spain as far as doctrine is concerned. If a French scholar had written a theological treatise in the style of Saadiah or Maimonides he probably would have delineated the same doctrines as one or another of the Spanish theologians. Perhaps in France the Jews would have taken greater umbrage over Maimonides' views on anthropomorphism. Even Rashi accepted simple statements that left one open to a Maimonidian charge that one is practically guilty of idolatry. No French scholar wrote a comprehensive halakhic compendium like Maimonides' *Mishneh Torah*, so again in the area of halakha we cannot be certain whether French

Jews practiced all facets of Judaism precisely as did Spanish
Jews. But we will see that aside from local custom that
evolved within the circumstances of living in northern France
and in a Christian civilization, Judaism was quite similar.
Again, the similarity must be seen from the perspective of
diversity. There was similarity, but not homogeneity. There
was a degree of conformity but not uniformity. There was an
effort to enforce hegemony over wide areas but local and contemporary authority prevailed.

B. *Marriage and Divorce*[33]

1. *Marriage*

Although the Jews of northern France accepted the enactments of R. Gershom to institute monogamy and require the consent of a woman for a husband to be able to divorce her, the
supremacy of male authority remained intact. R. Perez of Corbeil was outraged that Jewish men were becoming prone to beating their wives during the thirteenth century. It was not un-
common for this to happen among non-Jews and a theological encyclopedia of the time informs us, "A man may chastise his
wife and beat her [*verberare*] for her correction...." This
was stated despite clear statements in law to the contrary.
In consequence of his irritation R. Perez suggested an enactment to allow for a court to either compel a man under ban to
promise not to beat his wife, or to allow her to leave him and
compel him to pay her support. No action is recorded on
this.[34]

Child marriage was common here as in Spain, despite the
opposition of tradition. The French sages, however, felt that
the uncertainty of the times requires that a father marry off

his daughter when he is able rather than take the risk of not having a dowry to provide for her some years later. Another rationale was that women were scarce so it was important to take the bridegroom the father preferred whenever the bridegroom was ready, lest if rebuffed, being anxious about the availability of a mate, he would not wait.[35]

A marriage was celebrated any day of the week. R. Jacob Tam, without explanation, even allows a man to marry a woman on the Sabbath if he is childless and if it is a necessity owing to the circumstances of the time. The Hebrew term is "need of the hour" and implies some socio-political turmoil or economic depression. In any event it is an unusual decision and attests to the high importance given to marriage without delay owing undoubtedly to the uncertainty of the times.[36] The ritual was more or less that known in the Talmud. Blessings of betrothal were recited first and the bridegroom then formally betrothed the bride with the formula still in use, "You are hereby consecrated unto me with this ring, according to the law of Moses and Israel", and placed a simple ring upon her finger. Then the *ketubah* (marriage contract) was read and the bridegroom handed it to his bride. This document established his monetary contractual obligations to her and provided her with a modicum of security in the event of his death or his divorcing her. The ceremony concluded with seven blessings of marriage. This basic format: the combination of a betrothal and marriage ceremony, the presentation of a ring and the seven marriage berakhot is still in use. As we will see in the next volume a variety of changes have enveloped the institution of *ketubah*.[37] It is naturally difficult for a person currently to acclimitize oneself to the idea that the consummation of the marriage then took place in public. But this was so, and we hear R. Tam protesting it as indecent.[38]

As we have already seen in reference to Spanish Jews, a major objective of marriage was procreation. Nevertheless northern France provides a glimpse into one other aspect of Judaism: its relative flexibility. And so we find that a subject that recurs in discussion is the use of contraception for birth regulation.[39]

If an argument from silence is allowable, the literature of northern France points to high sexual morality. According to some who have intensively surveyed the sources there are no cases of incest reported, little sexual perversion, and only one reference to lesbianism.[40]

2. *Divorce*

In matters of divorce, too, male supremacy remained unaffected. There was concern for the interests of women, but this did not go so far as to provide them with initiatory rights. The courts would help a woman receive a divorce when they thought she genuinely deserves her freedom. But they had to operate aggressively against the husband. The husband was the only one with the power to execute the divorce.[41] Basically the procedures had remained the same since talmudic times and no innovations were introduced. Similarly the causes for which a husband may divorce his wife or for which a wife's suit for divorce may be granted remained essentially as they were in talmudic times. This meant he could practically divorce her at will. Although the husband possessed this almost absolute power to divorce his wife there were a few exceptions, but in France in our period no new innovations had been made to advance the status of women. Nevertheless, out of Germany came the decree of R. Gershom and this was more or less accepted in France. In effect because the absolute right of the husband had already been weakened by a variety of modifications which date to the Mishnah and Talmud, men sought rabbinic advice before divorcing their wives. In order to regularize this procedure the absolute right of husbands to divorce their wives was abolished around the year 1000 by a decree of a synod called by R. Gershom b. Judah of Mayence. We do not have a copy of this decree just as we do not have the text of his decree against polygamy. But the divorce item is cited in medieval sources where we read that "...just as the man does not put away his wife except of his own free will, so shall the woman not be put away except by her own consent". There is an even more restrictive enactment which says that no man in the Rhine communities "...shall be permitted to cast a writ of divorce to his wife without the consent of three communities..." under penalty of excommunication.[42] Obviously this would make divorce far more difficult for the man and would be important protection for the woman. Like his decree against polygamy which was also accepted in France, it gave a boost to the status of women. But it did not provide her with the power to divorce her husband.[43]

3. *General Status of Women*

The status of women was not only negatively affected in matters of domestic relations but also in matters related to religious ritual. As I have noted elsewhere women were treated tenderly and placed on a pedestal but were not accorded rights. As their economic power grew so did male willingness to offer more prerogatives. But in the style of the time women and men were segregated from one another at social events, including wedding celebrations. An eleventh century ruling (anonymous) forbids men and women to mingle, "whether at the meal, at the dancing, or at any other part...for at a happy occasion especially the sensual passions are aroused".[44]

C. *The Life-Cycle*

The Jews of northern France practiced the same rituals as Jews elsewhere. But while the basic observances were relatively universal there were diverse local customs that originated in different areas during different eras. The following life-cycle observances were normal, although details of observance may be expected to vary with geography and century.

1. *Circumcision*

Circumcision, the ritual which brings a male infant into the Covenant of Abraham is often performed in the synagogue. It is a fully developed and elaborated ceremonial during the eleventh century. A throne is set up for Elijah the Prophet who is believed to be present. The child is washed in warm water, robed in special linens as on a wedding day and the congregation rises for him. Then the ritual is performed.[45] While some scholars attribute the holding of the ritual in the synagogue to the eleventh century others claim it is as old as the ninth century. The use of the throne of Elijah is traced back to primitive superstitions in which offerings were made to gods of fortune who were the guardian deities of the home or of a new-born infant. The story that relates Elijah's reviving the child may have influenced his eventual replacement of the deities.

In any event the custom of setting up the throne of Elijah is another cogent example of innovation in ritual. What can

become a mere surgical act is infused with meaning. Firstly
it is an example of investing a ritual with more symbolism
and interrelating diverse theological conceptions. Thus the
belief in Elijah's ascension to heaven alive allows for his
re-entry for singular religious occasions making for his universal relationship with all Jews. The myth is that he attends
all circumcisions and visits all Passover Seders and is the
harbinger of the Messiah. He is guardian of the child because
he is guardian of the covenant, as expressed by Malachi (3:1
is taken to be Elijah), and thus the circumcision ritual binds
up the individual entering the covenant with the individual's
ultimate salvation in the messianic era. Both the beginning
and the end of theology is thereby embodied in the ritual.

Secondly this development in the circumcision ritual
points up how a non-Jewish idolatrous rite, the presentation
of gifts to a deity of fortune to win his favor, is "Judaized"
or adapted into Judaism and divested of the pagan implications. A close study of a large number of rituals in Judaism
would reveal this process recurring again and again.

Thirdly, it indicates how custom took hold in a given
place, and sometimes it is not known where or when precisely,
and spreads across vast areas of the world simply on the
strength of accepting a scholar's approval or initiative.
This characteristic is bound up with what I have written about
the strength of contemporary authority and the validity of
local custom.

It is apparent from the antiquity of the sources that
this observance of an Elijah throne was already prevalent in
geonic times. It was possibly even older. Thus, Pirke de R.
Eliezer, a product of a time no later than around 900 contains
the lore surrounding Elijah's throne and relates that "...the
sages instituted the custom that people should have a seat of

honor for the Messenger of the Covenant; for Elijah, may he be
remembered for good, is called the Messenger of the Covenant,
as it is said, 'And the Messenger of the Covenant, whom you
delight in, behold he comes...' (Malachi 3:1)." This surely
reveals that a throne of Elijah was an accepted eastern custom
long before 900.

2. *Naming Children*

Naming of boys was done at the circumcision, the naming
of girls on the fourth Sabbath after birth at morning worship.[46] Practices in this matter differed widely. Much
superstition was connected with it such as a name prefiguring
the person's character, or if one names an infant the same as
an adult the latter may die. On the other hand there was also
positive folklore, such as by giving a child the name of an
ancestor the memory of the ancestor is preserved. Superstitious elements were more prevalent among Ashkenaz Jews while
Sephardic Jews were less addicted to some of the more esoteric
ideas. Thus Sephardic Jews name children after living relations while Ashkenaz Jews do not. Sephardim even call their
children by the name of living fathers, although this is not
frequent.[47] There are a variety of restrictions upon naming
children, but these are localized and not a mandatory part of
Jewish religious practice. Thus, there are those who object
to naming children after a person who was killed or one who
died young, or after another child that died.[48] But these
notions along with many others are folkloristic and not really
halakhic or theological.

The naming of girls is done with the father called to the
Torah at Sabbath worship. The child is named and a prayer for
her welfare is said. In medieval times it was customary in
southern France, Hungary and Belgium to bring the baby girl

into the synagogue for the occasion. In sum, there have never been "uniform fixed regulations" in the matter of naming children. "Since these customs are governed by certain ideas and beliefs which not all people share in the same degree, it is not strange to find that the customs themselves differ so. Some people are more superstitious, others are more rational." This points up the fact that even in so rational a faith as Judaism often appears to be, many life-cycle observances which touch the heart of fear and anxiety tied to life and death are still rooted in superstition rather than faith.[49]

3. Death and Mourning

The religious observances of Judaism related to death, burial, grief, bereavement, mourning and memorializing the dead are basically post-scriptural. The practices upon which French religious observance, both informal custom and halakha are founded originate in the Mishnah and Talmud tractate Moed Katan (Minor Festival), a euphemism for the concept of mourning, and in a similarly named post-talmudic volume called Semahot ("Rejoicings"). The halakha is quite detailed. Some practices are also based upon early medieval superstition. Some are no longer observed in contemporary Judaism. Aspects of superstition expanded with the centuries and became even more pronounced after the eleventh century, especially in Germany.[50]

There is naturally a tendency to develop a greater degree of uniformity in a matter like death because people are in greater fear and anxiety in the face of great mystery. Therefore, as far as we can ascertain, in this subject there is no radical diversity. But in some places embellishments were added out of the superstitions that arose during medieval times when people were more prone to superstition. It may first be

noted that although Jews generally had their own cemeteries
they buried their dead during the fourteenth century in Christian cemeteries and this gives pause for reflection. Maimonides did not raise the issue at all in Egypt but that might be
because from time immemorial Jews in the east had their own
burial grounds. In the newer places of settlement in the west
it is apparent that there was an ambivalence on the subject.
It is quite possible that had the Jew ultimately not been
segregated in life, he would not have segregated himself in
death.[51]

Burial halakha went back to talmudic times and while many
practices are undoubtedly as old as biblical times, most are
creations, modifications or innovations made by the rabbis,
while others are later developments. One of the objectives
of the early halakha was a simplicity that would obviate the
shaming of the poor or prevent any necessity for large expen-
ditures of money.[52]

The basic custom was that the body was wrapped in a linen
shroud, a prayer shawl was wrapped about the deceased, and the
body was then placed in a coffin. The impact of local custom
and resultant variety is seen in the matter of the prayer
shawl. In some places it was not used because the rabbis felt
it had been too frequently a neglected mizvah during life and
consequently it was felt the deceased should not be wrapped in
it, an act which would have a taint of hypocrisy.[53]

The custom was followed of lowering the body into the
grave and the liturgical officiant saying the *kaddish* rather
than immediate mourners. Each person then took a little earth
and recited "He remembers we are dust" (Ps. 103:14), and cast
it behind him three times. Another custom was to pluck grass
and throw it over the shoulders while reciting "They from the
city shall flourish as the grass of the field" (Is. 26:19).

This was a liturgical invocation of immortality or resurrection.[54] Upon return home a week of mourning began.[55]

Mourning in Judaism consists of three stages: seven days of more intense observance, thirty days of relative intensity, and a full year of restraint from excessive levity. Mourning was considered to be an obligation of the Torah, reinforced in rabbinic literature. There are, of course, a large number of complex questions about how to count the three periods in cases of drownings or disappearances where one cannot be certain the person is dead. Other halakhic questions arise concerning infants, suicides and sinners. Maimonides, for instance, is quite stern regarding those, in his words, "who deviated from the practices of the congregation...in the performance of the precepts, observance of festivals, attendance at synagogue and house of study, but felt free to do as they pleased, as well as for epicureans, apostates...for these no mourning is observed". Similarly there are no funeral rites for suicides, and no mourning is observed. But in reference to this Maimonides sets a very interesting precedent: only if a person, for instance, pointed out that he is climbing up on a roof with the implication that he is going to jump, is he a suicide. But if a person is in a state of agitation and then later is found dead he is not presumed to be a suicide. Maimonides is probably the first scholar to have applied this aspect of psychology to the halakha of suicide. Later scholars are able, by building upon that, to declare that an emotionally wrought up or mentally-disturbed person is not a suicide, and thereby is not to be deprived of his burial and mourning rites.[56]

After the funeral, neighbors bring the first meal to the mourners. This invariably includes eggs. The explanation offered by the French compiler of *Mahzor Vitry* is that "mourning is like a wheel, ever recurring". But undoubtedly it goes beyond that, to the perception that the egg is the agent of regeneration and affirms faith in resurrection.[57]

The period of mourning is one in which sexual relations is forbidden, as is the application of cosmetics, shaving and cutting the hair or even wearing shoes. Similarly a mourner is not at all to engage in his economic activity but is to remain confined to his home for the seven-day period in a relatively meditative posture, not even conducting ordinary conversation.[58] The custom known in modern times of cutting a ribbon which is attached to a mourner's garment is a modern substitute for an ancient rending of the garment itself. This rending is done in the specific cases of those for whom one observes technical mourning. These are parents, brothers, sisters, children and spouse.[59] No mourning is conducted on the Sabbath or on festivals which are to be observed joyously.[60]

IV. DECLINE OF FRENCH JUDAISM

A. *The Crusades*

The eleventh century was one of great disruption in Europe, culminating in the great crusading zeal with which pope and barons hoped to overwhelm Islam and capture the rich economic prize of the east. In Clermont, France, Pope Urban II in 1095 issued his call for what became the First Crusade. Peter the Hermit began his preaching in France which inspired the multitudes to bravery and risk. But neither France nor the Jews of France suffered the consequences to which other European centers were subjected.[61] The only exception to this is an attack at

English-controlled Norman Rouen where the crusaders applied unassailable logic: "After traversing great distances, we desire to attack the enemies of God in the East, although the Jews, of all races the worst foe of God, are before our eyes. That's doing our work backward." The subsequent massacre of Jews gathered in the synagogue "without distinction of sex or age", spared "those who accepted Christianity...."[62]

Otherwise French Jewry suffered no more than the economic loss attendant upon the remission of debts for crusaders. The twelfth century, as we have seen, was a richly developing one for Judaism. It is wrong to think as some historians do that "1096 marked a turning point in Jewish history". It may have been significant for Rhineland communities, as we will see later on, but not at all in France.[63] Part of the reason might have been an agreement reached to urge German communities to assist Peter the Hermit on his march through the Rhineland. This notion is reinforced by the fact that nothing happened when he passed through in April. Ultimately Jews who had been compelled into forced baptism in Normandy were permitted by decree of King William II of England and Normandy to return to their faith. The basis of such royal action could easily be the church's general opposition to the forced conversion of Jews by violence.[64]

That there were many such Jewish apostates is evident from the eleventh century halakhic discussions referring to considerations of status of Jews and descendants of Jews who had been compelled to baptism and were returning to Judaism. Thus, Rashi in Troyes, took the position that an apostate "...is still under the jurisdiction of Jewish law....The general rule is: an apostate has the status of a Jew suspected of heresy."[65] The very nature of this discussion in the

medieval religious literature of Judaism points up a very
interesting and significant fact. Contrary to popular belief
there is no strict requirement for martyrdom in Judaism. It
is apparent that Jews had the right to save their lives through
the ritual of baptism. The two assumptions were that they
would live secretly as Jews, and that Christianity is not a
form of idolatry. The Jew was required to undergo martyrdom
rather than publicly submit himself to idolatry. Thus public
baptism, attendance at church, even genuflections to church
dignitaries were obviously not considered idolatrous.[66] Once
such converts reverted to Judaism they were not even to be
reminded of their prior lapse. They were even accorded a
higher status by some scholars than Jews who publicly dese-
crate the Sabbath who "have the same status as non-Jews".
This later notion was not the consensus, however, and was
never incorporated into Judaism.[67]

With it all, however, French Judaism flourished through
the twelfth century. The Second Crusade called by Pope Eugen-
ius III in 1146 again did not affect French Jews, nor did the
Third Crusade.[68] The famous theologian Bernard of Clairvaux
was a great preacher of the Second Crusade. He preached
against anti-Jewish activities, arguing, "They are living
symbols for us, reminding us always of the Lord's Passion.
For this reason they are dispersed....When the time is ripe
all Israel shall be saved." This was in contrast to Peter the
Venerable, abbot of the great monastery of Cluny and a highly
respected churchman, who also urged crusaders to do no violence to Jews, but wrote, "Let their life be spared them, but
their money taken away in order that, through Christian hands
helped by the money of blaspheming Jews the boldness of unbe-
lieving Saracens may be vanquished."[69] During the Third Crusade again no violence touched the French Jews despite unex-

pected riots in England at the coronation of Richard I in London, and except for a minor incident in the town of Bray. And despite the riots of England, Richard I, as King of Normandy, gave Jews as much protection there as they apparently enjoyed elsewhere in France. That Bernard of Clairvaux was largely credited for this is attested to by Ephraim of Bonn, who after referring to St. Bernard's activity, writes, "Were it not for the mercies of our Creator in sending us the aforementioned abbot and his epistles, Israel would have been left without remnant and vestige."[70]

B. *Factors in the Decline*

.If the Crusades did not destroy French Judaism, what did? The answer, to be sure, is complex. But it appears to be far more related to the intellectual-spiritual realm than the socio-political one. Perhaps there was involved envy over the wealth of French Jews, unabashedly described by Jewish historians as frequently derived from exploitation and usury. Another factor might be the tragic miscalculation by Jews involved in taking church ritual objects and other sacred relics as surety for loans.[71] But in the final analysis the decline of the French center of Judaism must be seen as multifaceted. As is so often the case, the character of a given personality may be a determining factor. In this case it may be the fact that three personalities complementing one another emerged at the same time. The first was Pope Innocent III, one of the greatest occupants of the Holy See, the first pope to call himself "Vicar of Christ" thus subjecting all salvation to the pope.[72] The second was King Louis IX of France, an exceptionally devoted son of the church. And the third was Nicholas Donin, an exceptionally devoted Jewish convert to the church.

Louis IX, styled "the Saint", reigned from 1226-1270, spanning the period of Jewish decline in France. Saint that he was, Louis, like other zealous religionists too often become, was active in persecuting heresy, seeking to overwhelm the Islamic infidel and reminding the Jew of his destiny to suffer.[73] His campaign against usury undermined the economic resources of French Jews. Nicholas Donin's campaign against the Talmud undermined the spiritual resources. Louis felt that usury is Jewish oppression of Christians. Donin argued the Talmud perverts Jewish faith. On the matter of Louis' efforts, emulated by French barons, a papal critique was issued, opposing oppression of Jews because "their fathers were made friends of God, and also their remnant shall be saved". "Such kindliness must be shown to Jews by Christians, as we hope might be shown to Christians who live in pagan lands."[74] The Church felt the Jews should live without usury. This would doubtlessly have been possible. But the Church apparently also felt they should live without their customary religious resources. And that was not possible.

The war against the Talmud, and by extension against all rabbinic literature, was instigated by Nicholas Donin, a Jew who was excommunicated by R. Yehiel of Paris and subsequently became a Christian, sponsored by Pope Gregory IX in 1236. The papal argument, possibly elaborated into thirty-five accusations by Nicholas Donin, in effect asserted that emphasis upon the Talmud as the source of Jewish religious practice is blasphemous against scripture, that talmudic material fosters anti-Christian ideas, blaspheming Jesus, and is morally offensive. The Dominican and Franciscan friars were to be the repositories of all the books to be gathered up in a general effort to deprive Jews of their literature, on March 3, 1240. All the books, presumably, of western Europe, for the papal letter was addressed to all the archbishops and kings of France, Germany, England and Spain, were to be funnelled to Paris and burned. A discussion of the contents of the books was initiated with rabbis given an opportunity to defend them. And in 1242 the great burning took place.[75]

It is clear, however, from the survival of the schools and the continued nurture of great scholars during the thirteenth century that not all the books were burned and that the burning in Paris may have been symbolic more than anything else. As the papal legate Odo saw it in 1248, the Talmuds had to be condemned again, and despite the fact that they may contain some good "...and hence no matter how much good they contain, they were, nevertheless, condemned by the authority of the councils, in the same way that heretics are condemned although they do not err in everything".[76] The Talmud therefore remained in condemnation indefinitely. The repeated efforts began to take their toll and intensive study, scholarship and research became impossible. Rabbis emigrated, the stream of foreign students that had filled the halls of the academies at Rameru, Dampierre and Paris ceased. Conversions to Christianity increased and men like Nicholas Donin, Theobold of Sens and Paul Christian (Pablo Christiani) became important avenues through which knowledge of Judaism passed to Christian scholars.[77]

All this was possible because it was the era of greater enforced segregation of Jews which resulted from the theological position of the reforming pope, Innocent III. These attitudes were canonized at the Fourth Lateran Council in 1215 and became the policy that more or less informed church relations with Jews until modern times. Innocent III ascended the papacy in 1198. Of him it has been said, "Few have equaled him in the capacity to administer, judge, negotiate, and decide in affairs

political and ecclesiastical involving all Europe."[78] As far
as Jews were concerned Innocent III initiated nothing new, but
he urged enforcement of old laws that were observed in the
breach, laws that intensified impoverishment, segregation and
degradation of Jews. Perhaps the single most effective instrument in this was the decree of the Fourth Lateran Council
that "Jews and Saracens of both sexes in every Christian prov-
ince and at all times shall be marked off in the eyes of the
public from other peoples through the character of their
dress". During the last three days before Easter and on Good
Friday they were not to go out in public at all since Christians are then in mourning. The Council had many other provisions of long-standing renewed. Buttressing it all was the
ancient theological doctrine that Jews were condemned to eternal servitude, as Augustine put it, as Esau was to serve Jacob
(Gen. 25:23), in expiation of their rejection and crucifixion
of Jesus. But though they were to remain in a state of humiliation and misery they were to be preserved in their diaspora
as living symbols of the truth of Jesus, ultimately to be converted before or at the Second Coming. Innocent III repeatedly referred to this theological premise: the perpetual servitude of the Jews for their guilt in Jesus' death. By canon
law, by repeated reiteration and by subliminal perception perhaps, this concept was translated into the ghettoization of the
Jew and the ultimate development of what appeared to be the
"natural" Jew, the East European of a different "ethnic" type,
different in dress, language, forms of entertainment, occupations, interests and in all the other amenities of culture and
civilization, the portrait often erroneously stereotyped as
the "shtetle" Jew of Poland, vintage eighteenth century, and
charged with being unassimilable.[79] This theological premise

was given muscle by Innocent III and theological credibility
by St. Thomas Aquinas (1225-1274).[80]

Possibly the demise of French Judaism is aptly summarized
in two statements. The first is from an anonymous Parisian
chronicle which states that in 1269 "...by royal order...the
Jews at Paris were ensigned with a circle of felt, in front
and in back on all the clothes which they wore".[81] The second
is from an ordinance of King Philip III, dated April 19, 1283.
Among other provisions renewing old laws, prohibiting both the
establishment and repair of new cemeteries or synagogues and
old ones, and ordaining the burning of left-over rabbinic
literature, he ordered: "Also, in our kingdom they may not
dwell or reside in small towns, among the rustics; rather they
must reside in large towns and in well-known locales, in which
they have been accustomed to dwell of yore."[82] If one cannot
die in a land, cemetery space being denied, one cannot ultimately live there. What Louis the Saint inaugurated, Philip
the Fair (IV) concluded.[83] Local expulsions of Jews took
place during the 1280's and 1290's and coincidentally Jewish
conversions to Christianity rose. Church doctrine, however,
could not serve as a premise for expulsion. Only economic
gain for an impoverished treasury, which intermittent warfare
caused Philip IV, could be a motive. The Jews were expelled
from all the land of France in 1306.[84] One might say there
was nothing personal in it, for in 1307 King Philip also
seized the wealth of the Knights of the Templars, a very
wealthy class of merchant-financiers. That there were Jews
in France to expell again and again during the fourteenth century was owing to the policy of Louis X who re-opened France
to the Jews in 1315, and successive kings who followed the
same ambivalent procedures. The expulsions and the segrega-

tion doomed religious life, however, and France was never again a great center of Judaism, not even recovering its glory of yore after emancipation of the Jews during the French Revolution.

CHAPTER 8

England: A Premature Experiment

I. THE SETTING[1]

A brick sculptured with a representation of the biblical
hero Samson driving the foxes into a field of corn (Judges 15:
4-5) dating to the first Roman settlement of England during
the first century A.D. was found. This might be a sign of
Jewish presence in England at that time. The historian De
Blossiers Tovey was reluctant to make that statement in anticipation of scholars arguing that Jews would not sculpture such
images because of the second commandment (Exodus 20:4). However, during the first century there was no such prohibition
on art in Judaism and therefore a Jew who settled in Great
Britain during the middle of that century with the first Roman
settlers might have sculptured that brick. Such settlers would
have been contemporaries of R. Eliezer the Great of Lydda who
even permitted Jews to supply artistic talent for idols if they
did it as a livelihood and not for religious reasons.[2] But if
there were Jews in England historians can describe Jewish religious life only after the Norman conquest in 1066, and then
most of the reliable data concerns economics.[3] It is clear
that the twelfth century was one of expansion for the Jewish
community in England which enjoyed prosperity and security,
controlling urban and rural real estate and building stone
mansions which became the envy of non-Jews and undoubtedly

contributed to the demise of the community.[4] A grand experiment at building an Anglo-Judaic center had an auspicious beginning but was early aborted.

According to known sources the first case of the "blood accusation" against Jews took place in England in 1144. The Jews of Norwich were accused of torturing a Christian child before Easter and of hanging him, crucifixion style, on Good Friday. The gory details of the torture are not calculated to assuage animosity.[5] This type of accusation included the charge that Jews did it in order to reenact the crucifixion. Similar events followed in Gloucester (1168), Bury St. Edmunds (1181) and elsewhere, and ultimately spread to the continent, at Blois in 1171.[6] The "blood libel" probably reached its fullest development in England in the famous incident of Little St. Hugh in Lincoln in 1255. An account of that is given by the historian Matthew of Paris which is entirely reminiscent of the account given of such ancient charges in the Jewish historian Josephus' work, *Against Apion*.[7] Matthew's account included details of how the victim was kept prisoner in a special chamber and was fattened up to be a sacrifice in the form of a crucifixion. Following the crucifixion, Matthew writes, the victim was disembowelled for use in magical arts. Little St. Hugh remained a permanent irritation for Jews of England because of the popular ballads associated with the alleged incident and the adoption of the legend by the author Geoffrey Chaucer for use in a prayer at the end of his "Prioress's Tale". This "ritual murder" charge, if nothing else, is a symptom of the popular feeling in England for Jews, and which made it feasible for Edward I to expel them in 1290.

There were at least twenty major communities with a fair number of Jews before the end of the twelfth century as we

learn from the "Northampton Donum" (1194), an assembly called
to decide how much the Jews should contribute toward an assessment to ransom King Richard I from the Emperor Henry VI.[8] All
the monetary tallages, tithes, and other transactions of the
Jews were recorded at and checked through the Exchequer of the
Jews.[9] It is in connection with this Exchequer that there was
a Jewish consultant whose title was *Presbyter Judaeorum*. Too
often the person holding this title has been considered a
"Chief Rabbi" of medieval England because of the clerical tone
of the title and because careless English scribes often called
him "sacerdos" and sometimes "pontifex" giving the connotation
of a sacred calling.[10] But the Presbyter was not a religious
functionary at all. The spiritual leader of medieval English
Jews like those elsewhere was called Rav or Rabbi and probably
Magister in Latin. This is seen in a document naming Magister
Benedictus of Lincoln in Latin, and in its parallel Hebrew
copy he is called Rav Berahyah de Nicole. Interestingly, too,
a 1273 record points to a Presbyter Hagin who was the son of
a Magister Moses; the name Hagin listed with no title, the
father Moses called Magister, further indicating the Presbyter
was not a Magister, and Magister was the title for the one who
was considered an English Rabbi, as in fact Magister Elias son
of Magister Moses was described, "a master of the Jewish law".[11]

There are no records that I am aware of for the presence
of Karaites in England. But a Canterbury document of 1240
refers to a *Dayan uMoreh Zedek* ("Judge and Teacher of Righteousness"). This is closest to the function of a medieval rabbi,
and one historian claims it is the only reference to a rabbi in
pre-expulsion England. That is a rash conclusion. I think
that happens to be the only reference to a Karaite "rabbi"
while "Magister" describes the others. There is no indication
that Karaite "rabbis" used that title but it is a title that

goes back to the first century Jews of the Dead Sea Scrolls and Karaites were closely related to that literature. Conceivably an English Karaite revived that title for himself.[12]

II. THE SYNAGOGUE AND JEWISH LEARNING

Knowledge of Jewish religious life is sparse. But there is sufficient information to provide an outline. As in France the Jews spoke French, in this case usually Norman-French and had French names. But although they were in many ways acculturated, the synagogue served as the center of Jewish life and Jews were taxed for its support.[13] Although they had the right since the days of Henry II to govern themselves by talmudic law, in criminal cases they were bound by royal courts and Jews served on the jury.[14]

Excommunications were called out in the synagogue, indicating a degree of communal control over the religious life of the individual as on the continent. From its pulpit were made announcements of common joy and sorrow and all proclamations of the civil authorities or the king's mandates. There is evidence of such mandates proclaimed for two or three Sabbaths in sequence.[15] The synagogue had several officials such as the executive head called either *bailluvas* or *parnas*, the *gabai* or treasurer, and at least two paid officials. One was the person who prepared meat for ritual use, the *shohet*, and the other was the *hazan* or reader, also called *chanteur*.[16] As on the continent there was not yet a salaried rabbi.

As far as the religio-cultural life is concerned, a little was produced of an original nature by English Jews. In general they drew inspiration and halakhic authority from continental scholars, but actual judicial decisions were made by an English

Bet Din which usually consisted of at least one "Master" (rabbi?) out of the three that formed the tribunal.[17] That many Jews were learned may be attested, although not definitively, by the Judaica libraries accumulated in England and left there at the time of the expulsion in 1290. Ephraim of Bonn writes of the books English Jews "had written in great numbers" which crusaders brought to the continent for sale among Jews there, and exuberantly indicates there were "none like them for their beauty and splendor".[18] There was a fine school of Jewish grammarians and exegetes during the twelfth century in England. Much copying and composing must therefore have gone on. The Jews of Cologne, Germany, for example, bought manuscripts looted at York and were excited by the beauty and the wide variety of the learned treatises of English libraries.[19]

Among books written in England during the thirteenth century was *Eẓ Hayyim* (*Tree of Life*), a compilation of the halakha, and including the liturgy then in use, along with some original hymns of the English synagogues. Also an important lexicon was composed there, as was a commentary on the Mishnah. There is a paucity of literary remains, but sufficient data to imply a preoccupation with poetry, exegesis, halakha and grammar. The extensive preoccupation with grammar and proper vowel punctuation indicates a school of masoretic studies in England. In turn this may point to a Karaite presence, for although Rabbanites also delved into this sphere of study, it was a Karaite specialty. It was from these grammarian-masorites that Roger Bacon learned his Hebrew during the thirteenth century.[20]

From time to time continental scholars came to England. Perhaps the most illustrious one was the biblical exegete Abraham Ibn Ezra (twelfth century).[21] In an introduction

to his work *Yesod Moreh* (*The Foundation of Religion*) Ibn Ezra
wrote, "I, Abraham, the Spaniard, son of Meir called Ibn Ezra,
began to compose this book and wrote it in the City of London,
in the island of Angleterre, in the month Tamuz. And it was
brought to an end in the month of Ab, in four weeks in the
year 4918 (1158) of the Creation."[22] Following this he wrote
his *Iggeret HaShabat* (*The Sabbath Letter*). Again he identifies
himself as being in England. He attributes this treatise to a
dream on a Sabbath Eve, the 14th of Tebet (December 7, 1158),
in which he is given a letter from the Sabbath personified,
informing him that he has a book in his collection that recom-
mends the profanation of the Sabbath Eve. He awakes, takes
the suspected book out into the moonlight and reads it. On
Genesis 1:5 he reads in the commentary that "when the morning
of the second day came then one whole day had passed for the
night is reckoned as part of the preceding day". This meant
the Sabbath would begin at dawn on Saturday morning, and Jews
who followed that, from the traditional point of view, would
be violating the Sabbath since it should begin at sunset on
Friday. Ibn Ezra then vows to write a treatise explaining the
beginning of the Sabbath on Friday at sunset.[23]

Very interesting also is Ibn Ezra's review of Jewish
studies in England. He surveys the variety of studies conducted there in the first chapter of his *Yesod*. He refers to
masoretic scholars, grammarians, and biblical exegetes who
concentrate on both Hebrew and Aramaic versions of scripture.
In each case he is critical of narrow specialization. He goes
on to describe the presence of talmudists, and again he indicates there are those given to specialize in halakha and those
who specialize in agadah. But, he concludes, to know the soul
and God, the angels and future world, one must study mathemat-

ics, logic, science and philosophy, and it is in these dis-
ciplines that he is rooting this book on religion. Perhaps
this teaches us more about Ibn Ezra, but it does give us a
sketch of twelfth-century learning in English Judaism. It was
diversified and plentiful and there were apparently a number
of scholars even if few have become historical figures.[24]
Among some better known is R. Benjamin, either of Cambridge
or Canterbury, who is mentioned in medieval rabbinic literature.[25] Another is R. Jacob of Orleans who lived in London
and met his death at the above-mentioned coronation of King
Richard I in September 1182.[26]

There is evidence that the authority of English rabbis
was as high as that of those on the continent. This again
bears out the validity of the thesis of contemporary and local
authority. This is illustrated by a citation in a medieval
halakhic work which deals with the prohibition of mixing two
different types of threads in a garment (Deut. 22:2). A certain R. Moses Cohen is asked whether *kanabos* is to be regarded
as forbidden for containing two types of threads. R. Moses
replies that "in all the lands of the diaspora they had the
custom of permitting it from the days of their ancestors, in
Germany, France, Angleterre and Provence where they all wear
wool sewn with *kanabos*".[27] With the continuous presence in
England either of resident or visiting scholars of note it is
not surprising that the educational system was well organized
and quite intensive from boyhood up. It was oriented to making the student familiar with the Aramaic translation of scripture in order to facilitate his entry into the study of rabbinic halakha. Apparently one son at least, of every family,
was to be "separated" and these were known as "the separated
ones", set apart for intensive Judaic study. Each one of

these studied for seven years. Adult studies, even for the elders of the congregations, were enjoined.[28]

Other famous English scholars were R. Menaḥem and R. Moses, both of London, thirteenth century.[29] In the light of the presence of these scholars and this educational system it is not surprising also that German ḥasidim had some influence in England as well. The name "Aaron son of the ḥasid R. Abraham" in English records would indicate that persons of that pietistic stripe also visited or settled. And this would further imply a diversity of religious life on that small island among its few thousand Jews that mirrored the full spectrum of the continent.[30]

III. RELIGIOUS OBSERVANCE; LITURGY AND DOCTRINE

Personal and public religious observance in Judaism covers a very broad area. There are the Sabbaths and festivals with a complex halakha of what may not be done, and in what way to positively celebrate and commemorate the occasions. There is the life-cycle group of observances and domestic relations which we have surveyed in Spain and in France. There are dietary practices, and a whole range of miscellany. Beyond doubt the religious guidance offered the adherent of Judaism on how to relate to his God and faith each day and for each occasion of life, is more intensive and extensive than other faiths. Although there is diversity in Jewish religious observance, the diversity is in particulars; in general, however, most medieval Jews subscribe to a basically homogeneous format of religious observance. As previously noted, we might say there is similarity without uniformity.

This same principle holds true for liturgy as for other observances. England's Jews had their own prayerbook, arranged in England and used in its synagogues.[31] The thirteenth century author of a significant compendium of halakha, *Hamanhig*, does not refer to an English ritual despite his visit to England, but that may be because it was compiled and published after his visit. In any event we know from a mystical work on liturgy of the thirteenth century that the well-known Judah the Ḥasid warned against the English who incur serious penalty in the next world because of "their additions to the Prayerbook, and omissions from it".[32]

There has been preserved the *Eẓ Ḥayyim*, a halakhic compendium by R. Jacob b. Judah of London who wrote it around 1287. Where he treats of the priestly benediction in this compendium he records the liturgy of thirteenth century England.[33] A variety of differences from the general liturgy prevalent in Europe is evident. For example it contains a full daily confession at the beginning of daily worship which is present in no other Jewish liturgy emanating from Europe.[34] Another interesting facet of the opening of the morning prayers is the wording of the prayer that expresses the belief in resurrection. Unlike our traditional texts which are relatively ambiguous, the English rite contains a very cogent affirmation of bodily resurrection, literally describing the rejoining of bones, tendons, flesh, skin and breath in the mode of the Prophet Ezekiel, even using the same words as the prophet to describe the process. English Jews apparently were among the most articulate on a problem that was full of ambiguity on the continent. And if, as I have noted earlier, the liturgy is a primary source of a religious group's theology, the English prayerbook offers a definitive statement on the doctrine of resurrection.[35] Furthermore the detailed daily confession emphasizes the belief of English Jews in the need for continuous repentance, giving evidence to their belief in the doctrine of reward and punishment as a primary one.

Undoubtedly, as in all other rituals, the New Year *Aḫinu Malkenu* prayer (Our Father, Our King) describes comprehensively the theology of the community.[36] This prayer articulates a wide variety of theological concerns, running the gamut of what Judaism sees as vital to the salvation of man and society. The opening verses may be summed up as including the following doctrinal assertions: a) man recognizes he is a sinner, and only on this premise he approaches God in prayer; b) God alone possesses sovereignty in the eyes of the Jews; c) what God grants is out of His grace and not because man deserves it. Following these three verses we find thirty-six verses of petition. These beseech God for every conceivable blessing required by man for enduring life. The worshipper prays for rescue from enemies, that God will annul any designs of adversaries, remove suffering and ill-health, will forgive sins, help him repent, send healing, and providentially provide his bodily needs as well as his spiritual requirements. In brief, God is the Source of all blessings. Providence is therefore a serious theological conception. Man is incapable of attaining his needs or wants, or achieving rescue from adversity or ultimate salvation without God. Whatever the philosophers may have said on the subject, this simple faith is what the Jew possessed, and for this reason R. Abraham b. David of Posquieres, Provence, took Maimonides of Egypt to task at precisely the time the prayerbook is being compiled in England.

That Judaism also contains a belief in vicarious salvation, that the death of some can atone for others is evident from the earliest of times, although it was also resisted from the earliest times. It was especially resisted after the rise

of Christianity but was never eliminated, and it is obvious
that it reappears in liturgy in the middle ages and still
constitutes part of divine worship. This is fully expressed
in this same prayer. The four closing stanzas of 'Aḃinu Malkenu reiterate the hope for God's grace in the absence of
man's worthiness for salvation, ending with "Our Father, our
King, answer us with Grace, for we have no deserving deeds;
act for us with loving charity and save us."[37]

We have discussed this passage at length because it is
one of those which varies considerably in the English ritual
and well demonstrates the religious independence of Jewish
communities. There are forty-two, instead of forty-four
stanzas, and the second half deviates considerably in text
and arrangement.[38] The English ritual does not begin with
the doctrine of grace but does end with it. It also contains
a stanza praying that God will "agree with those who advocate
our merit". This expresses the idea that in heaven there is
a "trial" of man to seal his fate for the coming year. He
is there attacked by prosecuting attorneys and defended by
defense attorneys. Here he prays for God's approval of the
arguments of the defense advocates.[39] The English ritual
contains another stanza not found in the traditional text
praying that God will grant His forgiveness and the accompany-
ing blessings beseeched for the year "for the sake of your
righteous messiah".[40]

The differences are not really "heterodox" if that word
may be used anachronistically, in the light of what was subsequently termed "orthodox". The liturgy neither rejects an
integral part of Judaism's theology nor innovates a new doctrine unknown to previous Judaism. Why did some of the German
pietists lash out against this ritual? It seems to me to be

only the consequence of the natural conservatism of the pietists coupled with a desire on the part of German scholars
to gain a hegemony which had been denied to rabbinic authorities throughout history, the most powerful group of all, the
geonim, as we have seen, not being able to acquire full universal authority.

IV. THE DEMISE OF ENGLISH JUDAISM

One of the ironic problems of English Jews was their
French acculturation which made them seem "foreign" once the
Anglo-Saxon and Norman strains coalesced to form the English
nationality. Not until it was too late, toward the end of the
thirteenth century, did Jews begin to acculturate to the new
English society and adopt English names and use the English
language. This foreignness of English Jews did not help when
it was reinforced by the strange conical hats they voluntarily
adopted as part of their costume, and all these things mixed
with the animosity against usury, envy of their stone houses
and wealth, ultimately reflecting itself in the popular willingness to believe and to spread the ritual murder accusations.[41] After the Fourth Lateran Council the Church encouraged a system of assimilation through conversion and especially toward the end of the thirteenth century the English
Church acted with alacrity. Edward I of England ordered in
1280 that the clergy is "to induce the Jews, by such means as
they, under the inspiration of the spirit of truth, may think
most efficient, to assemble and hear...the word of God preached
by the friars...." The Church favored this policy even earlier,
and on the basis of the hope to convert Jews Bishop Robert

Grosseteste, a famous medieval theologian, helped them avert
a local expulsion from Leicester from 1231 for over twenty
years. Grosseteste is often remembered for vigorously de-
nouncing Jewish usury, but this was not "anti-Jewish", as he
also denounced Christian usury and severely criticized Pope
Innocent IV for allowing Christians to take even higher
interest rates than those being received by Jews.[42]

This Grosseteste item in itself points up a very complex
question: why neither the Church nor the state was able to
find a solution to the problem of living with Jews. It was
not usury. Christians shared in that sin. It was not wealth.
Others had greater wealth; and anyhow Jews were usually expelled after having been impoverished. It could only have
been theological, or a combination of theological conviction
and an atavistic fear and anxiety. Deeply embedded in the
psyche of medieval theorists was the persuasion that one must
either abandon the theology of Jewish culpability for the
crucifixion, or act on its reality. I do not believe people
like Edward I or Philip the Fair of France really comprehended
why they were doing what they did. They rationalized their
radical surgery but never understood it. The Church understood its dilemma but was never able to liberate itself from
the theological enigma. This is why the Church legislated
protection for the Jews, and bishops and popes again and again
ordered mobs and agitators to desist from harming Jews. A
study of Pope Innocent III would serve as a microcosm of the
condition we are here considering.[43]

In any event, in England was enacted the first total mass
expulsion of Jews from an entire country, Edward I promulgating
on July 18, 1290, that by November 1 all Jews are to be gone
from his realm. There seems to be no evidence that the newly
emerging Parliament legislated. The lack of such legislation

was argued by Cromwell in the seventeenth century when he
asserted that Edward's act was "private". Though Judaism
thus officially remained outlawed, Jews were always returning
to English soil. Certainly Marranos were present during the
reign of Queen Elizabeth, and Shakespeare had much opportunity,
contrary to popular notion, to know Jews at first hand. But
while Jews did live there continuously, Judaism ceased to
function. There were Marrano places of worship, but these
were secret. There were no schools or scholars again until
the seventeenth century.

CHAPTER 9

Germany: Piety and Ritualism

I. PARAMETERS

French and German Judaisms were quite similar. In most
books one reads of the "Franco-German" center of Judaism. By
one of those arbitrary decisions it was necessary to make by
virtue of the nature of this book, I have separated France from
Germany. The two were geographically contiguous, but politi-
cally divergent. The Jews of France lived under separate kings
in lands that used a Romance language: those in Normandy for
awhile lived under the English king. The Jews of Germany lived
for the most part in what was then Lotharingia, West Germany or
the Rhineland, using a Germanic tongue, destined to develop a
different culture. These two geographic units which ultimately
evolved into the nation-states of France and Germany constituted the "Carolingian Empire" running more or less from Spain
to the Elbe river in the east and from the North Sea to central
Italy, fashioned by the great king Charlemagne who ruled 768-
814. The great empire was split in 843 by the Treaty of Verdun
with the foundations thereby set for the historical evolution
of France and Germany. Even if Jews were there, Judaism never
flourished in the Carolingian Empire. It was in eleventh and
twelfth century Champagne, Ile-de-France and Provence that
Judaism flowered in France. And in the Rhenish provinces of
Germany there developed a great center of Jewish learning dur-

ing the same centuries, spreading eastward through Franconia
to Bavaria, and Bohemia, lands later also known as parts of
Austria and Hungary. Judaism naturally did not emerge in a
vacuum nor by artificial insemination. Much of what transpired
in the complex historical unfolding of empire and church between 750 and 1450 had significant impact upon Judaism's evolution and the direction it finally took. Here we must be content with covering only selected aspects of Jewish religious
development.

Consequently we will survey the emergence of that religious scholarship in Judaism which created the seedbed of the
contemporary twentieth-century Judaism. We will see that it
was German scholars who laid the foundations of what became
East European "orthodoxy" and which, in its turn, served as
parent to successive nineteenth and twentieth century revolutions in Judaism leading to the unusual but significant version of Judaism known especially in North America. We will
also examine some aspects of what characterized German Judaism such as its minutiae in ritualism and a pietism ripe for
Kabalah.[1]

II. THE SETTING

The Carolingian Empire became possible through the successful efforts of Charles Martell of Austrasia (North-East Spain)
in stopping the Islamic advance in 727. But the Verdun agreement of 843 prevented it from becoming a world-empire successor
to the old Roman Empire and resulted also in the emergence of
a separate Jewish community in Germany. According to unveri-
fied legend Charlemagne was instrumental in establishing Jewish

learning in Germany when he invited R. Kalonymus from Lucca in Italy to settle in Mayence, Germany. In any event we have no sound historical knowledge prior to the eleventh century.[2] Germany served as the place of origin of Judaic learning in northern Europe. It also originated the legal status that disabled the Jews of central and eastern Europe from Frederick II, 1236, to the French Revolution. And even more paradoxically, that great point of origin of European Judaism which sent forth spiritual colonies to North and South America, Australia and South Africa, was also under Adolph Hitler during the twentieth century, the source of the demise of European Judaism.

It was in 1182 that Frederick I Barbarossa offered a charter of autonomy to the Jewish community of Ratisbon. In it he said, "...We rightly preserve his due to everyone of our loyal subjects, not only the adherents of the Christian faith, but also to those who differ from our faith and live in accordance with the rites of their ancestral tradition. We must provide for their persevering in their customs and secure peace for their persons and property...." The king goes on to lucidly enunciate the principle that the well-being of Jews was his responsibility. This theory also had another side to it: the Jews "belonged" to the sovereign, and were therefore subject to all the ramifications of being *servi camerae* or "serfs of the chamber", possessing only the civil or political rights granted or withheld by the sovereign. This had its disastrous effect upon Judaism in time. But in those early centuries it made for religious freedom, and relative security and prosperity. It made it possible, in short, for Judaism to become so enriched spiritually, and in scholarship, that socio-economic and political calamity was unable to shake it.[3] It is this spiritual impregnability which we are examining. This story begins with R. Kalonymus of Lucca (880-960) whose responsa are possibly the earliest surviving European rabbinic literature. We are not well-informed, however, of his life or his son's, R. Meshullam (910-985). But we know from the famous R. Gershom that R. Meshullam was a noted scholar in his day. He was also a liturgist and his sacred poetry became part of the liturgical ritual of Askenaz Judaism. We also have a number of his responsa. It was with reference to his poetry that R. Gershom permitted what some Spanish scholars and geonim were opposed to: the inclusion of newly composed poetry in the liturgy. This decision was instrumental in the evolution of the prayerbook as was inherited by twentieth-century Judaism.[4]

The next great scholar in Mayence was R. Judah son of R. Meir Hakohen (930-1010), also known as Rabbi Leontin and Sir Leon. This man was the teacher of R. Gershom, apparently a remarkable scholar whose halakhic opinions R. Gershom sometimes preferred over those of the geonim. This once again evidences for us the concept of rabbinic independence and local and contemporary authority. R. Gershom wrote that Sir Leon did not always agree with the Babylonian geonim "and his opinion was more acceptable to me than theirs".[5]

III. RELIGION AND LEARNING

A. *R. Gershom*

It was in this setting that R. Gershom (960-1028) studied and himself became a significant branch of the Judaic tree. Very little is known of his life. But the impression he made was so profound that he was given the honorific title "Rabbenu" Gershom, and toward the end of the twelfth century the literature begins to refer to him as "Light of the Diaspora" or "He who enlightens the Diaspora".[6] Although the talmudic commentary that goes by his name is really a compilation of later students at Mayence and consequently few literary remains testify to this greatness, his responsa exhibit his intellectual mastery and independence of judgment. Some of his views may have permanently altered the direction of European Judaism. We can only briefly survey a few.

1. *Apostasy*

Although it is difficult to say, it is within the realm of possibility that it was R. Gershom who changed for all time the direction of the sentiment of Judaism toward Christianity. Thus he permitted Jews both to accept ecclesiastical robes as security for loans despite their sacerdotal use which others claimed was enjoying the benefit of something related to idolatry, and to deal with Christians on their sacred days, both of which had been forbidden in talmudic times. R. Gershom simply rejected the notion that Christianity belongs in the category subsumed in talmudic literature under *aḃodah zarah* (idolatry).[7] In this same vein he liberally accepted Jews who had left the faith under compulsion back into the faith and even pronounced a ban upon anyone who used the temporary apostasy against them by reminding others of it, or insulting them over it. The only theological justification for R. Gershom to allow this kind of easy return to Judaism as if nothing had transpired is the notion that Christianity is a monotheistic faith. This teaching was later followed faithfully by Rashi.[8]

On the other hand the person who adopted Christianity and
had no intention of return to Judaism was penalized by the community with the loss of his right of inheritance. This notion
went back to R. Meshullam b. Kalonymus, a predecessor of R.
Gershom. The view was incorporated into the earliest halakhic
work we have from northern Europe, the *Sefer Hadinim* of R.
Judah Hakohen (980-1050).[9] R. Gershom accepted that view too
and this is not incongruous with his other views. The premise
upon which one enters a faith is that he is newly-born. The
gentile who becomes a Jew takes the name of Abraham as his
"father", for he now is as if born again. The same concept
holds true in Christianity. When one receives baptism one is
newly born and therefore is in a spiritual sense no longer the
progeny of his previous parent. The rabbinic argument, therefore, was that "an apostate is not called the 'seed' of his
father". But it had nothing to do with one's theological conception of the monotheistic status of Christianity.[10] For conversely if an apostate returned to Judaism he was again his
father's seed! Even a *kohen*, the remnant of the ancient
priestly group which was a hereditary one, still retained
certain inherited functions and prerogatives in Judaism as
"priestly seed", after the destruction of the Temple in Jerusalem. A priest-apostate could return to his priestly status.[11]

2. *Polygamy and Divorce*[12]

We have discussed the questions of marriage and divorce
and have explored the problem of polygamy in previous chapters.
Here it merely remains to recapitulate to set the matter in
historical perspective. Polygamy was permitted in most versions of Judaism since biblical times even if at times some
scholars required that the first wife consent to the husband's

taking a second.[13] The Qumran community, however, prohibited polygamy, remarriage after divorce, divorce, any second marriage even for a widower or a divorced man, or all of these or several of them, varying according to the views of different scholars.[14] Karaites prohibited polygamy, and whether R. Gershom was influenced by them or by Christianity will remain a matter of debate. We do not have his own discussion of the question. But contrary to the idea that Karaite views were not known in Germany we do have Genizah evidence that Frenchmen traveled to the Middle East and conversed with Karaites. Even if Karaites did not visit Germany, the information brought back by the international traders and travelers of Germany would be considerable. If we have learned anything about medieval society from the Genizah documents it is the great mobility and widespread international travel in which Jews engaged.[15]

We know for a fact that Jews traveled from the Mediterranean to Germany as well. The German Jews had an institution called *ḥerem hayishub*, a ban on settlement, which regulated who, and whether a newcomer could settle in a community. We find that a scholar in the east dissuaded another scholar from traveling to an unnamed land where the language was barbarous and Jews did not liberally admit their fellow-Jews to reside in a community at the risk of being placed under *ḥerem*, the ban or excommunication. This certainly helps us perceive the probability of Karaites or of Karaism being directly known in Germany.[16]

In any event, whatever influences were at work in the mind of R. Gershom, he led the thrust in Germany to ban polygamy in Judaism. Since we do not have his original text we do not know why he did it at that particular juncture. But it was very

soon accepted among all the European Jews, except those of
Spain, although it ran contrary to both Talmud and Bible, re-
inforcing the notion of rabbinic and contemporary authority
taking precedence over the past and even over biblical provisions.

The ordinance had its problems, however, and these were
further solved by rabbinic independence. What is a man to do
if his wife becomes a Christian and leaves him, and refuses to
be involved in the Jewish divorce proceedings? By another of
R. Gershom's enactments in halakha a man could not divorce his
wife without her consent. Shall he be permanently bound to her
and not permitted to remarry because of the polygamy ban of R.
Gershom? Interestingly enough, although women suffered greatly from the àgunah problem (being bound to a man whose death
cannot be proven reliably or who refuses to divorce her, or to
a brother-in-law who is an apostate and refuses both to exercise his levirate prerogative by marrying his widowed sister-
in-law or to waive his right by the ceremony of ḥaliẓah, all
of which items we have discussed earlier), the rabbis would
not shackle a man with it. Here again we see the male bias
coming forward. Later rabbis arranged to suspend the polygamy
ban in such cases, or even to further contravene R. Gershom by
allowing the husband to divorce his wife through the rabbinic
court without her consent and without her ever actually receiv-
ing the document.[17]

What all of these instances bring forward is the independence of rabbinic authority and the consequent flexibility of
Judaism. This made possible the adaptation of religious pre-
cept in all centuries irregardless of geography. Judaism was
thereby able to orientate itself to a Christian milieu, or to
an Islamic milieu, or to a secular milieu. What was true in
the matter of polygamy, the very heart of the institution of

the family being involved, was also true of divorce, another
significant facet of the same institution.

We have already surveyed certain aspects of divorce halakha and have broached the subject of injustice or at least inequality for women. R. Gershom sought at least one ameliora-
tion even if by contemporary standards, a twentieth-century
assessment would consider his action less than tokenism. In
his own day it was a veritable revolution. He arranged for
the prohibition of a husband under any circumstances to divorce
his wife against her will. The talmudic precident upon which
he based his action, although he certainly did not require
one, was that no *get* (religious divorce) is valid unless it is
executed in accordance with the regulations of a rabbinic
court. This meant that hereafter such rabbinic courts (three
rabbis usually) would require the consent of the wife and any
divorce issued without this would be null.[18]

3. *The Question of Religious Authority*

R. Gershom seems to have favored mandatory communal decision rather than scholarly interpretation leading to voluntary acceptance. Thus his activity was conducted under the
umbrella of synods, councils that met and ruled. Halakha or
religious life in general within Judaism had never been governed by synods before, whether in Palestine, Babylonia or
Spain. It must therefore have been the influence of the church
which brought this about. The information on particular synods
is scanty and many unprovable assumptions are made. But what
is clear is that a *takanah* is attributed to R. Gershom requir-
ing that the decision of a majority of a community be obeyed
by all. There are obviously advantages to this, but in the
realm of religious devotion and especially ritual it can be
stultifying.[19]

R. Gershom's view was not permanently enacted into Judaism because, as in so many other instances, other scholars disagreed. R. Tam in France, the leading scholar of the twelfth century reversed the trend from tight communal control or expanded central control of a federation of communities, by arguing for the supremacy of individual scholarship. It would take us too far afield to describe the arguments that prevailed all through medieval times for and against majority communal authority. We cannot pause to discuss specific historic events which prompted scholars to take one or the other point of view. Suffice it to say that until the twelfth century the view best personified by R. Gershom held sway, that decisions of importance in halakha, whether of civil or ritual nature, should be made by synods, and that these decisions be binding on all Jews of the area represented by the synods. After the twelfth century authority was temporarily restored to the individual scholar and R. Gershom's view was replaced by that of the Frenchman, R. Tam, who probably enjoyed an even greater universalized authority than R. Gershom. It would be anachronistic, but interesting, to wonder whether it was the individualistic libertarian French spirit that governed R. Tam as over against the authoratarian German approach that influenced R. Gershom.[20]

This French view was opposed in Germany, and we find that the outstanding scholar of the late thirteenth century, R. Meir b. Barukh of Rothenburg, sided with his German predecessors. There were a number of synods in Germany that continued the Gershomist system. Later, as we will see, in east Europe there were attempts at this form of governance in Judaism. But these attempts always ultimately failed. Historically Judaism always reverted to individualistic authority. It was true of all branches of Judaism in less or greater degree.[21]

Nevertheless the historical fact is that synods met and imposed practices upon Jews which may have been thought to be necessary by some authorities in their day, but which, because they carried the authority of a synod under pain of excommunication, acquired a mystique and a power that was not in consonance with the original spirit of Judaism. These *takanot* often became part of the minutiae of observance that rested heavily upon that German Judaism which we will shortly see became the seedbed of east European observance later raised to a level of "orthodoxy". Among such ritualistic impositions were: a) that a husband must not eat with his wife during her menstrual period before she undergoes purification; b) that a Jew must not cut his hair or shave his beard gentile-style; c) that one may not use the utensils of gentiles for Jewish wine or permit gentiles to assist in the preparation of Jewish wine; d) that one may not eat food cooked by gentiles.[22]

Some of the enactments were important and show positive and ethical judgment: a) that committing perjury regarding taxes renders one unfit to serve as a witness; b) that every Jew shall set aside time for study, and synagogue worship shall be conducted with proper decorum; c) that one may not clip coins. Coin clipping played a role in the expulsions of Jews from various places, especially England in 1290. R. Meir of Rothenburg believed it "brought about the destruction of our brethren in France and Britain". This activity, the clipping of coins, was a means of cheating on the value of currency in precious metals, and the crime was a charge often levied against Jews. It gave them much grief.[23] Another significant *takanah* issued in 1250 was one that indicates the danger in the whole Germanic approach. The effort to enforce centralized communal authority was maintained by the rather liberal

use of the power of excommunication, a power whose origin is
in the Talmud but, as we noted in an earlier chapter, was
rather expanded by the geonim. This power of excommunication
readily lends itself to abuse. By 1250 the Jews had come to
recognize that this weapon "threatened to become a Franken-
stein that would destroy them". And so at a synod at Mayence,
the birthplace of the concept of centralized power backed by
excommunication, the mutual power of both rabbis and community
councils to promulgate excommunications of individuals was
curbed. The two forces were required to agree on an excommunication. This would tend to neutralize them and in time
this weapon became harmless, obsolete, and almost unused.
One factor that tended to destroy the power altogether was
that despite the ruling of 1250 rabbis and communities at
times used it carelessly and at whim, and upon one another,
until it became such a mockery that it was no longer obeyed.[24]

The synod system continued in Germany. It is interesting
that one of the greatest rabbis of the thirteenth century, R.
Isaac b. Moses of Bohemia, author of *Or Zaruà*, one of the most
important halakhic compilations of the whole period, took
little part in the synodal enterprise. He lived for a long
time in Germany but he also studied in Paris. It is possible
he acquired an ecumenical viewpoint. In any case he went home
to Bohemia, possibly convinced that the French were right after
all.[25] Nevertheless the German system and the German emphasis
upon minutiae and pietism soon gained primacy, if not authora-
tative hegemony. The major figure in this development was R.
Meir ben Barukh of Rothenburg, a man whom one might consider
the "father" of seventeenth to twentieth century Judaism.
This Judaism became the criterion against which those who
battled reform and called themselves orthodox measured their
piety and halakha during the nineteenth century, and continue

to do so in the twentieth. But R. Meir also favored the authority of the individual rabbi and his right to independently interpret the Talmud.

B. *Rabbi Meir Ben Barukh, 1215-1293*

   1. *The Man and His Method*

R. Meir was born at Worms in 1215.[26] He gained great renown and became a magnet for many students. His disciples included the elite of halakhic scholarship who set their stamp upon Judaism for the next six hundred years. Among them were R. Asher b. Yehiel who carried German tradition to Spain, R. Mordecai b. Hillel who wrote a work which is a great repository of halakhic riches called by his name, *Mordecai*, and which became a major source for fourteenth century scholars. They, in turn, transmitted the views of R. Meir to the fifteenth century.[27] The major literary work of R. Meir himself was the great number of responsa he wrote, and is cited in the works of many others, often by the acronym *M'HaRaM* (*Morenu*, our teacher, *harav*, the master, Rabbi Meir).[28]

The thirteenth century in Germany was the period when Jews began to turn inward into themselves. Oppressive taxes and the rising merchant and banking classes, were impoverishing and supplanting them economically. Leisure resulted in more time for study and for religious devotion. Whatever the reasons, religious devotion led to greater mysticism or at least pietism. The European pietistic emphasis upon saintliness among Christians naturally affected Jews. Thus every utterance and action, every prayer, every ritualistic formula and every facet of the halakhic pattern became of extreme importance. The relationship between man and God was translated

into the confrontation of the soul with hell, and every iota
of religious behaviourism became of immense significance. R.
Meir was part of this milieu and was given to devotion to
minutiae and even ritualistic trivia. He had a disciple
called R. Samson b. Zadok who was, as one biographer called
him, a Boswell to R. Meir's Johnson. He copied down to the
minutest particular everything R. Meir said and his manner of
saying it, and described his mode of every religious observance, and how he intoned the prayers and berakhot. This account, in a book called *Tashbez* (the acronym for *Teshuvot
Shimshon ben Zadok*), became a very popular religious manual
during the following centuries and was one of the major links
in that chain which led from R. Meir to the orthodoxy of the
modern era.[29] Not only did R. Meir thus contribute to the
endless expansion of ritualistic minutiae becoming the norm
in European Judaism, he also contributed to a significant
ideological shift. He emphasized the halakhic authority of
past scholars. He maintained that there must be autonomy and
independence among contemporaries but negated the notion that
scholars of his own time and those who will arise subsequently
have the authority to contravene the earlier great halakhists,
the geonim, R. Hananel of Kairuwan, Alfasi, Maimonides, and
the French schools. His reliance upon the halakha of Maimonides naturally implies that the German heritage which was
handed on to become east European orthodoxy also included
fragments of eastern custom. He regarded the opinions of Maimonides as likely to be based upon better traditions and his
reasoning to be superior even in the absence of tradition.[30]
On the other hand R. Meir operated within a set of principles
that were certainly historically valid and are capable of providing great latitude for revision of religious practice.
Among these principles were: a) the rabbis of the Talmud

always protected the interests of the public; b) inter-group
relations and the security of Jews within a majority non-Jewish
society have to be given priority consideration even if it becomes necessary to innovate new halakha for which there is no
precedent.[31]

2. *Matters of Ritual*

In the light of what we have said about R. Meir, it becomes clear that he was a man who placed heavy emphasis upon
authority and yet left wedges open for revisionism in religious
practice. Nevertheless it was his pietistic and authority-
oriented side which governed him mostly during his lifetime
and became the legacy of future centuries of east European
Judaism. His meticulous ritualism is seen in the slightest
of deeds that became models for emulation, and were recorded
as sacred literature. Sometimes a beautiful custom might arise
from his ritualistic concerns. Thus it is thought that the
custom of eating a fruit of the new crop for the first time in
the season on the second night of Rosh HaShanah is derived from
R. Meir. It seems that he was caught between the differing
opinions of scholars on whether one should recite the berakha,
known as *sheheḥeyanu* ("who kept us alive"), thanking God for
allowing him to live to this joyous occasion, on the second
night, since he had already recited it the first night and it
was still the same occasion, Rosh HaShanah. Some scholars
maintained it is a superfluous recital on the second night and
the reciter is therefore using God's name in vain, violating
the third commandment. Others maintained it should be recited
because all the rituals of the first day should be precisely
duplicated on the second day of Rosh HaShanah. R. Meir therefore introduced the idea of drinking the first wine of the new
vintage that night, thus being required to recite the special

sheheḥeyanu which is always recited when one enjoys a "first".
In later times the new fruit was substituted.[32]

Yet, as has been shown by others, he was lenient in matters that affect waste and economy. For instance, in *kashrut*
(dietary practices) he permitted the use of meat that had remained unsalted for three days, which is contrary to halakha,
after the meat had remained unsalted, in order that it not be
wasted and the consumer or the retailer as the case may be
endure a loss. He was similarly lenient in matters that
touched upon humane considerations.[33]

A fuller study of the sources, however, shows that his
overscrupulousness in ritual grew while his leniency remained
aborted. And as his overscrupulous pietism dominated his religious views the heavier became the potential of this weighty
ritualism for dominating the future of Judaism.[34] In some respects his successors and the masses who followed them went
even further. Thus, as will be remembered from a previous
chapter, the separation of dairy and meat foods and utensils,
early became normative in Judaism. During the thirteenth century the question was directed to R. Meir as to whether, if a
pot which had been used for cooking meat was thoroughly washed
and then had a neutral vegetable soup cooked in it, and this
soup was then eaten, the consumer of the soup was permitted to
eat cheese after the soup without wiping his mouth and washing
his hands? This example is not produced here in a facetious
mood. It is a fair sampling of the type of thing we are discussing, that was of utmost concern in the schematics of piety
at that time, and was transmitted as legacy to future generations. The reply of R. Meir is in the affirmative.[35]

It is apparent that a man who lives a long time as did R.
Meir will often record contradictory views that reflect the
needs of a particular place or time. Thus in one responsum

he charges "women of our generation are loose in their manner
of life". And in another he defends liberality of settlement
and coercing a husband to divorce his wife who refuses to live
with him and has no concern that this will encourage rebel-
lious wives to proliferate, because "Heaven forfend, Jewish
daughters are not suspected of such malefaction." In general
it appears that women were in a state of tension over their
rights and perhaps for some liberation from male sexual domination. For in responsa dealing with domestic relations there
are a considerable number occasioned by men beating their
wives and wives deserting their husbands or refusing sexual
life to them. In one responsum the writer indicated "The
women of Regensburg were always arrogant in their relations
to their husbands and now are even more supercilious than
ever...." Why this was especially so in Regensburg is not
clarified.[36]

We have seen that R. Meir was considerate in matters
that affected human relations. Yet again we can discern a
contradictory strain. Thus, a childless widow was confronted
with the problem of having two brothers-in-law to perform the
levirate marriage, one in a distant country and therefore
possibly inaccessible, the other close at hand but an apostate.
R. Meir was asked whether she may accept ḥaliẓah, from the
apostate and he replied in the negative. This meant that un-
due hardship was placed upon the distant Jewish brother-in-law
to fulfill his obligation, or in the event he refuses, upon the
widow who will then be unable to remarry. Yet, possibly so
acrimonious had become the Jewish feeling for Christians in
general and apostates in particular toward the end of the
thirteenth century that R. Meir was no longer true to his own
perceptions in deciding such cases.[37]

3. *Implications of R. Meir's Later Life*

R. Meir was arrested and confined in several prisons successively while seeking to emigrate from Germany. In a town of Lombardy he was recognized and returned to Germany where Emperor Rudolph I imprisoned him from June 28, 1286 to his death on April 27, 1293. His body was not released for burial until 1307! We cannot, by virtue of the nature of this book, enter into the extremely controversial details of the history of the time, the documents that convey the information and the biographical particulars of R. Meir's last seven years.[38]

What is clear from this tragic ending to a great man's life is that a radical transformation took place in the condition of Jews in Germany. This condition had its temporary improvements during the fourteenth or fifteenth centuries, here or there. Like all historical conditions Jewish life was not subject to a one-track movement up or down, but traveled in concentric circles. The fact is discernible, however, that with the end of the thirteenth century also came the beginning of the decline of Judaism in Germany. R. Meir's arrest and imprisonment, according to some was the result of the determination of King Rudolph I to prove that under the institution of *servi camerae*, in which Jews were, in the German term *Kammerknechte*, serfs of the royal chamber, the sovereign was direct master of the persons and the property of the Jews.[39]

The following century brought French Jewish refugees to Germany. The costs to bribe the king to allow their settlement were enormous. The Black Death, 1348-1351, brought in its wake hitherto unrivaled suffering for European Jews. Pogroms began in Spain but became widespread and German Jews endured profound misery. A synod was held at Mayence in 1381 where the prominent leader was R. Moses b. Yekutiel, father

of the later significant scholar R. Jacob Molin. But spiritual
life was relatively mediocre. During the fifteenth century a
certain R. Seligmann Oppenheim made one more effort to central-
ize authority with himself as "Chief Rabbi". But as noted in
a previous chapter, such an office has no validity in Judaism
and the opposition of major scholars was aroused to defeat him.
As a matter of fact synods or councils that met over the next
two centuries were not really religious conferences. They
dealt with Jewish legal disabilities and persecution, and the
production of religious literature fell radically in quantity
and quality.[40]

According to some historians, and probably correctly so,
the demise of German Judaism is heralded in its last attempt
to restore its grandeur, a synod at Frankfort in 1603.[41] This
synod, however, is evidence that rabbinic *takanah*-power had
lost its potency. It is evidence that the communities were in
a state of internal religious disintegration. It is undoubtedly proper for the religious historian to ask whether the failure of the synod of 1603 was not due to the fact that there
was not one scholar there with the vision or the courage to
innovate. The total thrust was to restore outmoded impositions
of the past. Gentile massacres cannot be blamed for religious
mediocrity which emerges from a synod that is bent upon restoring the thirteenth century rather than inaugurating the seventeenth. There were ordinances against gentile wine, when long
ago the rabbis had declared Christianity was not idolatry and
a Christian's wine consequently not "idolatrous libation".
There was a ban on marrying one's fellow-Jew who bought wine
from a gentile and a rule to depose a rabbi who permits it or
does it himself. Obviously rabbinic independence was asserting itself in this matter. There was an ordinance against
rabbis officiating at any marriage of individuals who trans-

gress these ordinances, and one against buying milk from gentiles. There were ethical ordinances, too, aimed against use
of counterfeit money and stolen goods. But there was nothing
new or imaginative. The great scientific discoveries of the
recent era, the explorations, the renaissance, the rise of
Protestantism and Humanism, are all absent from the delibera-
tions as we know them from the sources available. As one
scholar has said, "...it was the last flicker before extinc-
tion".[42]

In the light of this deterioration of Jewish religious
life concomitant with a deterioration of the physical life of
Jews in Germany after the death of R. Meir, this may be the
place to make a cursory survey of the legal or juridical status
of Jews in Germany and precisely how this affected Judaism.

C. *Judaic Status*[43]

1. *The State*

It is significant that the medieval conception of the Jew
was a religious one, contrary to all the modern ambiguities
propounded in answer to the question, What is a Jew? The Jew
was one who adhered to a particular religious community that
shared the same doctrines, worship, and religious life, which
separated them from the religious life, doctrines and worship
of Christian society. Once a Jew converted to Christianity he
ceased to be a Jew in the eyes of the medieval church and state.
They correctly had no ethnic or racial hang-ups and when they
used the word "nation" of Jews they merely used it in the sense
of a separate community. This signified they were not part of
the civil organization from which they were excluded, in the
land in which they resided.[44] Jews were early given the right

to live in communities in accordance with their own civil laws
and to have full autonomy from the secular and ecclesiastical
courts.[45] The development of the *servi camerae* status to which
we have referred was not the fault alone of the ecclesiastical
concept of a "perpetual servitude" for the Jew in expiation of
the sin of crucifixion. The fact that theology and secular
juridical conceptions coalesced was perhaps unfortunate. It
made it easier for a bishop in Lombardy to arrange the arrest
of R. Meir and have him sent back to Rothenburg to undergo
imprisonment by Rudolph.

This conception of Jewish status arose only with Frederick
II in 1236 when he applied the phrase *servi camere nostre* ("our
chamber serfs") to the Jews. That it was not a legal theory
before is indicated by the absence of any discussion of it in
the great legal digest of 1224, or any discussion of the cor-
related theological concept of "perpetual servitude".[46] Again
in 1237 Frederick II "faithful to the duties of a Catholic
prince" as he styled his action, excluded Jews from any public
office because of the "perpetual servitude upon the Jews, as
punishment for their crime".[47] The apex was not yet reached
when each Jew had to pay an annual poll tax after 1342. But
perhaps the acme of degradation was finally described in the
Berliner Stadtbuch of 1397. There we read an article that explains or excuses why it is that Jews are allowed at all to
live in a Christian country. It introduces the laws pertaining to Jews and declares they believe in God the Creator but
are "...antagonists...of all Christendom, in that they brought
about the innocent death of Christ the true God...." It goes
on to provide four reasons why the Jews are allowed to live in
Christian lands: "First, that we have the law from them where-
with we have testimony to Christ. Second, for the sake of the
forefathers from whom Christ took...his humanity....Third, for

the sake of the Jews' conversion....Fourth, in remembrance of
Jesus Christ...."[48]

This was in great contrast to the self-image the Jews had,
by testimony of rabbinic scholars, in the twelfth century when
they regarded themselves as free men, possessing property,
freely able to move about.[49]

2. *The Church*

We have in our previous chapters and in this one from time
to time touched upon the role of the Church and of theological
doctrine upon the hardships endured by Jews and Judaism during
the middle ages. A scholarly debate has long gone on regarding
the relative blame to be placed upon the secular rulers and the
Church. For that matter, objectivity requires one investigate
to what extent the Jew himself shared in his humiliation. To
what extent could he have avoided riots, expulsions and separation into ghettos, had he not practiced usury, clipped coins,
taken Church ritual objects as surety, flaunted affluence and
enjoyed the status of knight for so long despite his not being
a Christian? These are undoubtedly insoluble historical enigmas.[50]

Undoubtedly Church policy was the logical consequence of
Church doctrine. And Church policy sometimes had the muscle
to effectuate itself. Sooner or later, at the very least, a
devoted prince like King Louis the Saint of France or Frederick
II of Germany, would supply the muscle for what he imagined
were sound theological reasons. To this extent canon law was
guilty. Furthermore, because the Church was a universal forum
and an ecumenical institution it created an international problem for the Jews. By 1275 in the southern German law digest
Schwabenspiegel we find that canon law had already become a
strong influence upon the secular law codes.[51] It need only

be said here in conclusion, that if the ultimate goal of the Church was to have the Jews recognize the error of their rejection of Jesus through the misery from which their God was not redeeming them, the Church failed. The Jew believed his misery was the consequence of the sins of his ancestors in Palestine during the first century, and did not include the crucifixion. They repeated this confession as we noted in an earlier chapter in every *musaph* worship. They looked forward to ultimate redemption, not through conversion, but as a result of ever-increasing pietism and meticulous and scrupulous attention to every detail of ritual and every word of prayer formulas. And so, as the end of R. Meir's life portended the coming demise of medieval German Judaism, so too his lifetime marks the beginning of a new strain in Judaism that ultimately led to Kabalah and new disasters embodied in Sabbatai Zvi, the pretender-redeemer.

IV. GERMAN MYSTICISM[52]

A. *The Background*

German Jews apparently did not indulge in the philosophic activity of the Spaniards. But they brought forth a different theological form under the influence of eastern geonic writings and under the impact of the harsh realities of the thirteenth century. This new religious form was called hasidism but its adherents, the hasidim, had nothing to do with either the hasidim of ancient times, at the time of the Maccabees, or the hasidim of the eighteenth century, except insofar as the name always signifies "pietism". While the kabalists of Spain during the pre-expulsion period and the later kabalists of Safed, whom we will discuss in the next chapter, were an esoteric sect, the ḥasidim were part of the common people and their ideas had an enduring impact upon folk-religion.[53]

During one creative century there were three major figures that gave rise to and shaped this mystical religious revival. These were Samuel the Ḥasid of the twelfth century, his son Yehudah the Ḥasid of Worms, ca. 1140-1217, and Eleazar ben Yehudah, ca. 1160-1238.[54] A major portion of the literary heritage comes from Eleazar who preserved the doctrine they believed went all the way back to Ezra (fifth century B.C.). But the most significant insights into the origins and doctrines of the movement are found in *Sefer Ḥasidim* (*Book of the Pious*), by Yehudah ben Samuel, known as "Yehudah the Ḥasid". Yehudah has been compared to his Christian contemporary, St. Francis of Assisi. Scholars vary regarding the role of contemporary Christian mysticism in the development of Jewish mysticism.[55] Be that as it may, there really is no unified systematic doctrine of German mysticism; only a mass of sometimes disconnected and even contradictory ideas, that fed into German Judaism from the old Merkabah mysticism which pictured God on a throne which one approaches after going through the *hekhalot*, the halls and corridors of the seven heavens. The *merkabah* is the throne-chariot envisioned by the prophet Ezekiel, which became the heart of ancient esoteric lore, of which we will have occasion to say a little more in our chapter on Kabalah.

These mystics called themselves Yorde Merkabah ("Riders of the Chariot") and have been described as people who were "able, by various manipulations, to enter into a state of auto-hypnosis, in which they declared they saw heaven open before them, and beheld its mysteries. It was believed that

he only could undertake this Merkaḅah ride who was in possession of all religious knowledge, observed all the commandments
and precepts and was almost superhuman in the purity of his
life." This older form of mysticism had a variety of routes
through which it could reach Germany. One was the *piyutim*,
the synagogue poems, written in the east and in Italy before
the eleventh century. As a matter of fact, it would not be
surprising at all if the opposition of many rabbis to including these poems and hymns in regular worship was not owing to
the disguised mystical content. Furthermore, as we saw above,
R. Gershom allowed these poems in Germany, basing himself upon
his contemporary R. Meshullam b. Kalonymus. But actually R.
Meshullam was a scion of that very family which may have been
the transmitters of the esoteric lore from generation to generation having received it from a certain Abu Aron of Bagdad.
Along with this element is also the German folk elements involving belief in witches and demons.[56]

B. *The Teaching of Ḥasidism*

1. *The Ideal*

Eschatological ideas were prominent in *Sefer Ḥasidim*.
These included all the elements we have surveyed earlier: the
nature of eternal bliss in heaven, redemption, bodily resurrection, reward and punishment, and such elements as are not found
in general eschatological literature as *ḥibbut hakeḅer*, the
"terrors of the grave" that overtake the dead within the first
days after burial.[57] The ḥasidim also had a theology of history based upon Genesis 8:18, "Thorns and thistles shall the
earth bring forth." "The earth" in the mind of Eleazar of
Worms signified human history, and the verse denoted the
"weeds", as he called them, that consistently operate to

frustrate God's purpose. This is what he called "profane history" whose origin is in the sin of Adam, the source of human inequality and of violence which in turn is the product of man's alienation from God.[58]

This brings us to the essence of ḥasidism. The alienation of man requires his reunion with God through the realization of a religious ideal. This achievement of religious perfection has no relationship, in ḥasidic thought, to intellectual attainment or to the acquisition of tradition.[59] In this sense indeed thirteenth century ḥasidism, in one way at least, became a direct mentor and precedent for eighteenth century ḥasidism. The ḥasid, the man who carries that honorific, is not necessarily a scholar or a man of any special worldly or intellectual achievements. He is simply a person who has been able to reach the goals of ḥasidut, "devoutness", saintliness, or superior piety.

There are two central characteristics of this thirteenth century ḥasid: a) asceticism, which renounces the material advantages and enjoyments of this world; b) altruism, through which the pious person indulges in self-abnegation to an extreme.

The asceticism of ḥasidut is a total turning away from the activities or pleasures of ordinary life, whether profane speech or playing with children, to mention only two curious unrelated examples as evidence of the wide spectrum ḥasidism included. It is in essence the very opposite of at least one strain in talmudic thought, that *derekh èreẓ*, the ordinary worldly life, should be brought into close conformity with the life of study and intellectual pursuit. In *Sefer Ḥasidim* the devout is urged to the pinnacle of spiritual attainment to be reached by *àzivat derekh èreẓ*, "the abandonment of the worldly way".[60] The talmudic teacher believed in a harmony of the worldly and the spiritual. For him, if man is to be immersed in the worldly it means he is to live an animalistic physical existence, but to be devoted utterly to the spiritual is a form of futile piety which cannot bring to fruition God's purposes for the world. A particular facet of the ḥasid's re-nunciation of the world is his willingness to bear disgrace and humiliation, much beyond the "turn the other cheek" of popular phrase.[61]

"The essence of ḥasidut is to act in all things not on, but within the line of strict justice--that is to say, not to insist in one's own interest on the letter of the Torah...." This quotation from *Sefer Ḥasidim* depicts the idea taken from older literature, that the pious person does not necessarily stand on the letter of a law to gain personal advantage, that although the law grants him such advantage he will waive his rights in the interest of others.[62] This talmudic principle of *lifnim m'shurat hadin* (within the line of justice) meant the opposite of what the words lead one to believe. It did not mean staying *within* the law, but going well beyond it in order to exceed its requirements and practice an even greater humanitarianism and spirituality. German mysticism laid greatest stress upon this as the way to saintliness. But it also implied that what is permitted by the halakha may be sin-ful and merits punishment. This is a conception utterly anti-thetical to the general halakhic system of Judaism (whether rabbinic or karaitic, ancient or medieval) where what was im-moral could never be considered halakhic and what was halakhic was beyond reproach.[63]

This pietism reaches a crescendo when Eleazar writes that when a ḥasid enters his true state,

> The soul is full of love of God and bound with
> ropes of love....And the lover thinks not of
> his advantage in the world, he does not care
> about the pleasures of his wife or of his sons
> and daughters, but all this is as nothing to
> him, everything except that he may do the will
> of his Creator....[64]

Unlike what some scholars say about this hasidic ideal resembling the ascetic ideal of the monk, I would remind the reader that it did not include a vow of sexual abstinence, nor was celibacy ever considered by the spiritual leaders of hasidism. But it was perhaps reminiscent of a monkish attitude in the sense that it did not expect every Jew to be a hasid.

2. *Prayer, Magic and Penitence*

The masses came to look upon the hasid as someone so unusual that he could command powerful forces. This implied his magical powers. And ultimately this is how Yehudah the Hasid appears in the legendary literature. To this literature is also attributed the origins of the legend of the *golem*, an automaton or artificial imitation of a human, which became the servant of its creator and carried out his orders.[65] Only as long as the divine name, written on a slip of paper, was in its mouth (or on its forehead, as the legend may vary) could the *golem* function. It could become destructive and then the paper was removed and it turned into an inert mass. The first person to whom such a *golem* was attributed was Samuel, the father of Yehudah the Hasid, aside from parallels in the Talmud.[66] It may be noted that these esoteric activities did not improve the public relations image of the medieval Jews. They were accused of magic and sorcery out of their own literature. From their own pietistic legends they could be charged with

possessing demonic power capable of uprooting Christian
society. This naturally made it easier to associate the Jew
with Satan the moving force of all diabolic magic.[67] Even
Jews engaged in rational intellectualism accepted the beliefs
in demons, evil spirits and the like and only rare exceptions
denied their existence. Thus Rashi even imagined them to be
among the living specimens preserved on Noah's ark during the
great flood.[68] But it was not only the Jews of the north who
accepted these notions. Some scholars think because Maimonides and Ibn Ezra denied the reality of demons the Jews of the
southern Mohammedan lands did not believe these things. But
that is not wholly accurate. Scholars of Islamic lands believed in demons, as did even later enlightened humanistic
scholars like Menasseh ben Israel.[69]

Prayer was closely allied to magical forces. Prayer was
dealt with in terms of special attention to the number of
words and the numerical value of words, parts of sentences
and whole passages of liturgy. These in turn were linked with
names and attributes of God and angels. Prayer was seen to
be the mystical ladder upon which man ascends to heaven. Certain formulae were created to engage in mystical meditation
that would perhaps serve two purposes: have magical influence,
or create a profound condition of *kavanah*, "intention" or
really "mental concentration", a concept which became significant in later Kabalah and ḥasidism. In this doctrine words
take on a very real and all-important vitality. Hence the
correct phrase is of immense significance. These words were
the potent forces the ḥasid sent up the prayer ladder to do
their work with the Lord. The ḥasid also engaged in ecstatics,
as is described by a thirteenth century disciple, R. Moses
Tachau. He writes that they directed strong intention upon
the use of divine names, and, "Then a man is seized by terror

and his body sinks to the ground. The barrier in front of his
soul falls....When the power of the name recedes does he awaken
and return with a confused mind to his former state. This is
exactly what the magicians do who practice the exorcism of the
demons...."[70]

Along with this new approach to prayer went a new emphasis
upon penitence. But it is also clear that we have here extensive Christian influence. Penitence is restitution for offend-
ing God. Such penitentiary acts ranged from a variety of forms
of fasting to voluntary wandering. For very serious infractions of the Torah the hasidim adopted such penitential acts as
sitting in the snow or ice for an hour every day during the
winter, or to expose oneself to ants and bees in the summer.
There is the story, for example, of a hasid who lay down on
the doorstep of the synagogue at the time of prayer each day
for a year so that all who come to pray will have to walk over
him as they enter, and as each person stepped upon him he re-
joiced for the opportunity of making reparation to God for his
deadly sin. What had been his sin? He washed away ink on a
piece of parchment and later discovered he had erased the name
of God.[71]

There were other concepts embellished from simpler older
ideas, especially mystical notions regarding the nature of God,
His holiness, and function, ideas that come under the heading
of theosophy.[72] The hasidim developed a very vigorous view of
the *immanence* of God and from this it is quite easily discernible why the northern scholars saw no problem in pantheistic
notions that were anthropomorphic as well, and therefore rejected the rationalism of Maimonides. From their point of
view God is closer to His creatures than the creature is to
itself. This doctrine of immanence is described in the "Song

of Unity" which was present in prayerbooks for many centuries
until the present. One "Song of Unity" was written for each
day of the week. They express rhapsodically God's total in-
volvement in the world.[73] This is also expressed in the *Shir*
HaKavod ("The Hymn of Glory") long chanted at the conclusion
of Sabbath morning worship, and still is in many rituals.
Written by Yehudah the Ḥasid the opening couplets exhibit the
central mystical notions of ḥasidism,

> I will chant sweet hymns and compose songs;
> For my soul pants after Thee.
> My soul longs to be beneath the shadow
>   of your hand,
> To know all Thy secret mysteries.
> Even while I speak of Thy glory
> My heart yearns for Thy love.

There are very direct images of God in the poem. He is seen
as an old man with hoary head and as a youth with raven hair,
and as a warrior armed for battle.[74]

It may be instructive to offer at least two examples of
the *gematriot*, the system of mystical numerical theology if we
may call it that. The ḥasidim discovered that Psalm 136 has
the refrain "for His mercy is forever" twenty-six times and
that the four-letter name of the Lord, the tetragrammaton,
consisting of the Hebrew letters *Yod* (numerically taken as 10
since it is the tenth letter of the alphabet), *Hay* (five),
Vav (six), *Hay* (five) also amounts to twenty-six. They therefore saw themselves in direct contact with deity when reciting
the psalm and so they originated the custom of standing for
its recital. Perhaps a more significant one of many that can
be cited from their writings is the response found in the *kaddish*, the "sanctification" doxology said at certain intervals
during the worship ritual and now well-known as a mourner's

prayer. The line which is used as a response is "Let His
great name be praised forever and forever", consisting of
seven words in Aramaic, the language in which it was formulated. The mystics saw in this cosmic significance. For
aside from the normal emphasis placed upon the number seven
in all mystical and occult circles, and aside from the fact
that the world was created in seven days, the first verse of
the Bible consists of seven words in Hebrew, "In the beginning
God created the heavens and the earth." Thus, according to
the ḥasidim, to praise God with these words is to participate
in the miracle of creation.[75]

V. THE DEMISE OF JUDAISM IN GERMANY[76]

A. *The Tragedy*

The realities of German history, that a medley of nation-
alities and tribes had not yet found the way to a national
state, meant that no single action in one area or by one
monarch would affect all Jews in Germany. Sporadic local outbreaks, however, were relatively commonplace, and were usually
commemorated in liturgical poems. None compared to a widespread massacre in Franconia, Bavaria and Austria in 1298 during which the great halakhist Mordecai b. Hillel was killed at
Nuremberg. The fourteenth century saw new mass outbreaks in
1336-37, and after the Black Death of 1348-49 the mass slaugh-
ter was unprecedented in terms of both the area over which it
took place and the numbers of people destroyed.

There were complicated aspects in these events and any
generalization about why they took place would of necessity

be an oversimplification. There was in process a spreading
social revolution. Peasants and workers who were not in debt
to Jews were allowed to commit barbarities by the passivity
of burghers and aristocrats who were. On the other hand,
cities like Ratisbon and Vienna protected their Jews from the
mobs and Germanic sections such as Bohemia, Moravia and north-
east German provinces were relatively free of disturbances.
Few Jews converted and consequently no German "Marrano" element emerged. Many Jews fled to Poland, however, where they
were protected by the royal power.

Although it is estimated that three hundred German communities were ruined, and great centers of learning ceased to
exist, these massacres did not entirely terminate the presence
of Judaism in Germany. Furthermore, in many communities from
which they had been driven Jews applied for and gained re-
admission. But during the fifteenth century the situation
deteriorated, even ending in tragedy in a place like Vienna
which hitherto had a good record. Jews were also accused of
siding with Hussites, who were a heretical sect which engendered much animosity. Here a mass *auto-da-fé* was perpetuated
against Jews, many children were converted and sent to monas-
teries and convents, and Jews were banished from Austria. Increasingly expulsions decimated the remaining communities, and
when in 1520 Rothenburg banished its Jews, Jewish learning and
spiritual life, which had flourished for six hundred years,
came to an end in Germany.

"Viewed in retrospect, however, we must not believe that
during the last three medieval centuries all Jews constantly
lived in fear and trepidation about assailants lurking around
the corner. When telescoped into a single list of pogroms and
expulsions, the attacks on Jews appear indeed as an uninterrupted succession of catastrophes."[77] Actually while one seg-

ment suffered others did not. Portugal and Provence did not suffer when Spain did, and during the fourteenth century when German Jews suffered their several attacks, Jews of Spain, Sicily, southern France, the Papal States, Bohemia, Hungary and Poland were relatively undisturbed. Judaism flourished in some places while under attack in others. Many a Jew lived out his life without witnessing personal suffering. Many a community existed for centuries without anti-Jewish riots. The suffering was great but should not be overexaggerated, and Jewish history should not be written as a lachrymose experience.

B. *Summary*

What we have seen is that Judaism consisted of great variety. While halakha as religious guidance and talmudics as major intellectual curriculum were relatively normative, Jews indulged in esoteric studies, in mystical ideas and in the occult and ecstatic aspects of religious behaviourism. The atmosphere in Christian Europe of the twelfth century after the inaugral of the crusades was one of religious enthusiasm and pietism, stressing the duty of the faithful to engage in self-sacrifice, and what was true in the Christian milieu had its impact upon Judaism. But it should not be thought that hasidism was revolutionary. It merely shifted an emphasis for its own devotees from talmudics to the esoteric, from living by halakha to going far beyond it. Most especially in prayers the focus was transferred from the concept of understanding the content to a preoccupation which fixed formulae and numerical exactitude. They moved from the hope that God will hear and respond, to the notion that the right number of words, the right words said in precisely the correct

fashion can have a potency of their own and achieve the response. Thus magic was interwoven with religion. But the
basic theology of traditional Judaism had not been radically
transformed. A certain balance of emphasis was shifted but
not the principles of faith. The concepts hasidism emphasized
in the new balance were all old, taken from talmudic agadah
and material contained in the many *midrashim* accumulated and
compiled since the editing of the Talmud.[78]

Finally, there can be no question but that this element,
along with R. Meir of Rothenburg's regimen of detailed ritualistic fastidiousness went along with the German Jew to Poland.
It became an ingrained aspect, albeit moderated in certain respects, of east European folk religion. As we will see, much
of the spirit of thirteenth century Germany emerged in the
mystic tendencies of eighteenth century Poland, Galicia and
Hungary. The thirteenth and fourteenth centuries led to
Kabalah. The fifteenth century led to Poland and to the consolidation of Judaism circa 1650. Both of these phenomena
will now be examined.

CHAPTER 10

Kabalah[1]

I. WHAT IS KABALAH?

The word Kabalah itself has a simple meaning: tradition.
Originally it is found as a term denoting any religious knowledge not in the Torah, and includes the rabbinic material. But
after around 1200 it begins to signify the mystical meanings
and concepts which were transmitted from generation to generation. The term has taken on a mystique. It exudes an esoteric
and exotic, and sometimes even an eerie sense of the irrational.
It is therefore important to know what it is. This will also
assist us in perceiving what precisely it supplies to the
thought and practice of Judaism.

Some define mysticism as a form of religion which emphasizes "immediate awareness of relation with God...religion in
its most acute, intense and living stage".[2] Generally in religion man seeks to close the gap between himself and God
through living in accord with God's communication with man,
His revelation, and communicating in turn with God through
prayer. Mysticism, however, finds this to be inadequate and
strives for an immediately more direct contact between man and
God. Thus the mystic sees revelation as a moment of history,
as all classical religion does, but he also regards it as a
real possibility that it can be constantly intuitively re-
enacted.[3]

The mystic understands all the historical aspects of religion as symbols of events that are repeated in his soul. Thus the exodus from Egypt is merely an outward occurrence of the liberation each individual must experience from the Egypt of his inner self. In this awareness of symbolism there is an aspect of mysticism in all religion. Few hardy intellectual spirits are capable of an exclusively rational faith, and for this reason the elements of myth re-enter Judaism from time to time. Then it is that the great debates ensue over the validity of anthropomorphism and ideas that border on pantheism.

What should be clear, and would become clear to one who studies Judaism in depth is that philosophical rationalism is not necessarily a reaction to mysticism, and mysticism is not necessarily a reaction to rationalism. Drawing dichotomies in Judaism, as in every faith or culture, has its perils. A cursory glance at Judaism's evolution will bring to light a perennially two-track development: rationalism *and* mysticism; not either one or the other. During the heyday of rabbinic intellectualism, evidenced in the Talmud, the same rational halakhists spoke the mystifying agadic statements that are the natural successors to mysticism in the Bible and intertestamental literature, and the historic predecessors of medieval mysticism which came to be called Kabalah. This mingling of the mystical and the rational was highlighted in R. Joseph ben Ephraim Karo of the sixteenth century. The same continued to be true during the centuries since then: the rationalist who was truly religious was mystical; the mystic who sought to preserve traditional values and forms pursued a rationalist halakhic course. Where formal or technical mysticism--or as it is called in Judaism, Kabalah--is different is in its adoption of esoteric forms of observance to bring about certain calculated spiritual results.

Let us look back at the historical incident, the exodus
of Israel from Egypt. In Jewish theology this is the premise
upon which God relates to the Jew, in return for which favor
God stakes His right to demand of the Jew that he live by
Torah.[4] What the mystic does is interpret that event for himself personally, and in the process re-interpret it. He asks
himself, What does "Egypt" mean? What does "bring forth"
mean? How does that relate to *me, now, here*? The Passover
Hagadah which delineates the ritual of the first Passover
night includes a passage which says "In every generation a man
is obligated to see himself as having gone forth from Egypt."[5]
The mystic interprets that not only in historic terms and commemorates the communion Seder rite, but also sees it as a
great challenge to liberate himself from corruption and deca-
dence, what he terms the "Egypt" in us. In Kabalah this is
not really an offense to the country, Egypt, for "Egypt"
ceases to be a country in historical time and becomes a concept, a symbol of the source of enslavement. Thus Egypt becomes greed, temptation, and whatever other base values that
prevent the individual from standing at his personal Sinai to
receive the Torah, to live by God's word.

It should be realized that although the idea expressed
in the above-quoted Passover ritual is not precisely the same
as the mystic's, it is also mystical. And it was propounded
in the acme of ancient halakhic rationalism, the Mishnah. Obviously, if a person is to fulfill the biblical verse upon
which the rite is based, "...because of that which the Lord
did for me when I came forth from Egypt" (Ex. 13:8), he can
only do so symbolically. He did not go forth from Egypt.
Egypt, the mystic therefore says, quite within the parameters
of the biblical doctrine, is a symbol. Like any symbol it
retains its original form: there was a country of that name,

Israel was in bondage there, and God liberated her. But then
like any symbol it is a representation of something that is
hidden and inexpressible. And that every mystic works out for
himself.

What we have here sketchily said about the doctrine of the
Exodus, holds true for any doctrine one may select. The whole
world, as one scholar has put it is a *corpus symbolicum*, for
the kabalist, and in the end every reality and every doctrine
is bound up with creation. And in turn it is in creation that
lies the ultimate mystery of the Godhead.[6]

The major contribution of mysticism may therefore be, not
in the forms it evolved nor in the esoteric and exotic aspects
of its world of imagery, but in a theological emphasis it
brought into medieval Judaism. This emphasis is the sense of
mystery, in its essential ancient meaning.[7] This transforms
a miẓvah or a halakha into a sacrament, terminology not as
frequently applied in Judaism as it ought to be. For the
mystic the halakha-become-sacrament still does not signify
that salvation is possible only through the proper observance
of certain rites in a specified manner, but it invests the
rites of Judaism with richness of meaning, color, drama and
poetry. Even more, as has been pointed out by others, "Every
miẓvah became an event of cosmic importance, an act which had
a bearing upon the dynamics of the universe."[8] Some of the
elements brought into Jewish ritual by Kabalah have remained
in it, and are part of contemporary Judaism, as we will see
later.

We have discussed the problem of *gematriot*, numerical
values given to terms, and the addiction to overfastidious
concern for the smallest detail of relatively inconsequential
rituals. These are among the dangers in the kabalistic way.
But all ritualism can become mere stilted formalism without

the redeeming virtue of being part of a cosmic drama. The challenge, therefore, of maintaining religious equilibrium between meaning and action exists in both the rationalist and the mystic spheres.

It was inevitable that this sense of the mystery of God in history and the cosmic significance of every halakha would intrude itself into the world of prayer.[9] Many prayers found in the Jewish liturgy are products of mystics, from the German hasidim discussed in the last chapter to the kabalists of Safed soon to be examined. Such additions to the liturgy continued well into modern times and were adopted by the modern hasidic movement.

Possibly the problem of evil in the world is a good illustration of the chasm between rational philosophy and Kabalah. Philosophers, as we have seen, have said evil is either the fault of man's free will or it is mysterious, its inequities to be balanced in the afterlife. The philosophers may not have satisfied the yearnings and the anxieties of believers. But the kabalists came no closer. They saw evil as very real, a concrete force in the form of demons and evil spirits populating the world. It was necessary through a variety of rituals to frustrate and overpower them. Many of the practices as we have seen, in the life-cycle ritual of Judaism revert to medieval superstitions that were condoned by Kabalah. Spirit-possession was one of those that was most disconcerting, and as a result, exorcism became a significant aspect of east European hasidic Judaism. That demons were a real danger to humans was an old belief. It is found in the Talmud, in Church literature and throughout medieval literature.[10] The kabalist response to suffering and misfortune was hardly any more curative than the philosophical.

II. A BRIEF RÉSUMÉ OF THE EVOLUTION OF JEWISH MYSTICISM

The origins of Jewish mysticism are without doubt in the Bible, the foremost historian Heinrich Graetz, notwithstanding.[11] Psalmists and prophets exhibit unmistakable signs of the mystic. Eschatological literature is mystical. The midrashic agadah and agadah embedded in the pages of Talmud is mystical. Perhaps this literature is not all "technically" kabalistic, but some of it certainly is, dealing in symbols and numbers, in magical formulae and the supernatural population, and similar facets that come alive in later Kabalah. To discuss all this "founding" literature of Kabalah is not really germane to our chapter. But a very brief review will be useful.

The notions of the Bible involving an anthropomorphic deity are the source of much mysticism. God speaks, hears, intrudes, becomes angry, loves, hates, like a human being. Maimonides labored to eliminate all thought of anthropomorphism. This was the reason for the stoutest opposition to him. And perhaps his overzealous Aristotelian rationalism with its emphasis upon the superior intellect was precisely the goad required for the perennial mysticism of Judaism to emerge from the shadows and shift the balance. Maimonides wrote his *Guide* at the end of the twelfth century. The opposition to him burned throughout the thirteenth, and during that century German hasidism made great inroads. An early kabalistic book, *Bahir*, began to play a role, and soon after that, as we will see later, the *Zohar*. Kabalah restored the anthropomorphic deity and its validation for credibility was no less an authority than thé Bible.

The sudden manifestation of deity in unusual form such as the visions of Isaiah 6 and Ezekiel 1, and the very notion

of prophecy, that God spoke with a human being, that a person
directly encountered God, is certainly not to be rejected as a
mystical experience.[12] The talmudic literature is replete with
puzzling passages and with a highly developed angelology and
demonology and discussions of many-lettered names of God, all
subjects of Kabalah.[13] It was from the first chapter of
Ezekiel, the chariot vision, that a major element of Kabalah
was drawn.[14] The mystic hoped to become a "*merkabah*-rider",
and thus penetrate the profoundest mysteries of the Godhead.
The most rational of early rabbinical scholars are found to be
mystics and dabbling in the enigmas of Ezekiel's vision.[15]
Following this came the *hekhalot* mysticism, which explored the
halls and palaces of the heavens on the way to the divine
throne on the chariot.[16] The geonim were versed in mystical
lore despite their rationalist intellectualism.[17] Not only
did the chariot vision have this impact upon Judaism. The
first chapter of Genesis, the creation story, with all the
cosmological ramifications of how an infinite and incorporeal
deity can create finite matter, was also a major subject of
mysticism from the earliest times. The road that led from
Genesis and Ezekiel to the speculations found in Tosefta and
Talmud undoubtedly ran through Enoch and other apocalyptic
writings of the apocrypha dated to the first century B.C. and
first century A.D.[18] Furthermore, there were relationships
between Palestinian mysticism and that of Philo who lived in
the heart of the Hellenistic diaspora.[19]

There is a straight line of mysticism in Judaism from its
very beginnings down into the middle ages. Then there appeared what scholars have been unsure of as far as authorship
and dating is concerned, the *Sefer Yeẓirah* (*Book of Creation*).[20] This book specializes in the meaning of the manip-

ulation of the letters of the alphabet by God in the creation
of the cosmos. It takes up one of the significant kabalistic
ideas for the first time: the doctrine of a succession of ten
sefirot through the process of *hamshakhah*, emanations. This
doctrine of emanation teaches that the *sefirot* are the inter-
mediary stages between God and creation, and avers that all
existing things therefore are radiations from God. Thus all
things are of God, and God is in all things as a flame is related to its candle. The ten *sefirot* signify spiritual "in-
strumentalities" rather than anything of a spatial sense.
These ten *sefirot* are: 1) the spirit, voice and word of God;
2) the air that comes from the spirit containing the inscribed
twenty-two letters of the Hebrew alphabet; 3) water condensed
from the air and in it is the chaos of which the earth is made;
4) the fire derived from water and of which the celestial glory
is composed including the heavenly population of Seraphim and
other angels; the next six *sefirot* are composed of the four
cardinal points of the compass and height and depth, that is,
six dimensions of space.[21]

Sefer Yezirah teaches that the "spirit of God" produced
the letters, and the letters are the prime cause of the
material world. Thus all emanations are from a unified divine
source. "God is at one and the same time both the matter and
form of the universe" as one scholar has put it.[22] Although
this book provided the entry into the major kabalistic discussion of cosmogomy and the complex doctrines related to the
relationship of the *sefirot* and emanations, it was eclipsed by
its successor, the Zohar. But before going on to look at that
work, a glance at a contemporary of the author of the Zohar
will help round out our survey.

III. ABRAHAM ABULAFIA AND HIS TEACHINGS[23]

The Zohar stands out as the best-known of all kabalistic writings. It represents Kabalah at its full flowering in Spain. In our earlier chapter on Judaism in Spain we touched upon the cross-currents there of an emerging mysticism. From about 1200 to 1350 Spanish and Provencial mysticism flourished and became the well from which future centuries of mysticism were watered, having an important influence upon Judaism right up to the twentieth century. This Kabalah was marked by an ambivalence between traditionalism and revolutionary thought. And the Zohar was not the only stream of mystical tradition. The revolutions were not candidly regarded as such. They were seen as the proper interpretation of ancient lore, or were presented as mystical revelations. One of the significant kabalists who transmitted what he called new revelations, was Abraham Abulafia, a contemporary of the author of the Zohar.[24]

In a booklet containing the relevant material of the famous debate referred to in a previous chapter between R. Moses ben Naḥman (Naḥmanides) and Pablo Christiani in 1263 in Barcelona, Abulafia read that Naḥmanides had said: "When the time of the end will have come the Messiah will at God's command come to the Pope and ask of him the liberation of his people, and only then will the Messiah be considered really to have come...." Abulafia went to the Pope, Nicholas III, but apparently the Pope died before Abulafia could appear before him and claim to be the Messiah.[25]

Other than messianic pretensions Abulafia's major characteristics were in ecstasy and prophecy. Abulafia's prescription for reaching ecstasy was to fully and exclusively concentrate in meditation upon the Name of God, the source of all existence. He saw letters of the alphabet combining as music

notes do for a listener. Coming from different instruments
played by two hands a wide variety of notes form a unified
whole. So the combination of greatly varying letters, each
carrying its own message combine to produce the revelation in
a state of ecstasy.[26] This brings about the union of the intellect and divinity which, in Abulafia's view was also that
of Maimonides, and constituted the nature of prophecy. Nevertheless, one cannot escape the similarity between Abulafia's
emphasis upon single-minded meditation upon one central medium
--in this case, the Name--and Indian mysticism, or his emphasis upon posture and breathing and Yoga.[27]

Abulafia has himself described the road to prophetic
ecstasy: "...Cleanse the body and choose a lonely house where
none shall hear thy voice...it is best if thou completest it
during the night. In the hour when thou preparest thyself to
speak with the Creator and thou wishest Him to reveal His
might to thee, be careful to abstract all thy thought from
the vanities of this world." Abulafia suggests the ecstatic
wear his prayershawl and tefilin to be filled "with awe of the
Shekhinah which is near thee". He should wear white garments,
kindle many lights and have at hand ink, pen and a table.
"Now begin to combine a few or many letters, to permute and
combine them until thy heart be warm...and when thou seest
that by combination of letters thou canst grasp new things
which by human tradition or by thyself thou wouldst not be
able to know..." that is the time for utmost exertion of mind
and heart upon thoughts of God and angels. As the aspiring
prophet reaches the height of his meditative efforts, Abulafia
tells him, "Thy whole body will be seized by an extremely
strong trembling, so that thou wilt think that surely thou art
about to die, because thy soul, overjoyed with its knowledge,